ISSUE 22   n+1   SPRING 2015

CONVICTION

THE INTELLECTUAL SITUATION

1 **Meh!-lennials**
On generational analysis

THE PEOPLE AND THE POLICE

7 **On Becoming More Human**   LAWRENCE JACKSON
Not dying is not living

10 **Seeing Through Police**   MARK GREIF
The donut is equivocal

19 **Hands Up**   COSME DEL ROSARIO-BELL, ELIAS RODRIQUES, DOREEN ST. FÉLIX, AND DAYNA TORTORICI
A round table on police violence

FICTION

63 **Two Stories**   CHRISTINE SMALLWOOD
Stewards and Hand Jobs

"Compelling snapshots of how Americans live, move, and work." Kirkus

CITY BY CITY

Dispatches from the American Metropolis

Edited by Keith Gessen and Stephen Squibb

May 2015

n+1
FSG

that they wouldn't otherwise have access to at an entry-level job—this requires extra programming and occasionally redundant work. But regardless of what an intern does, an internship requires capacity for management that many small operations lack. Often interns become their own job-producers, making up their own tasks and responsibilities. If you do not have the resources necessary for this, then you are not looking for an intern. You are looking for a paid entry-level employee.

—*Aaron Braun*

On the Level

Dear Editors,

In his profile of Juiceboxxx ("The Next Next Level"), Leon Neyfakh nicely captures the melancholy of pursuing an artistic vision into one's late twenties, despite little economic reward. But by identifying his subject as "a guy who couldn't be anything other than what he was," Neyfakh grants Juice an aesthetic purity that's surprisingly blind to how congruent the Juiceboxxx routine is with recent artistic trends.

I've seen Juiceboxxx shows a handful of times in the last decade, always with at least one other act that mixes stubborn experimentalism and willfully tacky pop. This has even included other rappers born of the basement noise scene, whose insistence that they're dead serious only deepens the irony of their personas. In fact, these acts are in line with plenty of contemporary art, from the classrooms of RISD to the Whitney Biennial. It's easy to picture Juice's "Thunder Zone" energy drink on display alongside works similarly toying with America's consumerist information pileup.

What Neyfakh misses, then, in his context-free admiration for Juice's vision, is the chance to wonder why, in the first couple decades of the new millennium, a young musician dropout would become not a folkie or a punk or a grunger but an unpopular rap-rocker spewing F-bomb-laced positivity. Can the layered irony of his relationship to the commercial cultural behemoth be understood as Jamesonian "blank parody"? As a reaction, maybe only semiconscious, to the failure of explicitly oppositional musical poses to do much more than expand the menu of cultural consumption? And what do we make of an artist emerging from an underground scene who seems to want so desperately to sell out? He runs in circles that are often aggressively antisuccess (tourmates Extreme Animals have VHS-only releases), and yet he refuses to break character, insisting everyone call him Juiceboxxx—and on spelling it like that! It's as though he feels that, at any moment, around some corner in Bed-Stuy, his connection to superstardom is coming, and he'd better be ready, tracksuit and all. Is this the next next level? The contradictions of the Juiceboxxx act tell us something about our time, but I'm still not quite sure what.

—*Benjamin Remsen*

ESSAYS

PHILIP CONNORS **Confirmation** 31
Love and basketball

KRISTIN DOMBEK **Both Ways** 101
The Help Desk for those in distress

GABRIEL WINANT **We Found Love in a Hopeless Place** 111
Affect theory for activists

JORDAN KISNER **Thin Places** 131
Where do I start and stop, is what I want to know

TRANSLATION

ALEJANDRO ALMAZÁN **Dispatches from Guerrero** 85
Season of the dead

REVIEWS

DAYNA TORTORICI **On Elena Ferrante** 155
BRANDON HARRIS **On Bill Gunn and Spike Lee** 172

LETTERS 187

Interns, Juiceboxxx, Lewis Lapham

NUMBER 22
SPRING 2015

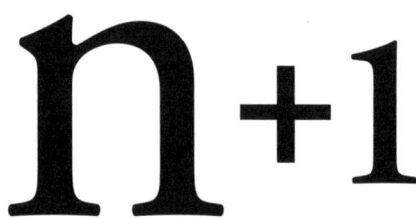

n+1 is published three times a year by n+1 Foundation, 68 Jay St. #405, Brooklyn, NY 11201. Single issues are available for $14.95; subscriptions for $36; in Canada and other international, $55. Send correspondence and submissions to editors@nplusonemag.com. *n+1* is distributed by Ingram and Ubiquity, Disticor in Canada, and Antenne in the UK and Europe. To place an ad write to ads@nplusonemag.com. *n+1*, Number Twenty-Two © 2015 n+1 Foundation, Inc. ISSN 1549-0033. ISBN 978-0-9890782-8-3.

EDITORIAL

Editors
NIKIL SAVAL
DAYNA TORTORICI

Senior Editors
KEITH GESSEN
CHAD HARBACH
CHARLES PETERSEN

Associate Editors
RICHARD BECK
LAURA CREMER
MOIRA DONEGAN
EMMA JANASKIE
NAMARA SMITH

Contributing Editors
MARK GREIF
ELIZABETH GUMPORT
MARCO ROTH

Founding Editors
KEITH GESSEN
MARK GREIF
CHAD HARBACH
BENJAMIN KUNKEL
ALLISON LORENTZEN
MARCO ROTH

Special Projects
STEPHEN SQUIBB
EMILY WANG

ART AND DESIGN

Design
DAN O. WILLIAMS

Art Editor
MARGAUX WILLIAMSON

Online Art Editors
IAN EPSTEIN
SU WU

FOUNDATION

Business Manager
COSME DEL ROSARIO-BELL

Program Coordinator
JOSEPHINE LIVINGSTONE

Managing Editor
DAYNA TORTORICI

Deputy Managing Editor
LAURA CREMER

Board
RONALD BARUSCH
KEITH GESSEN
JEREMY GLICK
MARK GREIF
CHAD HARBACH
DUSHKO PETROVICH
NIKIL SAVAL
DAYNA TORTORICI

WWW.NPLUSONEMAG.COM

THE INTELLECTUAL SITUATION

A Diary

Meh!-lennials

WE LIVE IN AN AGE OF CEASELESS GENERAtional analysis. Among certain classes, especially business elites, it is considered a sign of profound insight to speak only in terms of youth and its consumer preferences. The jargon once endemic to *Ad Age* (which coined the term "Generation Y") now peppers style sections and business books, earnest organizing meetings and talk shows, such that no one of any age can open a newspaper or a website without reading about the "millennials"—people born between 1982 and 2004—and their doings, interests, and needs.

It seems not to matter to the proliferation of writing about millennials that so much of it has been internally contradictory. In the year 2000, the sinister David Brooks said that stats suggested the boomers were raising friendly, sociable, and altruistic kids. In 2012, Jean Twenge at the *Atlantic* retaliated with fresh stats that revealed them to be inveterate narcissists profoundly uninterested in social problems. "Politicians: Millennials Won't Vote Because They Hate You" declaimed *Bloomberg*, prompting an older *Huffington Post* correspondent to wonder ruefully, "Millennials: Why Do They Hate Us?" All this despite evidence that millennials vote in the same numbers as young people of previous generations. Millennials, according to *Business Insider*, are disaffected with workplace authority and value flexibility, but an IBM study written up in the *Washington Post* suggests that in this respect, too, millennials are indistinguishable from other generations. Reading around, you can form a picture of millennials either as great disrupters, creating massive discontinuities in civilization, or as essentially the same as everyone else. In this way generational analysis resembles astrology: ascribe any quality to a certain sign and your claims are guaranteed to be neither true nor false.

It's easy, of course, to make fun of generational analysis. For many years generations have been the favored category of social pseudoscientists, not to mention marketing gurus and breathless lifestyle journalists. But much of the oxymoronic character of millennial-speak derives from its pairing claims to statistical rigor with an utterly unscientific fondness for making wild predictions. Behind this is a confusion of logic, according to which the present desires of humans create the future: once you know what young people want, you know what tomorrow will be like (and how to make a buck off it). Institutions, classes, and environments play hardly any role in this view. One influential example is Richard Florida's theory of the "creative class," which imagined the salvation of postindustrial cities resulting from young people choosing to live in them. If millennials like cities, the thinking went, then cities will be rejuvenated. In 2012, Florida sheepishly qualified some points of this theory in a new introduction to 2002's *The Rise of the Creative Class*, but his original thesis was so persuasive that it's still regarded as common knowledge. Meanwhile, the cities that banked on this kind of thinking, like St. Louis or Baltimore, have foundered spectacularly.

The abundance of such lazy analysis may seem reason enough to dismiss "generations" as a meaningful tool for understanding history. What are generations, one might say, but an ingenious marketing rubric we have come to treat as natural? But the fact remains that generations capture everyday divides that everyone recognizes intuitively. People are born into spans of time, into worlds that precede them and survive them. If it makes sense to segment history into periods, it follows that those periods have something to do with the people growing up and dying within them. Edmund Wilson plausibly referred to the "generation" that made the Russian Revolution in *To the Finland Station*, and it was broadly true, in 1961, that a "new generation of Americans"—"tempered by war, disciplined by a hard and bitter peace"—were more vocal than the "silent" group that preceded them. The Chinese born into the waning years of the disastrous Cultural Revolution shared an urge to question their government, and today's millennials, innocent of cold war–era hysterics, find fewer toxic clouds trailing the word *socialism*. Though one can't predict the future from these data, it does make sense to consider generations when thinking of how social change takes place. Generations seem to do *something*, but it's not clear what or how.

How useful is generational analysis, then? Traces of its utility were first identified in 1927 by the sociologist Karl Mannheim, whose essay "The Problem of Generations" remains the best account of its virtues. For Mannheim, a generation was something like a social class: an objective, structuring social fact. If the objective aspects of class were economic, those of generations were biological. But it would be a mistake, Mannheim argued, to attempt to deduce from the cyclical facts of birth and death the very "secret of history," as many positivist thinkers of his time did (and as business types do today). The subjective experience of a generation would also be important, as well as variable and unpredictable. Instead of thinking in terms of generational cycles as naturally important, Mannheim imagined how a particular generation could come to be important.

Much of Mannheim's focus fell on the importance of "youth" in the analysis of generations. In stable communities (such as the European peasantry of the Middle Ages), youth is a simple biological distinction—the quality of being not yet old. But in times of social instability, youth becomes a source of difficulty, a problem. Mannheim was thinking of revolutionary eras, such as the early 19th century, when the movement from countryside to city was accelerating, and the status society of the restored monarchies was buffeted by a nascent bourgeoisie. It was a classic moment when the young people of a certain period became (in Mannheim's terminology) an "actual generation": "We shall therefore speak of a *generation as an actuality* only when a concrete bond is created between members of a generation by their being exposed to the social and intellectual symptoms of a process of dynamic de-stabilization." Generations tend to get made by the people in them and by the times they live in when a span of time is felt by a biological cohort as one of crisis.

But millennials grew up not self-making but defined and redefined by people several decades older. When the term was coined in 1991 by demographers William Strauss and Neil Howe, a great deal of hope was placed in millennials (the oldest of whom were around 8, and not especially responsive to polls). Nurtured by caring parents, Strauss and Howe argued, this new generation would be civic-minded and ethical. Not only would they be less interested in TV than their parents, but "what programs Millennials do watch will be sanitized and laden with moral lessons." This hopeful portrait was a reaction to its time. It was the close of the Reagan era, when the once socially minded boomers were seen (even by themselves) as having become irremediable narcissists, and twentysomethings were portrayed as Patrick Bateman–type sociopaths. A crazy messianism attached itself to the youth: millennials were going to save this involuntary, belligerent, and vacuous country from itself. And in the years that followed, proliferating urban farms and community-supported agriculture and bike-shares—all faithfully chronicled in *GOOD*, the echt-millennial, nonprofit-loving magazine of the larger, for-profit Good Worldwide Inc.—began, if you squinted and cherry-picked, to prove the point. The religious fervor peaked with the election of Obama in 2008—proof, it seemed, that millennials would change the world (66 percent of 18- to 29-year-olds who voted voted for Obama, though nearly half that group declined to vote at all).

Subsequently, the narrative changed. As the economy went into free fall, the fascination with millennials reached a new intensity, and the think pieces proliferated. And, increasingly, the think pieces disagreed. Who are the millennials, and how do we explain their behavior? What do they stand for? (As if 100 million people ever stood for a uniform thing.) The answers differed greatly depending on the writer and the poll, but the pitch of anxiety was constant. Much of the obsession came from the business world—from the older, wealthy, mostly white decision makers who longed for a master key to understanding the needs and attitudes of the young people who would make and consume their products. For their analysis, these businessfolk looked to the major media institutions—which, racked by the recession, in a panic to figure out the internet, and acutely aware that no one under 90 read the newspaper, were themselves obsessed with what young people wanted. So the papers and magazines catered to their loyal readership—wealthy older people—by feeding them piece after piece about millennials, who seemed less promising than they once had.

In 2010, parents across America emailed the *New York Times Magazine* article "What Is It About 20-Somethings?" to the adult children living in their basements. "The question pops up everywhere," the article went, "underlying concerns about 'failure to launch' and 'boomerang kids.' . . . It's happening all over, in all sorts of families, not just young people moving back home but also young people taking longer to reach adulthood overall. It's a development that predates the current economic doldrums, and"—here things get serious—"no one knows yet what the impact will be—on the prospects of the young men and women; on the parents on whom so many of them depend; on society, built on the expectation of an orderly progression in which kids finish school, grow up, start careers, make a family and eventually retire to live on pensions supported by the next crop of kids." Meanwhile, millennials were looking up *pension* in the dictionary. In 2012, a record 21.6 million adults between 18 and 31 lived with their parents, prompting almost that many essays about the millennial crisis. ("It's Official: The Boomerang Kids Won't Leave," the *Times Magazine* confirmed in 2014.)

Of course the kids stay home because they can't get jobs that pay rent. But the function of millennial-speak is to disguise structural causes (the lack of jobs) as human desires (the kids want to stay home), and to justify further measures (make hiring and firing easier) in terms of those desires. This is why millennials are constantly figured as happily zigzagging from job to job, fleeing long-term employment, luxuriating in the intense anxiety of a precariousness said to be uniquely theirs. If they (we?) don't like a job, what use is there in organizing or demanding more from it? Just quit and move on, we're told, and so we tell ourselves the same. (Another paradoxical statistic: a majority of millennials look fondly on unions, but are also less likely than previous generations to join or form one.) Having been told for decades that they are creative snowflakes, "knowledge workers" laboring in a new kind of capitalism, younger cohorts have been encouraged to recognize themselves as operating in a wholly different, less fair economy than that of their parents—which is one way of ensuring that such an economy actually comes into being. In this way articles that worry over the socialization of millennials function as a way of socializing them into an unequal society.

This self-fulfilling prophecy has turned out to be tremendously useful to ruling classes who find the remaining institutions of the welfare state frustrating. Because, after all, it's not just executives who dislike the strictures of seniority and job security, they can explain—*it's also the millennials*, who crave freedom and flexibility. An incomplete and accordingly corrosive image of society has developed out of this analysis, in which a class conflict gets portrayed as a war between the generations: everywhere the image of the autonomous, free-spirited millennial is being deployed against the geriatric, self-protective boomer. If teachers' unions' work protects seniority, this is said to hamper the desire of young teachers to flit in and out of jobs; meanwhile, it licenses charter school expansion. If older Greek or Italian workers protect job security, this is said to hamper the ability of the young to find work—and therefore justifies the expansion of contract and part-time work. Across Europe and the US today, the benefits fought for by older workers—especially in the public sector—have been represented as "unfair" to the youth, and the young are being mobilized against labor protections that they themselves have been taught not to hope for. What is taking place is a great expropriation of the futures of young and old, the roots of which are deeper and older than we are permitted to believe. Calling it a generation gap only swells the chasm opening up beneath our feet. +

SISKIYOU
Nervous

ERIC CHENAUX
Skullsplitter

GODSPEED YOU! BLACK EMPEROR
'Asunder, Sweet and Other Distress'

MATANA ROBERTS
Coin Coin Chapter Three: river run thee

COLIN STETSON AND SARAH NEUFELD
Never were the way she was

AVEC LE SOLEIL SORTANT DE SA BOUCHE
Zubberdust!

OUGHT
More Than Any Other Day

HISS TRACTS
Shortwave Nights

LAST EX
Last Ex

CONSTELLATION
cstrecords.com

Artwork by Michael Drebert for Siskiyou *Nervous*

All titles on 180gLP, CD, MP3 & FLAC

SOJOURNER TRUTH PARSONS, *I'M THIRSTY*. 2014, ACRYLIC AND MIXED MEDIA ON CANVAS, 30 × 24". COURTESY OF THE JESSICA BRADLEY GALLERY.

POLITICS
The People and the Police

LAWRENCE JACKSON
On Becoming More Human

A version of this speech was prepared for a student rally at Emory University on December 4, 2014, in the wake of national protests over the killings of Michael Brown and Eric Garner.

I AM PROUD THAT YOU HAVE CONVENED THIS assembly for a much-needed discussion. We are talking about an issue personally important to me. I am a 46-year-old black American man, and I myself have survived some extraordinarily violent encounters with the police. I have had two friends killed in encounters with the police. I am inspired by the willingness of young people like yourselves to march and risk arrest to bring justice to American streets and work to repair the nation's troubles. But I also worry that few gains will come of our work. I worry that the main beneficiaries will be a self-enriching group—those of whom it was once said, in the 1970s, that their "livelihood depended on finding continuous instances of racial discrimination."

Last week, as I walked to campus, I listened to the news broadcast *Democracy Now!*, which has offered some of the most balanced and probing reportage there is on the public killings of Michael Brown in Ferguson, Missouri; Kajieme Powell in St. Louis; Eric Garner in Staten Island; Tamir Rice in Cleveland; Akai Gurley in East New York; Rumain Brisbon in Phoenix; and Trayvon Martin in Sanford, Florida. But listening to these reports, I felt it was insincere of people to express shock when confronting the fact that lethal police violence toward black men is endemic to American society. As a teacher, I wondered how it was possible for the *Democracy Now!* panelists to have missed that lesson in school. On another level, I was even more flabbergasted to hear, again and again, that the policemen and policewomen and emergency medical technicians had failed to recognize or appreciate the *humanity* of their African American male victims.

I'd like to follow up on that. I think you have to have a shared collective memory of the past to recognize another human being. But if we can't remember the Watts Riots of 1965, which burned for six days after a police officer struck a woman in the head with a nightstick, or the 1992 Los Angeles Riots, which followed the brutal police beating of Rodney King and videotaped shooting of 15-year-old Latasha Harlins, what makes us so confident that we know a human being, or that we recognize or think deeply about humanity?

People seem surprised that police officers like Daniel Pantaleo and Timothy Loehmann, who had been cited multiple times for poor performance or sued for abusive actions even before they murdered unarmed Americans, are still employed and carrying out their duties with measured, mundane brutality.

To those who are surprised, I ask what you think the typical policeman is doing, and why municipal budgets have expanded to hire more policemen and fewer teachers. We live in a nation that has chronically high unemployment for black men, and whose fastest-growing economic sector is somewhere between the fingernail parlor and the speculative-financial-services industry. The job of the policemen or the district attorney is not to regulate and control the behavior of investment banks or, as you all are well aware, even to uphold the law on this campus; we are a private university with a private police force whose primary job is to ensure the safety of the campus residents. The most fundamental job of the working-class police in the United States is to regulate the behavior of people like themselves (typically a half-step but almost never a full step below): a sometimes idle, sometimes job-seeking population in cities like New York, Cleveland, and Atlanta that is visibly black and Latino.

I think we misstep if we assume that our crisis is one of police reform, training, or instruction. The police in the United States are a reflection of the funding priorities of its elites. They are expressing the will of our best and brightest, which is us and our classmates.

Let me tell you about one of the greatest disappointments in my life. I was raised in a city that closed down its major industries during my childhood and young adulthood, resulting in an exodus of taxpayers. A famous quarterback once refused to fulfill his contractual obligations to play football in my hometown; it wasn't the kind of place where an ambitious, elite person wanted to go. But by the time I had finished third grade I understood the United States could be invaded by the Soviet Union any day, or that, even more likely, the siren that rang all through the city might finally call us to the basements of our houses, where we would try to survive a nuclear attack. I disliked the Russians the way one dislikes a sports rival, and I wanted to see them defeated. But I hoped that the giant war promising both victory and defeat would never come.

In 1989, when the Wall fell, the distant halves of Germany reunited, and we declared victory in a war against the Soviet Union that had been unofficially declared in 1946, I imagined our world would shortly change. I had always admired the sparkling, affluent suburbs as a child in the 1970s; politicians had told us we couldn't have better lives in our cities, because it was so crucial to devote the national budget to massive military spending—to fund the wars in Vietnam and dozens of other places, to create space-age weapons and their equally fantastic delivery systems, including the ships and planes of the Navy and Air Force. When the US declared victory in this history-ending war to end war, I expected that at least some government spending would be redirected inward. To rebuild the underfunded public schools I had attended; to pay and reward good teachers and self-sacrificing doctors; to create neighborhood recreation centers; to fund after-school programs and athletics, neighborhood hospitals and parks; to provide treatment centers and clinics for the visibly ill people crowding the streets; to resurface our roads and build effective transportation systems; to provide a banking system that offered affordable loans, so that when I turned 16 the small businesses in my neighborhood could be run by people who lived in my neighborhood, who would hire me after school or in the summer; to make the technology available so that the radio station I liked could stay on the air after dark; and, yes, to pay the person we used to call "Officer Friendly" in the '70s to walk his leisurely patrol around the neighborhood, acting like he cared about the people who lived there.

But none of this happened, you all. In fact, the opposite happened. After a brief and very minor drop in the 1990s, people for the next complete generation argued that military spending should be not just what it had been, but even greater, and that our lives in the cities should be even less like the lives of people in the suburbs. They argued that war was now endless, in fact—a part of the human condition. We should have a war on drugs, one that would push the incarcerated population past 2 million. We should no longer build schools in the cities but prisons, detention centers for "wilding" juveniles, and hire as many police as possible on the shoestring budgets of local governments. All the amenities that I had dreamed of, that I connected to the American way of life, were to be the unregulated province of private companies.

And throughout the nation, a brand-new model for urban revitalization was trumpeted. It was based in New York City, where the police—who had always been aggressive, sparking massive riots in 1943 and 1964 for shooting unarmed black men—were praised for finally getting tough on crime. The New York Police Department got tough by a policy known as "stop and frisk," and millions of young black and Latino men were violently seized, searched, and detained, and had their information stored in police files. These men, like Abner Louima, Amadou Diallo, and Sean Bell, had no constitutional rights. But New York's streets shone with glitter and gold for people with money to spend there. I don't believe it is at all far-fetched to say that we as individuals have made some unadvised choices about who gets to be human, but some very significant choices were made for us, too.

And let's be frank. Our own pursuit of "humanity" is weak-kneed and insincere. My suspicion, based on the students I recognize among you, is that you are among the few even taking humanities courses in the college. Our crowd today is not seven thousand strong, perhaps because our undergraduate student body, and really most American elite college students, are disinclined to major in the humanities, to take more than an obligatory course. We aren't strongly inclined to think too hard about issues—or even the language—of fairness and justice. Our concerns lie more generally with rationalizing and computing our privilege and our hopes of individual enrichment. And if we don't, on our own campus, take the humanities so seriously, why would we believe that retraining the police and giving them added technological equipment like cameras, like from that old movie, *Robocop*—or, more frighteningly, that other old movie, *The Terminator*—would help them appreciate human life more perceptively? Increased surveillance, tape-recorded representations of life, played back and rewound and remixed over and over again, digitally and virtually, will only remind jurors of an imitation of life, but it won't revive the real thing. Rather than die knowing my death had been recorded by the camera, I would just rather not die. And rather than not die, I would like to choose to live.

Two final points about change and sacrifice. Many of us today hope to take our protest to the streets, to join in national solidarity and to be on the right side of history. But I suggest that if you want to make a decisive change, you should not exclude the place where you can see the obvious fruits of your victory: your own campus and among your own classmates.

Second, I am certain that every one of us has the capacity to find very useful, very necessary employment. However, it might not be lucrative. Which is to say that while we might earn enough to eat, put a roof over our heads, and pay off our debt, the jobs that are at our fingertips require us to be servants of the public. We would be vulnerable, we would be humans, taking a public bus, being forced to share, having to reconcile our differences with strangers from all walks of life, perhaps purchasing only the things that we could afford right then, not on credit or future leverage but cash on the barrelhead just like the poor, no longer among the elites we know at this school, and perhaps not so wealthy. Perhaps not wealthy at all. We might be disappointed because we were not sharply upwardly mobile. We would have to face, for a period at least, that we had failed the American dream. We didn't earn more than our parents, we didn't have a larger home or a more exclusive social circle or wield more political or economic power. We weren't living under the bright glare of glamorous reward. But it is at least possible that of the 21 million Americans enrolled in college, we have here among us some special abilities that have to be harnessed, developed, and then set free. It is quite possible that we have the capacity to engage in some special discussions, and to put into language what is in crucially short supply in America's public places. One of our real challenges is whether or not we will freely make our voices, and our knowledge, and our skills and our learning about humanity available to the other citizens of this land. Those of you at this rally must help your fellow classmates, teachers, and administrators make choices that will benefit not the ranking, not the endowment, not the stock market, not the numbers, but the people, but humanity.

If we do that, we might well have created the reform that all of us here understand is so desperately needed if our country is to survive and thrive. We might have helped to create the conditions for justice in the land. We might have truly become human. +

MARK GREIF
Seeing Through Police

A SURPRISE OF BEING AROUND POLICE IS how much they touch you. They touch you without consent and in both seemingly friendly and unfriendly ways. The friendly touch is the first surprise. A policeman allowing protesters to cross the street touches you on the arm or back as you cross. Face to face, police will put a hand on your shoulder, from the front, intimate as a dog putting his paw up. It is unnerving. Women say male police know very well how to touch, even in public sight, in ways that are professional and neutral, and also in ways that are humiliating and sexual, with no demonstrable distinction dividing the two. The police know, and you know. Like a reversal of electric polarity from protective to hostile, this conversion of mood does not only follow the policeman's individual initiative. It traces something like an atmospheric charge among police in groups, their silent experience of a phenomenon, their habitual tactics in response.

In confrontations on a curb (when you stay on your sidewalk, because the public street is forbidden except to police), they may press lightly on your collarbone, "holding you back," just measuring out the distance with their arms. You can even be held up in this way, if you relax. Shoving you requires a separate, additional level of their energy. Batons and gloves extend the police field of touch, insulating them from the brutality that their arms and hands will do. A gray-haired professor of history I know put his hand on the top rail of a metal police barrier, at a protest, as one will do when standing still. An officer forbade him to touch it. All macho, the historian refused to move his hand. The policeman smashed it with his baton, splitting the flesh but not breaking the bone. That was a conflict over the reciprocation of touch: the rail and the baton were proxies. The unspoken rule is that the citizen must never return touch.

Singling out an individual for arrest, the next escalation is to grab the citizen's body at the neck or shoulders—attacking from the front, black-gloved fingers grip the face, while from behind, the palm shocks the base of the skull—pushing at the fulcrum of the neck to hurl the person down. Sometimes the cop's left hand pulls up or tears at the arrestee's shirt or outermost garment while pushing with the right hand. A poet in his forties I know was thrown to the ground like this because he stepped outside a crosswalk at the beginning of a march. Other officers swarm the downed man or woman and pull at arms and legs, and kneel on the back or the neck or head, or mash the face into the pavement under their palm while cuffs go on. The final escalation is punching, beating, or kicking. Sometimes this is reserved for the arrestee on the ground who is already restrained, as a form of punctuation. Sometimes it is done in the van or on the way to it. Police are more likely to do this when they believe they cannot easily be recorded with cameras.

The purpose of touching by police is to make persons touchable. Touch readies more touch. The restraints in civilization on attacking anyone, especially a citizen who portends no harm or threat, are fairly high. For most forms of violence that breach civilized norms, even if it is one's art or profession, steps of habituation are needed. The "sudden" violent arrest at a protest is almost never sudden if you have been watching the officer and the longer sequence. The process of change in an officer who brings someone down is not oriented to the target, but seems interior, oriented to the self; in the expressions that pass over the face—usually in an instant of stepping back, at the end of an interaction or negotiation—you can detect a change of availability that prefaces the attack. It very often seems to surprise nearby officers, even astonish or trouble them, but they still know to capture whichever citizens wind up on the ground (sometimes the wrong ones, as the trailing officers seem to cuff bystanders who happen to get knocked down indirectly in the attack).

POLICE ARE DIFFERENT THINGS to different people. Not because each person has his or her own subjective view on the constabulary, but because the meanings of the functions of police vary with a citizen's identity, as one or another possible target or beneficiary of policing.

What are the exemplary police activities, in ordinary vernacular? "Directing traffic." This function of restricting and encouraging movement through a city may be the very oldest job of police. The most manpower and work time are still devoted to it. Police maintain a spatial order. What is traffic? Certain neighborhoods contain certain types of people and behavior. Others contain others. Various subjects must move through corridors of the city and redistribute themselves over the course of the day and night, but they must not unsettle police's fundamental sense of who belongs where. Today, when police accused of racial bias in their traffic stops and pedestrian searches are asked to justify themselves, they speak with pride of the fact that they do not just stop and question black people, but also white people caught in black neighborhoods and rich people cruising in poor neighborhoods. This, to their minds, is parity. They don't recognize their role in making up the boundaries of these neighborhoods in the first place, or why not all neighborhoods are functionally the same.

"Catching criminals." This is the activity police truly like to identify with, however little of their time it occupies. Occasionally, police stumble on red-handed robbers or thugs fleeing an assault. But the bulk of "catching" people lies in traversing the city as necessary to find someone on the word of someone else. Police act as go-betweens for antagonists who may even be practically within arm's reach—yelling outside their cars in a fender bender, or giving opposite accounts of a domestic dispute. Real "investigation"—the glorious business of tracing an unidentified malefactor after the fact of a crime, without just finding out who did it from the witnesses closest at hand—is an activity that does exist in police departments, but only among a tiny number of specialized personnel who don't even have to wear uniforms.

When police identify crimes against the city, state, or law, rather than against an affronted person—the so-called victimless crimes of illicit possession, unlicensed work, or unlicensed sale—they perform the essential police function of distributing crime. The legislature declares certain objects and unlicensed commerce illegal; the police then go and distribute these violations. Street drugs are made illegal (prescription drugs are fine), hidden and unlicensed weapons are illegal (carried by people on unsafe streets, which is to say the poor), flawed cars are illegal (busted taillight, broken muffler, unpaid insurance). Thus police spend a large part of their time distributing crime to the sorts of people who seem likely to be criminals—the poor and marginal—and the prediction is prophetic: these people turn out to *be* criminals as soon as they are stopped and forced to turn out the contents of their pockets or glove boxes. Leave them alone, and most would never be "criminal" at all. The majority of violations technically listed in the tables of the law are of no interest to uniformed police. People who break laws in business are unlikely to be detected or sought out, and when their violations are disclosed—leading to the awkwardness of having to reach a settlement—they are dealt with by regulatory agencies, guilds, or accrediting bodies, and at the far extreme by civil-court proceedings and court-mandated money exchanges. Very rarely are police or criminal justice brought in.

The most admirable and defensible of the exemplary police activities may be "keeping the peace." It is also the least discussed, the least subject to written laws and directives, and the least specific. In a democracy of equal citizens, people will inevitably come into conflict, even through no fault or crime of one party or the other. Someone will take advantage or threaten. The role of the police here is to pacify—and pacification, in a civil democracy, is no bad thing intrinsically. It is a vital, valuable thing.

But one mode of "keeping the peace"—enforcing racial terror—may be the very worst thing police do habitually. This exemplary function, unofficial or officially denied though universally known, owns no single familiar phrase. In recent decades, African Americans have made proverbial the facetious offenses that police seem to be pursuing: "driving while black," "shopping while black," "walking while black." Only a limited number of Southern police forces can trace their lineage directly to slave patrols, but interethnic conflict after the Great Migration effectively nationalized Jim Crow policing through the 20th century. Police departments' role in racial terror has survived even where racism has waned and their forces have integrated nonwhite officers. It may have been replicated in foreign municipalities, as in London policing of Caribbean and South Asian populations, and Paris policing of North Africans in the *banlieues*. Racial terror creates enormous complications for any ordinary theory of what American police do, for it carves a fundamental division between the experience of African American and non–African American citizens and the expectations they have of police.

I WOULD LIKE TO ADD another essential function of police: being seen.

If you want sometime to sympathize with police, watch young ones when they don't know they're being observed. The young cop stands on a corner, squinting in bright winter sun. Pedestrians approach from every side: they ask questions, ask for directions, talk without introduction, boring him, because he is part of the street like a stop sign. Or, as one does with a stop sign, they ignore and veer around him (sometimes deliberately, pointedly, despising him for his uniform).

You can see how hard it must be to ready a face for each of these people that will look authoritative rather than deferential. Between encounters, you can watch the front fall, strained by all these obligations. That is why our comic picture of a moment of rest for the harried policeman requires him to take off his patrolman's hat and wipe the perspiration from his face, as if smoothing down the instrument that's put to such exhausting work.

The basic ambition of a policeman is to ceaselessly project force, stolidity, seriousness, intimidation. But that's impossible. Policing contains daily humiliations at each inevitable failure of the policeman's front. The uniform itself, the badge in its widest sense, with the luster of all shields meant to dazzle, is meant to maintain this front regardless of the individual inside. But the uniform can never succeed. You would need Robocop. There is something in the cladness of police, their preoccupation with holding the uniform together, that makes us aware of all their armor's shortcomings, or inspires one to imagine these human beings naked, their uniforms taken away. The traditional English name for the mana with which police are invested is surely awe. Erving Goffman, in his famous conceptualizations of front, face, and performance, recalled Kurt Riezler's point that the inevitable obverse of awe is shame.

The coupling of awe and shame among police comes out in our awareness of police symmetry and asymmetry. A shield is worn on the peak of the hat, while a second one covers the heart. The gun descends from one side of the utility belt, and, traditionally, the nightstick hangs from the other. Sometimes a flashlight substitutes. Looking at individual police, they almost always seem lopsided. The belt pulls down on one side. The blouse comes undone. They are constantly hiking up their pants. The regulation shoes are the same as those of nurses, waiters, and mail carriers. Heaviness gathers at the waist, in a sedentary, slow, caloric job. There is something in police that droops.

The symbol of police in this dimension in North America is the donut. The donut is equivocal. It is not loved as apple pie is. It has no national standing as apple pie does. It has a local message only. Donuts, like other deep-fried delicacies, do not travel well.

Yet donuts have our rueful affection. Really, it is the pursuit of coffee that drives police to donut shops. Donuts confirm what they will not admit with their badge and gun, that they are the ones who must be awake all the time, in public, in the extremely boring job of sitting in a place, either to assure passersby and the public that they *are* sitting there, watching, or to ensure that other people *don't* sit there. So they are living traffic cones. Traffic cones, too, would drink coffee and eat donuts to stay awake.

Most surprising, perhaps, is that to spend time looking at police is to see that the law is not a true resource for them. A rationale, yes, but a thin one. Police lack law. I hadn't noticed this until I really started watching them, thinking about what I saw, reading research done on them. The original television version of *Law & Order* split each episode into two parts. First, policing; second, courtroom proceedings. It took me years to notice that the title was backward. Police are order. This explains the police perception of, and anathema toward, any symbol of disorder or mess. In their daily practice, police pledge at every level to clean up dirt. The cliché from Mary Douglas's *Purity and Danger*, her cross-cultural study of the constitution of dirt and taboo, holds up here: What we call dirt is only "matter out of place."

It is always hard to remind or convince police that their stated loyalty is to the Constitution. It's not their fault, really, so much as it is the fault of a municipal organization of authority that keeps legal and political thinking at a level "above their pay grade." A bad consequence is that it's quite difficult to make police feel responsible for civil rights violations or unjust laws, since rights and the law of the polity are not theirs to know or decide. The police reformer David Harris describes the experience of a friend in the Oakland Police Department that crystallizes a general truth:

> In 2001, Captain Ron Davis, a twenty-year veteran ... led an in-service training session on racial profiling. ... Davis began by asking the assembled officers a simple question: "What is your job?" ... "What I want to know," he asked, "is, what is your mission, and the mission of your department? To what are you dedicating your time, day after day?"

Most of the answers were variations on "fighting crime": "Catching bad guys"; "Getting criminals off the street"; "Keeping the streets safe from predators"; "Chasing crooks"; "Taking down the guys that need to be taken down"; "Responding to 911 emergencies"; "Helping the department achieve its goals"; "Carrying out the chief's orders." ... Then he asked, "What does your oath say? When you graduated from the academy and became a cop, you all raised your hand and took an oath. What did you swear to do?" ... Silence. ... Eventually, an officer gave Davis the answer he sought: "We swear to uphold the law and the Constitution." Another officer spoke up. "Well, sure, that's the oath," he said, "but everyone knows what this job is really about."

I'm not sure anybody knows. Not us, but also not police themselves, not politicians, and not political theorists.

PART OF THE REASON police seem at present unreformable is that they have no intelligible place in the philosophy of democracy. It's possible they never have. When our theories of democracy took shape, police as we know them were a minor tertiary agency and an afterthought. If police don't take stock of the Constitution, I sometimes wonder, might it be because our Constitution can't conceive of them?

Police as a word and concept exists in Europe from the 15th and 16th centuries forward, as a word for the administrative state management of population and territory—*Polizeiwissenschaft*, for the incipient German bureaucracies. Modern Anglo-American police forces date to the urban development of private hired watchmen and guards for merchant or guild-professional spaces. Benjamin Franklin helped reorganize and rationalize one such force in Philadelphia before the American Revolution, as he relates in his *Autobiography*. The major urban institutionalization of police occurred in London under Robert Peel in 1829 in the Metropolitan Police Department (yielding officers nicknamed "bobbies," for their founder, and the traditional abbreviation for the department, "the Met").

This metropolitan form of police organization marked a dividing line with the tradition in Europe. On the Continent, crown monarchs had kept even the prosaic functions of policing tied to the sovereign. This meant that the European tradition, emanating from France, wove military power, spying, and control of the poor in with urban regulation and penal justice. First abolished by the Revolution, police surveillance was reconstituted a decade later under Napoleon. In *Discipline and Punish*, Foucault described the position of European police with the 1768 motto of Vattel: "'By means of a wise police, the sovereign accustoms the people to order and obedience.'"

Police and *policy* are cognate: our liberal political tradition has focused on the second. The most revealing juncture in classical liberalism for police theory may come in a rare discussion from Adam Smith, in the 1763 lecture given the title "Of Police." For Smith, what matters to civil government as "police" only possesses sufficient dignity when it speaks to what we would call economic policy. The constabulary is acknowledged as a necessity for its execution of the criminal law but is beneath political notice:

> Police is the second general division of jurisprudence. The name is French, and is originally derived from the Greek πολιτεία [*politeia*], which properly signified the policey of civil government, but now it only means the regulation of the inferiour parts of government, viz. cleanliness, security, and cheapness or plenty. The two former, to witt, the proper method of carrying dirt from the streets, and the execution of justice, so far as it regards regulations for preventing crimes or the method of keeping a city guard, tho' usefull, are too mean to be considered in a general discourse of this kind.

"The proper method of carrying dirt from the streets" and "the method of keeping a city guard": twin practicalities.

Liberal and social contract theories of democracy—those that begin from Hobbes and Locke and that form the official philosophical background to the American Republic that was constituted in 1787—do have a central place for punishment, but not for police. This is perhaps because, on a strong version of contract theory, police ought not to exist. How could democratic agreement fail to be self-enforcing in its daily practice if the agreement is real, sustained by each individual's consent? Social-contract theory does include the discouragement and rectification of error after definite breaches of the contract, as punishment will address the convicted wrongdoer who either gave in to the temptation of self-interest or was perverted to it by some personal flaw. But the right agency for requital is penal law. Crime and punishment belong to judicial proceedings and courts, where the cause can be unfolded after the fact. There is no location alongside or outside the citizens and their contract for a supplementary force or additional locus of authority and violence, for mediation or interruption. There is no place for any intervening agency with political standing, only as a kind of collector or picker-upper of persons—hence, an agency very much like that of a trash picker or one who carries dirt from the streets, as Smith proposed.

With the growth of the role of police in democratic societies, a theory of their presence and place in government has simply not emerged in proportion to their power and variable function. The only really worthwhile thing we have is empirical description, from the late 20th-century field of police sociology—and this research has been most useful in dispelling illusions, not creating comprehensive philosophy. An impressive number of practical things have been studied and yielded surprising findings on such topics as work hours, organization, decision making, dramaturgy, constituencies, professional attitudes, and differential application of the law to people of different identities and situations. The radical theorist Mark Neocleous described the results in 2000:

> Both the "law and order" lobby and its Left critics have failed to take on board the implications of a mass of research on the police. . . . The overwhelming majority of calls for police assistance are "service" rather than crime related: in an average year only 15 to 20 percent of all the calls to the police are about crime, and what is initially reported by the police as a crime is often found to be not a crime by the responding police officer. Studies have shown that less than a third of time spent on duty is on crime-related work; that approximately eight out of ten incidents handled by patrols by a range of different police departments are regarded by the police themselves as non-criminal matters; that the percentage of police effort devoted to traditional criminal law matters probably does not exceed 10 percent; that as little as 6 percent of a patrol officer's time is spent on incidents finally defined as "criminal"; and that only a very small number of criminal offenses are discovered by the police themselves. Moreover, most of the time the police do not use the criminal law to restore order. In the USA police officers make an average of one arrest every two weeks; one study found that among 156 officers assigned to a high-crime area of New York City, 40 per cent did not make a single felony arrest in a year.

The disillusioning thrust of this work on the usual mandate for police—stopping crime—had already been distilled forty years ago by the most famous and influential sociologist of police, Egon Bittner. As he put it in 1974: "When one looks at what policemen actually do, one finds that criminal law enforcement is something that most of them do with the frequency located somewhere between virtually never and very rarely." The work that followed from this knowledge, also identified with Bittner, inscribed this ironic mode in the theory itself. What even the most original sociology of police seems to show, again and again, is that police are paradoxical and their strictures unworkable. They don't fit philosophically. As a stopgap profession poised between other philosophically grounded institutions, police are "impossible." Perhaps police ought not to exist, thinking theoretically, since their behavior is inadequately supported by the democratic social order's explicit justifications. Yet they must exist, practically—despite their errors—precisely because they have proved themselves in democracy as both "first responders" and a "last resort," a mobilization of nondefinition and nonfixity for all sorts of situations: the agency thrown at anything in society that can't be accommodated or that we don't want to see. Bittner's formulation haunts the field as the only really original and lasting philosophical contribution to our understanding of what police are:

> I propose to explain the function of police by drawing attention to what their existence makes available in society that, all things being equal, would not be otherwise available. . . .

> My thesis is that police are empowered and required to impose or, as the case may be, coerce a provisional solution upon emergent problems without having to brook or defer to opposition of any kind, and that further, their competence to intervene extends to every kind of emergency, without any exceptions whatsoever.

And that's all they are—that's their essence. "The assessment whether the service the police are uniquely competent to provide is on balance desirable or not, in terms of, let us say, the aspirations of a democratic polity, is beyond the scope of the argument," Bittner adds drily.

The key term from his definition may well be "impose," or "coerce"—and the sine qua non for Bittner's picture of police becomes availability of force (or even violence).

Surprisingly, the damning body of Bittner's work has been embraced by police chiefs, perhaps because it furnishes executives with the only plausible apology in the face of continual criticism. One major professional association now gives out its annual Egon Bittner Award—not ironically, but in earnest—to a municipal chief who has survived more than fifteen years of service.

IMAGINE WE DID WANT to find the place of police in a democratic polity. What version of their role can be desirable for democracy?

One genuinely useful function of police is the way they lift accidents, events, and gatherings into vision. Police make things visible. They enhance situations, but no one mistakes them for the main show. The officers are a blue aniline dye poured into channels of society, down alleyways and interstates, sketching in blueprint the lines of public space, how we distribute assembly, how we distribute dispersion, how we distribute crime, how we distribute safety. One knows to walk toward where police are standing, where they mark the significance of something else: a parade, a concert, a demonstration, or an arrest, an abuse, an accident. One can go to enjoy them—to watch their offer of theater and ritual to daily occurrences, as they establish a space of eventfulness—or to watchdog them, to make sure that their handling of people can't occur invisibly and unaccounted for.

Secrecy by police in any public place always identifies them as suspect. Yet police departments hold tightly to their capacities for secrecy and claim them to be necessary for their heroic function of detection and investigation. Insofar as detection of crime is what police *wish* their job were about, police are likely always to strain for greater secrecy and silence.

Where sight disappears, in the paddy wagon and the police station, abuse becomes possible. (And indeed these are the sorts of places, along with jails, that a democratic police might seek to eradicate or open up.) One knows the hush that occurs in a crowd when an arrestee disappears into the closed, windowless wagon; the citizen has temporarily disappeared from the democratic public (until arraignment, the space of salvation by habeas corpus—then one looks for marks on the face, marks on the wrists and the body, from abuse). This is one of those gaps into which citizens fall where democracy can disappear.

Yet the real rival of sight is not just secrecy but touch, which registers itself only between bodies that know what has actually been done but can't prove it by other means. Police possess touch; citizens should possess sight. A question is why a third element that could stand between sight and touch doesn't come much more to the fore: talk. Talk is the actual basis of a democracy. It is the specifically democratic dimension of human relations. It restores the assurance of neighborliness. Talk is what police mostly do in encountering the public. Yet one doesn't think of police as talkers and listeners first, but as bullies. What happens when citizens and police talk in the fateful encounter? *How* do they talk? And if they don't talk, why not?

SUPPOSE WE SAY THIS: Police are negotiators, but without access to contract, law, or eloquence. Their medium is not law. They do not always use memorable or wholly coherent words. Usually they confront situations of conflict they did not cause, but which they are required to enter as third parties. There, they become deliberately distracting, grandstanding observers, turning the attention of other parties away from each other and toward themselves.

When you look at them this way, focusing on the middle range between space-holding inaction and violent attack, you can see how negotiating is actually what the police do unendingly, habitually—but unfamiliarly, because in some way they refuse to recognize or care about the original goals of the relevant parties. They bring a separate set of criteria to bear, and not always an appealing one. Is this chargeable? Should this person be removed or transported temporarily? How soon can I leave, and how do I scare these citizens a bit so they won't come into conflict again and police won't need to come back? Police negotiate without a unitary reference or goal—other than to end the necessity for their being present, unless they're in a location they want to forbid the use of to others. And they are always asking themselves a separate question, of whether to lift a person out of the horizontal conflict and into the vertical mechanism of criminal justice—a process they will not ultimately be responsible for, and which they won't have to enter into themselves.

Even minor infractions and victimless crimes become negotiations between cop and citizen over the reach of a law that stands beyond both of them. Here the negotiated outcome may be a "warning": "OK, I'm going to let you go with a warning." A warning is ostensibly a name for something official. Yet the "warning" is not known to the statute book. It does not exist as a juridical category. It is one of the major categories of police thinking, and one that we might want to preserve rather than object to for its arbitrariness or uneven application. It is a key moment when police, without breaking "front" or admitting deficiency, acknowledge that a negotiation has been in some sense won by the citizen.

LET'S MAKE THE BEST CASE for police: police exist so we can see them on the corner or the subway platform, so that we know, when we move in public, that no other person can take from us unseen, to rob us or molest us without defense. Police exist sometimes just to mark a lane closure (by standing in it) or road construction (by standing in front of it) or a town fair (by standing at its entrance). They announce eventfulness, and in some way their mere presence stands against danger.

Of course we feel different if we think the danger they might think they see is us. Or if we resemble their idea of obstruction, or of a notable event. When police eye African Americans, harass African Americans, obstruct the movements of African Americans, and wind up drawing their guns and murdering African Americans—which even in the 21st century they do with regularity, no matter the police department or region of the United States—it's first because America still sees racially. Kidnapping an African labor force to build the country is still the country's unrepented sin, concomitant with the annihilation of Native Americans. The mad but ingenious mechanism of coding the difference between free and slave by "color," not by an actual spectrum of tans but "white" and "black"—as metaphysical as day and night, bright and dark, noble and base—still lingers. Police, as votaries of sight and seeing, sustain this way of looking at every citizen of recognizable African ancestry.

What differentiates a place that seems clean, orderly, and peaceful, from the same location with items out of place, mixed up, confusing, noisy, and conflictual, isn't just aesthetic norms in the neighborhoods police come from, but what they think that "we" want, by how "the public" sees. But who are we? The police sociologist Peter K. Manning, one of the best ethnographers of police behavior, has strongly made the point that one thing police tacitly depend on most is how they think their client citizens view them as they undertake patrols and arrests. Yet many of the formalizations they use to imagine such "law-abiding citizens," "good people," "the public," as they rigidly enact an absent standard of order, alienate them from the actual citizenry. The idea about which police possess the least clarity is what "good people" want and how we want to be treated.

Violence, too, is given to police as a technique they alone can use in the service of preserving the general nonviolence of society, wherein citizens need never use violence legitimately against one another—they route it through police, so to speak. But this formal device, too, winds up defining police by their application of violence.

Police are left to instigate violence as a means of resolving any social deadlock, to add violence to situations they feel to be ambiguous. But if we can really see, and see through, police, we may see that this becomes a way of injecting *testing* violence into the heart of society in a public way. Police test what violence we, as citizens, will allow, and against whom. Small comfort, perhaps, since there is no guarantee that we will oppose the wicked things that police may show us. Our neighbors may support that wickedness. We may have no idea how to fix it. Still, police violence differs from forms of violence and domination that have no visible presence or public check. The police measure out in public what the society will tolerate, even to our shame. +

> The police were designed to respond to citizen demands and requirements for service as much because this represented prevention or deterrence of the sources of crime as because the police were intended to act symbolically as one citizen would to another in time of need. The symbolic centrality of police action as standing for the collective concern of people, one for another, cannot and should not be underestimated. Law has grown up as a means of formalizing the conditions under which the police *must* act and *cannot* act but does not provide the basis on which they do or should act.

COSME DEL ROSARIO-BELL,
ELIAS RODRIQUES, DOREEN ST. FÉLIX,
AND DAYNA TORTORICI
Hands Up

The following conversation took place on Sunday, November 23, 2014, in response to the murders of 28-year-old Akai Gurley, in New York, and 12-year-old Tamir Rice, in Cleveland. The following week, a grand jury in Ferguson, Missouri, decided not to indict officer Darren Wilson for the murder of 18-year-old Michael Brown.

Akai Gurley, Omnipresence, Gentrification

COSME DEL ROSARIO-BELL: I assume you heard about this guy who got shot on Thursday night, Akai Gurley. He and his girlfriend are leaving her apartment in a project in East New York called the Pink Houses, and the elevator doesn't work. So they take the stairs. At the same time that he's about to enter the poorly lit stairwell, two rookie cops are doing what's called a vertical patrol. This entails going to the top of a project-housing building and working their way down via the staircase—and one of the cops was doing it with his gun drawn and flashlight out. When one cop saw a shadow move on the landing below, he shot immediately and hit Gurley in the chest. Who knows why, but the cops shot this dude and then left.

DAYNA TORTORICI: Police Commissioner Bratton used the quick reflex as an excuse. Like it was an accident—he used the phrase "accidental discharge"—because there was no verbal exchange.

ELIAS RODRIQUES: But that's what safeties are for! That's why you have a safety on a gun! You don't pull the safety off until you're ready to shoot someone!

DOREEN ST. FÉLIX: There's also the whole problem of the practice of vertical patrol in the first place. These cops have their weapons drawn when they're going down the staircase.

DEL ROSARIO-BELL: According to Bratton, there's no official protocol on when you're allowed to patrol with your gun out. It's up to the discretion of the cop. But at the same time, he implied that the cop would need to have reasonable cause to have his gun out—there would need to be a reasonable expectation of danger. But still, Bratton's press conference was so strange. He kept saying "accidental discharge."

ST. FÉLIX: Akai Gurley went around a corner in a way that made this policeman nervous. Fifteen years ago, Amadou Diallo pulled out his wallet and the cop saw a phantom Negro weapon.

DEL ROSARIO-BELL: I think that the term *furtive movement* was created to explain why white people are shooting black men. What does that even mean? Why would you even need a term like *furtive movement* to insert into police lingo? It implies a small or sly, threatening movement. So—anything.

ST. FÉLIX: Yes. That slippage is institutionalized even in case law, where probable cause is defined as more than a suspicion but less than certainty. Time and again we find that probable cause is grounded in action closer to a whim or a hunch.

This is part of a larger, structural conversation about racialized housing and segregation in New York City. One reason I think white people might feel they can't comment on police brutality is because they don't see it on the daily basis on which it occurs. Because they don't live in these neighborhoods, it's invisible to them. The only apparent reason the police come to these neighborhoods is to patrol and protect, but if you study the chronology of how a lot of these shootings take place, it's totally the other way around: black men and women are just walking around, and they're perceived as being dangerous by the police, and that's when the "interaction"—to speak like Bratton—takes place. Brutal policing happens casually. It's a lot more mundane than media theater around certain fatal policing instances makes it seem.

DEL ROSARIO-BELL: In St. Louis, the week before the young leaders in Ferguson made a national call for outside support, this guy, Vonderrit Myers, was in a pretty nice St. Louis neighborhood, Shaw. He bought a sandwich and was walking down the block with his friends when an off-duty cop saw him and decided, "These guys look dangerous, I'm gonna follow them." So they ran, because they were being followed by some random dude in a car. He was shot eight times, six in the back of the legs. Seventeen shots total were fired. The officer said Myers was shooting at him. Even if he had a gun, that situation was created by a cop deciding to escalate the situation by hunting them down.

TORTORICI: The police bring violence to nonviolent situations for reasons that are not logical. People are just being singled out and harassed.

RODRIQUES: And what is the point? To what end? What the fuck do you gain from doing this?

DEL ROSARIO-BELL: I guess what's implied is that these spaces, these public black spaces, are violent—to say nothing of how violence is created by state-sanctioned racism, state-sanctioned white-supremacist cordoning off of poor and black folk in areas of poor opportunity. All of the details of the Akai Gurley killing were evidence of how the state just don't give a fuck about poor black people. Their housing: "We're not going to fix the lights in their building because, fuck it, they don't pay any money for it. We are not going to send experienced cops to protect them because, fuck it, we don't actually care if we are actually protecting them. We're not protecting them, we're policing them." Even when Bratton was saying it, it didn't make any sense. He was like, "Well, we need to send cops to patrol violence in 'high-impact zones.'" Then why are you sending two dudes who just left the academy eighteen months ago?

RODRIQUES: These places are a state blind spot: no one has to give a shit because for the most part no one is seeing it. It would be a different thing if the police stopped and shot a dude walking through Grand Central. But so much of this happens in this New York blind spot, where people—and by people I really mean people whose voices are, let's say, heard, or have the power to be heard—don't see or interact with them. Which is not to make some naive claim that if everyone saw this violence everyone would want to stop it. I know better; that's not how people work.

ST. FÉLIX: We've been talking about hiding, visibility, lighting, and illumination . . . Um, "Omnipresence," I don't know if you have heard about it.

Everyone laughs.

DEL ROSARIO-BELL: Motherfuckers have more lights outside of the project than in the stairwell!

ST. FÉLIX: Exactly, exactly. And so . . .

TORTORICI: Wait, can you explain what Omnipresence is?

ST. FÉLIX: Omnipresence is a new iteration of a centuries-old system of policing in which police officers are set up in high-crime areas to be omnipresent, to surveil. To be sentinels. I think one part of Omnipresence is that police stand on corners 24-7, just being there, and then another thing is having lights shine in from the outside of the housing project. They're very bright during the night, and you can't sleep because these floodlights are entering your bedroom, entering your bathroom. And they're also just really loud, because the generators set up to keep them running hum through the night.

DEL ROSARIO-BELL: Nobody's investing money to put in good, unobtrusive lighting in public housing so that people can walk through the projects without being afraid. No, it's: Put up these big-ass, loud, super-bright NYPD-branded lights, and then put a cop car on every other block, with the lights flashing, plus cops on foot.

ST. FÉLIX: This is why we fail if we say that police brutality is a black issue. Because the NYPD's ability to do these things is implicitly—they never say it, but it is—to protect whiteness. So if you are policing blackness, the policing doesn't occur in a vacuum. You're doing it because black people are considered dangerous to white people.

Take gentrification. It's not a coincidence that stop-and-frisk numbers went up super, super high in the late '90s to the '00s, as a lot of out-of-staters started moving into communities on the border of the projects. You move into Bed-Stuy, but a couple blocks down there's Marcy Houses. The migration of white people to typically urban black areas tends to increase police presence, and therefore brutality, on the borders, all in the name of increasing safety for ostensibly white residents. Gentrification is really violent, and yet is described in mostly passive ways ... If we think about policing as traumatic—as literal removal of black people from their homes, making them feel that their homes are never truly their homes, that they are always a place to be policed—I think that's where we might see that white communities are complicit in police brutality and in the new methods that are being used.

RODRIQUES: Well, newish. Making black people feel that they are always being policed is not uncommon, just to think even of police forces post–Fugitive Slave Act of 1850, right? Maybe it's just because I am teaching Harriet Ann Jacobs's *Incidents in the Life of a Slave Girl*: there's one chapter where she's talking about her brother who's trying to escape slavery and how he's just looking around, constantly worried that wherever he goes, he'll see, somewhere, a sign with his face on it saying ESCAPED SLAVE. Since the Fugitive Slave Act had passed, there was nowhere that was safe for him. Or for freed black men, for that matter.

Copwatch, the Panthers

DEL ROSARIO-BELL: I'm part of an organization called Copwatch, which is a volunteer group that watches and films police patrols. On the one hand it's very direct and very hands-on, which feels really good. So you're out, you're patrolling, doing what cops do, except against the cops. When people see you and recognize what you're doing, they're like, "That's what's up. We're glad you're out here." Visibility is really powerful. But at the same time it's the most passive active thing you could possibly do. We roll up to stops and do as much as possible to not do anything that will actually do something.

RODRIQUES: What would be a more active act you could do?

DEL ROSARIO-BELL: Like putting hands on these cops, physically stopping these cops? Actually protecting people. Because all we can do is film it, maybe try to give whoever is involved some tips. For example: "You don't have to answer that question." But you can get in trouble for giving people advice and information, so a lot of the time we'll be like [*speaking loudly*], "Hey, Elias, does that guy have to answer that question?" And you'd be like, "No, I don't think he does! He doesn't have to answer that question." Because overstepping that boundary can land you in jail. Like it did me!

TORTORICI: What happened?

DEL ROSARIO-BELL: It was completely innocuous. So we approach a traffic checkpoint on 145th Street in Harlem, coming across the 145th Street Bridge from the Bronx into Manhattan. The cops are randomly pulling people over—checking their license, checking their registration—and they have like four, five cars lined up at a time. So we go up and start filming, and the cops say, "You gotta go down to the end of the block." We're on a public sidewalk, so we basically say, "No. We're not gonna leave." It was very quick: a few minutes of back-and-forth, and they arrested us. It was fairly routine, and it wasn't too violent; we did everything we trained ourselves to do. And we got arrested.

ST. FÉLIX: Makes me think of the surveillance state. In videotaping the cops, you're sort of flipping the relationship of who watches whom. But that reversal can only happen around the type of policing that's visible on the street. I'm thinking of how surveillance never seems to be in service of protecting black people, especially black women; the intentional lack of policing around issues that affect black women is instrumentalized through police brutality.

For example, two black girls, teenagers, were found hog-tied on the side of the highway in Florida this past September, and the police search for their killers, not to mention the country's attention, has been pitiful. Oklahoma police officer Daniel Holtzclaw is a serial rapist who attacked black women in his custody for years unchecked. Forty percent of the people who are missing in America are people of color, and of that percentage, which doesn't account for unreported cases, black women constitute the majority. Sixty-four thousand black women and girls have been reported missing since 2010.

About a month ago, Carlesha Freeland-Gaither was kidnapped in Philadelphia. She happened to be walking through a wealthy white neighborhood, which was next to a "good" high school, and so the kidnapping was caught on the school's security camera. She was found within twenty-four hours. I remember, I was on Twitter a lot—I mean, I am always on Twitter—and in that moment a lot of the black feminists I follow thought, "Thank God she was walking by this particular high school and not the high school in the ghetto," because that high school isn't outfitted with those cameras. Nobody would even have known that she was missing, let alone would she be found. Some of the violence that is enacted on black women—I will speak for myself as a black woman—by the police is actually their lack of policing.

TORTORICI: Negligence.

DEL ROSARIO-BELL: I don't know about this particular situation, but I don't like the word negligence. It's almost like an "oops." These are not mistakes, these are decisions. Whenever I walk by projects I think, "Yo, this is punishment." It's not just that city planners tried to do some social good and messed up and kind of forgot about it. No, they're letting housing projects turn into these violent, bad places to live. That is a decision. Somebody is deciding to cut funding, someone is deciding to cut food stamps.

The system isn't broken, it is working exactly as intended. Even if that is not completely correct, I am at that point. I am not here for any fucking reformist fucking bullshit—"Nah, we just need to pass a bill, we just need to outfit all cops with body cameras."

TORTORICI: I hear that. At the same time, I get frustrated whenever I hear white male radicals make that argument, "Revolution or nothing." I think: You can say that because you feel so safe! This is about safety for people. I think it's pretty revolutionary to demand safety.

It's also crazy to me that people are discouraged, even in casual conversation with friends, from expressing what they don't like about something unless they propose a solution. As if you were having an argument over what to eat for dinner: "If we're not having chicken, what do you want to make?"

DEL ROSARIO-BELL: As if the chicken that you don't like isn't a product of hundreds of years of dedicated and deliberate work by white supremacists! And you then have to be like, "Oh, I have the perfect recipe for this turkey!" Like one person is supposed to have a ready alternative to something that has been created and re-created, and reinscribed and remade, over and over again.

TORTORICI: But then when people do have solutions, they are branded as terrorists. If you read the Black Panther Ten-Point Program from 1966, number seven is "An Immediate End to Police Brutality and Murder of Black People," and the right to self-defense against police violence. Like Copwatch with guns, with interception.

DEL ROSARIO-BELL: Copwatch does come from that legacy, of Huey P. Newton going around in his neighborhood with an unloaded shotgun and a law book. The Panthers would roll around their hood, with an unloaded shotgun and a law book, and come across police interactions, flip to a page, and speak up. Saying, "Nope. They can't do that!"

TORTORICI: Which makes sense, since the onus is on citizens to know their rights. Cops don't obey the law. But also, speaking of "terrorists," the fact that last year, in 2013, Assata Shakur became the first woman on the FBI's top ten most-wanted-terrorists list. She's living in Cuba under political asylum, but the FBI raised the bounty, basically, on her head, to $2 million. Anybody can go kidnap her, a former political prisoner, or kill her, for $2 million.

DEL ROSARIO-BELL: Modern day, modern day . . .

TORTORICI: Fugitive Slave Act? Kinda, yeah.

DEL ROSARIO-BELL: Also: How do you expect black men to have the answer to how to replace an entire system that is oppressing them and their sisters, when very obviously this system is so ingrained in them that they're policing people on the streets themselves?

Black Boys Can't Be Black Boys

ST. FÉLIX: Last Saturday, a black boy, a child, Tamir Rice, 12 years old, was killed in Cleveland. He had an airsoft gun. The person who called 911 said twice: "I think this person's gun is probably fake." I don't know why, if you thought the gun is fake, you would call 911. But at any rate the police shot him twice in the stomach, and he died this morning. Even me, I had been naively operating under the assumption that a 12-year-old is almost unilaterally seen as a child, a preadolescent. Yet he was already being boxed into the "suspicious black male" narrative. I think if we're going to chip away and get to the specific communities that are at risk by police brutality, we're talking specifically about youth, we're talking about kids. Michael Brown was 18. Vonderrit Myers was 18. John Crawford was 22, I think.

DEL ROSARIO-BELL: Ramarley Graham was 18.

ST. FÉLIX: Right. And so what I experience as someone who talks a lot to activists within the black community is a generational difference. When black people make it, by the grace of God, past the age of 25, they do whatever they do, they reach their middle-life stage where they forget what it's like to be a teenager. So many illegal activities are sanctioned when we think about teenager-dom. You smoke weed.

RODRIQUES: Drink underage.

ST. FÉLIX: Exactly. Because you're a teenager and you're not supposed to be making rational decisions. But then, how does that—

DEL ROSARIO-BELL: Get thrown out the window?

ST. FÉLIX: Yeah! That tacit, "Oh, you're free, you're doing your own thing."

DEL ROSARIO-BELL: "Kids!"

TORTORICI: "Boys will be boys!"

ST. FÉLIX: But black boys can't be black boys! NPR had this barbershop series a couple of years ago with black men looking back—they were in their forties—and they were like, "Damn, all these things my mother and my father told me to do in the presence of whiteness and police to keep myself alive . . ." This expectation of how black teenagers should behave and how they should comport their bodies is untenable.

RODRIQUES: I think about how impulsive I was as a kid, yet I was expected to act like a calm, grown-ass man. If I thought someone was going to threaten me, I might run, you know? I'm fucking worried, I'm a kid, I don't know what's going on. I don't take that long to think about things because I'm not very calm. I'm 14 or 15, I make irrational or dumb decisions. In the face of fear, I only become more irrational. And I should be allowed to be unreasonable. I shouldn't be worried that this might result in my death. When I was growing up, people said, "You shouldn't run from the cops, you might get shot in the back." It's true, but if I am a 14-year-old and I think that I'm fast and I'm worried that I'm going to die, I'm just going to bolt.

DEL ROSARIO-BELL: Black youth are always being seen as irrational and wild, but if you imagine how intelligent you have to be to navigate, not only your personality and what you say but your body in these different spaces . . . when you're with your friends, you have to act a certain way so you don't get punked. When you're in front of white people, you have to act a certain way so that they don't think you're violent or threatening. The amount of social and physical intelligence that a 14-year-old is required to have is paralyzing and incredible in the worst way.

Just thinking of myself growing up: I have a white mom, and she was kind of oblivious to this stuff, which meant I never had "the talk"—the talk that black mothers have with their children about how to not get killed by cops. And so I was sort of blissfully unaware of how dangerous things were for me. I guess I had other things going for me—being light skinned, going to a diverse school—but I'm thinking now, wow. I was saved from so much of that preemptive policing, just because my mom didn't know what the fuck was going on. I remember being able to consider myself as a person and as a body very freely as a kid, without these constraints, and that's because my mom was oblivious and my dad was being a present-but-not-present dad. A lot of kids don't get that.

ST. FÉLIX: This touches on unspoken intentions of respectability politics, on the ways you're taught to choreograph your innocence to the outside, to make your body seem not guilty, and how that can also be read as assuming stereotypically white affectations. It's an assurance that says, "Listen, I'm more like you than I am like other black people," and explicitly does not say, "I am like blackness."

Turning 14 was critical for me in terms of performing this choreography, if subconsciously, because I got a scholarship to go to a fancy school on the Upper East Side. I don't think I'd ever been past Times Square before then—I'm from Canarsie. It's only now, looking back eight years later, that I realize that I was aggressively stopped and frisked, sometimes sexually harassed, all the time by the police, and that was probably because my attempt to choreograph innocence seemed suspect to them. How twisted, because my parents taught me that to protect myself I had to know how to play white.

Playing white is like when animals play dead. The performance is meant to trick your predators into thinking you're not prey. But it doesn't trick, and nothing works. And knowing how to play white meant I didn't have the knowledge to know what was even happening to me by the police. When I turned 21 last year and was protesting Ray Kelly at my school, then I realized, "Shit! This thing was happening to me."

RODRIQUES: I don't know what it would mean to be safe and black. I don't mean "to be safe" in the way of "nonthreatening to other people," I mean "safe from possible violence." My image of safe is white. I think of a nice, white family in the suburbs. And I say this as somebody who frequently claims to be really happy that he is black. At the same time I don't know if I will ever stop feeling unsafe. I don't know if I can feel safe and be black.

ST. FÉLIX: Sometimes I find myself shielding myself with white bodies to feel safe. I have friends of all different groups of people, but I experience a surfeit of body creativity, of doing whatever I want with my body, if I'm surrounded by white girls. When I mean safety, I also mean freedom of expression. It's not just about not being seen as dangerous—it's about being seen as a happy person, someone who can be approached, and someone who can be quirky. Quirk is the fullest reckless freedom white people traffic in . . . It's the quirky-industrial complex.

Quirkiness is white bodies expressing the immense space the state and culture carves out for them to be free and safe. Safety is always at the expense of policing black bodies, because again, neither whiteness nor blackness exists in a vacuum. If quirkiness is eccentricity or white-girl-weird, then it's about making new movements, tics—and they can be affectations—that are peculiar but never seen as threatening. Black people are often forced to keep making old movements, in our bodies, speech, the way we live, because the space for whiteness to see us as safe if we're unpredictable barely exists.

It is not just a matter of you being dangerous, it's that that potential is rarely seen in white bodies. How does that affect me and the way that I comport myself? Am I limiting my creativity?

RODRIQUES: In relation to the freedom one has when surrounded by white bodies, I have never been stopped and frisked while with somebody who is white. When I'm alone, there are all of these things that go through my mind. How do I present myself? How do I walk? Then, if I get stopped, I'm like, "Fuck, I fucked up and I wasn't looking unsketchy enough." You don't have to think about that when you are surrounded by these threat-diffusing factors.

TORTORICI: That's really intense, what you're describing—the sense that if you're stopped, you've failed yourself, you've failed your performance. It's not like, "Oh shit, I'm getting stopped." You almost forget why you are performing, and the failure to perform adequately feels like a personal failure.

Ferguson and the Art of Protest

TORTORICI: You went down to Ferguson last month. What happened when you were there?

DEL ROSARIO-BELL: Nothing too crazy. The cops were on their best behavior, given the previous months and the media presence on that particular weekend. But there were some showdowns with riot cops, for sure. A tank thing. Blatant intimidation by police toward regular folk. It was so tense! But then, you know, we were able to leave. It felt good, it felt terrifying, but those kids who are there every day, that's what they're dealing with. Though we are dealing with the same thing in New York, it's not different—that's what needs to be the common thread. Eric Garner, Mike Brown—it's a list, a list of people who need to be individually memorialized, sure, but we can't see their deaths as separate, specific incidents. They need to be seen together and given a collective importance.

The other thing is that in St. Louis, in Shaw, in Ferguson, the people on the front lines are kids. And they get it. They're putting their bodies on the line. People are so afraid to put their bodies on the line, and I understand! I don't want to die. But if there's anything to be taken away from the kids in Ferguson who are leading those protests, it's that they get it, they know they're at risk of dying, and they're going to do it anyway. And they're 16.

ST. FÉLIX: That's a radical mode of self-care. Not to say that people who aren't protesting aren't caring for themselves, but one of the ways that you can, when your life is under siege, is to go out against the threat.

Trauma is a huge effect of being a policed person, whether she is protesting against that policing or not. I mean, by the fact that she continues to live, she is protesting. But trauma isn't often talked about in public-health circles like this. Because you're still going to work, taking care of your kids, doing what you have to do, but you're still traumatized.

DEL ROSARIO-BELL: But then we also have to recognize that these communities are amazing at taking care of one another, in spite of being attacked from all sides. The fact that black bodies are facing trauma every day, and yet somehow people are still fighting and people are still living. It's sad that we have to be so good at celebrating, and it's sad that we have to be so good at taking care of one another, even when people say that we're not! But shout-out to acknowledging that even if Darren Wilson doesn't get indicted, people will keep figuring out ways to be OK in spite of the trauma that they face.

RODRIQUES: I think you're right. One of the things I think a lot about in moments like this is this classic Teaching Tolerance resource that says, "Don't always talk about the oppressed as victims. Teach that they are also agents, be positive and teach how they keep themselves and one another alive and give one another support."

DEL ROSARIO-BELL: When I was in Ferguson, some of the most amazing forms of protest we saw were these kids just partying at the police station, in front of the police station, chanting, freestyling. And then later these kids were doing the most incredible improvised avant-garde hip-hop performance pieces that were both memorializing the death of Mike Brown and obviously very cathartic. There's an awesome hip-hop artist collective in New York called Rebel Diaz that was in Ferguson that weekend; they brought their portable sound systems, and the kids who were there loved it. They were playing beats and these kids were just bugging out, only feet away from the front line of cops protecting the Ferguson Police Department.

At one point, in the dark, a bit down the road from the main crowd, the group of kids started freestyling about Mike Brown. Some of them laid on the street, laying bandannas over their faces as if they were all dead, while the others kept rapping . . . It was beautiful, and haunting, and really crazy—an impromptu, deep, amazing, and powerful celebration, memorializing and cathartic, directly in front of this stone-faced system. +

ENRIQUE MARTÍNEZ CELAYA, *THE MAP*. 2009, OIL AND WAX ON CANVAS, 66 × 72".
PRIVATE COLLECTION, LONDON, UNITED KINGDOM.

CONFIRMATION
Philip Connors

THE YEAR I TURNED 13, my first as a townie, I often withdrew into the realm of fantasy, as uprooted children will. In one of my recurring dream lives I became a local basketball legend, escaping the shadow of my father's hard-court heroics. In another I became fantastically rich, escaping forever the shame of my family's poverty. I found validation for both of these dreams in the attentions of one old man.

A basketball hoop stood on one end of the tennis courts in Currie, Minnesota—a railroad spur town, population 350, to which the railroad no longer ran—and I would shoot there for hours, practicing my midrange jumper and my crossover dribble in an effort to realize the more immediately attainable of my fantasies. It was nice to have a proper court on which to practice after the years I'd spent shooting at a netless rim hung on the side of a barn. On the farm I'd chased the ball all over the property, even—I should say especially—when I made a shot that would have swished; now there was not just a net on the rim but a chain-link fence around the court, which did a lot to make up for the fact of my family's downward mobility. Every time I went there, the old man across the street came out to watch.

I enjoyed the audience for several reasons, chief among them the Cadillac parked in his driveway. It was a real beauty, the newest model, creamy white and always polished to a gleam; I'd seen no other car like it in our part of the world. Of a gap-toothed codger with a rusty Ford Granada, I suppose I'd have been suspicious, but the aura surrounding that Cadillac lent the old man instant gravitas. I pretended I didn't notice he was there, sitting in his lawn chair, watching me, but every dribble between my legs or behind my back was meant to impress him. As I passed by on my way home he would call me over. He'd open a beer for himself and a Coca-Cola for me, and we'd sit with them in his yard, drinking and making small talk. He told stories about how he'd coached the boys' basketball team in the 1950s, back when the town had its own high school, and before he embarked on a banking career from which he was poised to retire any year. The school building had been turned into a mushroom farm—windows blacked out, security bars installed—which gave it the look of an institution where children were imprisoned and tortured.

Kind of ironic that the old school became a place to grow mushrooms, he said. Different product, same process: keep 'em in the dark and feed 'em full of shit.

He often said funny, irreverent things like that, one of the reasons I came to like him so much. Our town was touchy in inverse proportion to its size—the words "God's country" were often invoked with a shrill pride—and to hear a town elder talk shit, literal shit, about the place was a bracing shock. He endeared himself further by telling me that he wished he'd had a player like me, back when he'd been a coach. His praise buttressed my hope of one day playing college hoops. That possibility remained six years away, but I found time to dream of it daily. In my seventh-grade art class I drew versions of the Georgetown Bulldog, the Louisville Cardinal, nothing but the mascots of powerhouse schools. I wallpapered my bedroom in cutouts from *Sports Illustrated*: Dr. J, Magic Johnson, Andrew Toney, Larry Bird, all of them frozen in poses of balletic grace on the walls above me as I lulled myself toward sleep by lying in bed, lofting a ball toward the ceiling, trying to achieve the perfect backspin on my fingertip release. I was going to be a shooting guard, one of those stone-cold marksmen, utterly without conscience, who made their name bombing away from distance.

My father had been the high school player of the year in Lubbock, Texas, 1969, and my grandmother had made a scrapbook of newspaper clippings about every game he'd ever played from freshman year on. I often pulled this talisman from the hope chest in my parents' bedroom, awed by his numbers and the photos of a lithe white boy who could dunk and shoot the jumper both. As I held it in my hands I couldn't help but dream of the day when the local paper would write about me. My father always told me how I could have played better during C-squad games; he focused on the passes I hadn't thrown crisply enough, the shot I'd rushed when I should've taken my time. He thought our team was poorly coached and if he didn't tell me these things, I'd never learn. He always prefaced his critique by saying he wanted me to get better, but I wanted him to tell me, as so many others had, that I was already good.

When I stopped by after shooting hoops the old man always smiled at me, a smile that twinkled with the handiwork of the best dentistry money could buy. I'd given him a show of all my best moves, minus the defenders and the teammates with whom I'd have shared the court in an actual game, and he liked what he saw. He liked it so much he always gave me a $20 bill. At first I'd turn away, pretend I couldn't accept it; I was a country boy new to townie ways, but I was smart enough to know that it was unseemly to take his money without refusing it at least once. He would wait a while, then slip it in the pocket of my shorts with a tenderness I mistook for generosity.

You keep that to yourself, he said. If word gets out I'll have every kid in town knocking on my door. I have more money than I'll ever need. One thing about getting old, you realize friends are more important than money.

He gave my thigh a squeeze.

I think we could be friends, he said.

I began to stop by without an excuse. He would invite me into the kitchen, offer me a seat, and call his wife, a willowy woman with a Pall Mall voice and a nimbus of purple-tinted hair. In all the years I sat at her kitchen table I would never see her smile, but I knew she appreciated my visits because her eyebrows rose just a smidgen when she saw me. She allowed herself no other expression of delight.

While she prepared a snack for me, she'd say things about the old man, how he spent too much time at the bar downtown, or how he hadn't made himself a meal in thirty years. The old man, defenseless against the charges but defiant nonetheless, would then direct a comment at me about her subpar cooking or the better company offered him by the men who drank at the Legion Club. Eventually she'd retire to the living room and her rocking chair and cigarettes and crossword puzzles, and the old man would start in on stories about serving in the Marines during World War II. He'd been at the invasion of Iwo Jima, had seen things he would never forget—ghastly things, his buddies blown apart by machine-gun fire, men bleeding to death in the mud, crying like little girls. For a moment his eyes got real spooky. Then he leaned close to me and talked in a conspiratorial hush about the whore he'd met in the Philippines, how she was by far the most thrilling woman he'd ever known, despite the fact that she couldn't speak English.

She was fluent in the language of love, he whispered.

He laughed and winked at me. My face burned, and the rest of me felt twitchy, as if tickled by invisible hands.

OUR ENTANGLEMENT was already sort of weird, and would get much weirder, but its most peculiar feature was in place from the beginning, the sort of detail you could never get away with in a short story. I'd only gotten to know him because we'd been forced to move to town—and he was the man who'd forced our move to town. More than a decade earlier, he'd extended my father a loan to buy equipment and seeds and rent a small corn and soybean farm about three miles east of Currie; he was, therefore, the same old man who'd signed off on the decision to close the books on the loan, ending my family's little experiment in the Jeffersonian dream. My father found work at a hardware store, my mother in an optometry clinic, and we rented a little house in Currie—just a short walk from the old man's place.

We lived there less than two years before the landlord told us he wanted us gone. This time I hoped we'd move to some other part of the country entirely, but in fact we only moved fifteen miles to Tracy, the town where my parents worked and I went to school—a railroad town, population two thousand, through which the train still ran. When my father broke the news, he accentuated the positive by telling me I wouldn't have to ride the school bus for an hour in the morning anymore. I could use the extra time to sleep in.

I didn't care about sleeping in. Being closer to a school I hated was no prize; I wanted to be gone. I'd read enough of a certain kind of book—the dime-store western—to begin to understand that in America you moved on from failure by moving on down the road. I was, by all appearances, an unremarkable kid, thin and bespectacled, an untutored country boy lacking the native toughness of your typical untutored country boy. Most of my clothes were hand-me-downs from my uncles, a bit frayed at the hems, never quite the right fit. In the school lunch line I used a special ticket, blue instead of green, that signified my family's "low-income" status. I was what you might call white trash of the northern variety—a little cleaner than the average sample—and these class markers shadowed my school days and inflamed in me an anger born of shame. I wanted to move someplace where no one knew me, where the stink of my family's failure might be misidentified as an exotic cologne.

When I told the old man we were leaving Currie, he looked as if he might cry.

He told me he felt lucky we were friends. A man reaches an age when he doesn't think he'll make new friends, and the ones he has start dying. Your world starts shrinking. That's why he loved me so much. I was something apart from all that.

I didn't know what to say, so said nothing. As he walked me to the door he opened his wallet and studied it for a moment. Then he plucked a bill and slipped it in my pants pocket. He cupped my cheeks in the palms of his hands.

Stop and visit sometime, he said. It would mean a lot to me.

He bent forward and kissed me on the lips, almost the way my grandmother did, but not quite.

I waited until I reached the end of the block to look at what he'd given me. I'd never seen Ulysses S. Grant on a piece of money before. It was the crispest bill I'd ever touched, and I held on to it for a few weeks—fondling it in the privacy of my bedroom, sniffing the exotic, newly minted fragrance of it—before I worked up the nerve to use it for a can of Dr Pepper and a box of Little Debbie snack cakes at a convenience store in Tracy. The lady behind the counter looked at me strangely when I gave it to her. She held it up to the light and studied it. I tried hard to look nonchalant, as if I was a regular spender of big bills.

Every Sunday my family drove back to Currie for mass at Immaculate Heart of Mary church. With my hair slicked back and one of my uncles' castoff ties knotted at my neck, I led the way down the outside aisle, beneath the stained-glass renderings of the stations of the cross, to the very first pew. I hated being on display to the entire congregation, with nothing to look at but the lectern and the altar—no distractions but the backs of the altar boys' heads, and dandruff like a sprinkle of sea salt on the collars of their robes. Sometimes I was one of them, which made the service pass more quickly. Otherwise I found it a kind of mental and physical torture. The pews were built not for comfort but for penance, and Jesus seemed nearly as remote as the moon—an icon on a cross, back of the altar and high on the wall, way too good to be true from the stories I'd been told.

After church we ate breakfast with my father's cousins and their friends at the café downtown. I'd inhale my meal and excuse myself to play pool in the bowling alley next door, or bowl on the eight-lane alley where the chrome ashtrays still held mounds of butts from the night before. Months of Sundays passed this way, until I got to thinking about the old man and his money, how I missed both it and him, his smile, his friendliness, his curiosity about me. He'd spoken to me as an adult, and I hadn't found a replacement for that—wouldn't for some time to come—and I certainly hadn't found a replacement for his gifts of cash.

It took me a while to work up the nerve, but eventually I asked my parents whether I could walk up to the old man's house and pay him a visit. I didn't want them to know about all the money he'd given me; until then I'd thought it best not to mention him. Now I lied and said that when we'd lived in Currie, he'd come over to the park a couple of times to give me pointers on my jump shot. I wanted to drop in and tell him thanks because his advice had helped.

Before my mother granted permission, she took me aside and cautioned me about the old man's drinking. She'd been a bartender at the municipal liquor store when money got tight on the farm, until the night she was threatened with a pool cue, after which my father made her quit—but not before she'd learned the drink of choice for everyone in town. She told me the old man had been such a lush that his liver had begun to fail. He was in the hospital for months. Everyone assumed he was a goner. For a few years he'd stopped drinking, but my mother had heard he was back at it, despite a warning from the doctors. If I suspected him of being drunk on a Sunday morning, she wanted to be the first to know.

Blackberry brandy, she said. That was his thing. Terrible stuff, sweet as cough syrup.

If she was hoping to warn me off, she could not have failed more completely. News of the old man's drinking habit only made him more intriguing and mysterious, more of the bad guy I hoped to become one day. I was deep into a phase of adolescent reinvention meant to scrub any trace of the child I'd been. Growing up on a farm had taught me many things, first among them the fact that I wasn't cut out to be a farmer. Ten minutes in the granary or the hayloft had been sufficient to trigger my asthma. My tractor-driving lessons had ended in shame when I smashed into the Quonset hut my first time alone behind the wheel. Castrating pigs with my father had left me nauseated: there was just no way that slicing the testicles off a screaming hog was ever going to fall within my comfort zone.

Moving to Currie had revealed to me a previously untapped talent for juvenile delinquency: egging old ladies' cars in the church parking lot, sipping Black Velvet in the woods by the river. Moving to Tracy only expanded my opportunities for mischief. My newest friend, Troy, was the youngest son of the couple who owned the Red Owl. I bagged groceries there with him in the evenings after school, and every once in a while he dipped into the safe for money to buy a fifth of vodka from one of his older brother's friends. Sometimes I'd stay the night at his place, and since his parents traveled a lot we were given ample opportunity to test our skill at drinking games while AC/DC roared on the stereo, the sound track of my life in those years, along with Ratt and Black Sabbath.

This was around the time my parents got deep into Amway, and my father became convinced that he could both honor God and become filthy rich. In the mail he received magazines resembling some weird adult yearbook filled with head shots of smiling couples, the photos arranged in groups by the level their subjects had obtained within the Amway hierarchy. The levels were named after jewels—ruby, sapphire, on up to diamond—and in the companion text many of the couples told heartwarming tales of their emergence from bankruptcy and marital strife through the simple miracle of selling household cleaning products to family and friends, who were then recruited to sell household cleaning products to their family and friends. No tales of hardship appeared but those of hardship overcome. My father had met a bunch of diamond-level big shots at Amway meetings, and he was understandably taken with their lifestyles: the fancy cars, the backyard pools, the very real diamonds glittering on the women's ears and fingers. I'd often find long lists of names on the kitchen table, local couples to whom he meant to "show the plan" and eventually "sponsor into the family," creating a downline of distributors who would make him and his upline sponsors millionaires. He listened to motivational speakers on tape whenever we drove very far in the car, men—never women—preaching the Amway gospel, and boiled to its essence the message was this: if you turned your life over to the Risen Lord Jesus Christ, then He would watch over you, becoming in the process both your savior and your friend. People who developed a personal bond with Him were pretty much destined to become rich, as long as they cultivated a wealth mentality. Bringing people into the Amway fold was similar to what the apostles had been up to a couple thousand years earlier, trolling for souls to save, but now instead of turning away from material things the faithful were encouraged to embrace them. Amway—short for American Way—was the very embodiment of the American dream, and it was no secret that Jesus loved America more than any other nation on earth. On long car trips to Amway "family reunions," we listened to a band called the Goads, who put the Amway message to music in songs such as "I Heard It Through My Upline" (set to the tune of Marvin Gaye's "I Heard It Through the Grapevine") and "I'm Going Diamond" (a rip-off of the Pointer Sisters' "I'm So Excited").

Back when we'd lived on the farm, my parents had listened to Sly and the Family Stone, Fleetwood Mac, the Beach Boys—music unheard in our house any longer, unless I put it on the turntable myself. They'd once hosted parties where all their friends got drunk and said funny things and played volleyball barefoot while wearing their hats at goofy angles. They were young, and it was the Seventies, but now the Seventies were over. Reagan had proclaimed morning in America, and the parties had stopped. Hangovers were no longer cool in this new dawn. My parents had even parted with their copy of *The Joy of Sex*, my favorite book of the hundred or so we owned, half of them Louis L'Amour novels. I mostly blamed Amway for the loss of everything fun and attractive in their lives. Now it was all work and church and boring sitcoms on the boob tube after dinner. I'd overheard one of my skeptical relatives call Amway a cleverly designed pyramid scheme built on a foundation of Christian sanctimony. Those words gave me the courage I needed to take a stand. With money I made bagging groceries at the Red Owl, I became a brand fanatic. I bought Crest toothpaste and Tide detergent and did my laundry separately from the rest of the family's, to avoid using Amway products. This pointless insurrection left my father baffled. If I needed some token way of asserting my individuality, he said, then fine. Go for it. Waste your money on Tide.

Maybe my parents hoped my friendly interest in the old man meant my personality wasn't entirely deformed by pubescent angst, as it must have appeared to them it was, not untruthfully. Maybe they thought my spending time with him would reveal to me the glories of becoming rich, and I would see the logic of their longing for upward mobility. In reality I doubt they thought much about it at all, concerned as they were about a whole host of other problems in their lives, not least the strain of money worries on their marriage. Whatever their reasons, they gave their blessing for me to walk the five blocks from the café to the old man's house each Sunday morning, while they gossiped with my father's cousins over hash browns and eggs. They agreed to pick me up when they finished breakfast, but they never entered the old man's house. They signaled from the driveway with a honk of the horn.

WE FOLLOWED THE SAME routine each Sunday. His wife poured me a glass of juice and a mug of instant hot cocoa. She made scrambled eggs and bacon while the old man asked what was new in my life. One time, when his wife left the kitchen, he started teasing me about girls.

A young buck like you must have them lined up three-deep, just dying to be asked out, he said. You must have to fight them off with a stick.

I blushed, as much with shame as anything. As far as I could tell, no girls were interested in me. He said that was the impression girls liked to give. I had to show interest in them, and they'd reciprocate.

I'd bet half my life savings you won't be a virgin next year, he said, not with those eyes. Unless you've already taken care of that.

He winked at me.

Once you get your driver's license, he said, I'm sure it won't be long before your backseat is covered in pecker tracks.

I looked at my eggs and tried not to think about being a virgin. I had no clue when I'd join the ranks of the premarital fornicators, or with whom, nor could I imagine what pecker tracks were. The girl on whom I had a secret crush had caught me, in one of our classes together, picking my scalp to form a little snowdrift of dandruff on my desk. She told me it was the grossest thing she'd ever seen. I can only guess how gross she would have found my masturbatory fantasies of her finding me in the bathtub, my hands bound behind my back, a tiny washcloth covering my erect cock—her plaything, to do with as she pleased, and indeed she pleased in these fantasies, again and again, the naughty little nympho. But then the fantasy was over and the bathwater was cold, and I'd climb out of the tub and confront in the mirror a face speckled with ever-shifting constellations of pimples. It seemed beyond the realm of the possible that any girl would kiss me if her chin were forced to make contact with mine.

A horn sounded in the driveway, the family car. The old man helped me put my coat on, real chivalrous-like, while I held out my arms. The chivalry lasted roughly three seconds. As I zipped up the coat, he slipped his hand in my pants pocket. It lingered there longer than was required to leave a bill.

You got a banana tucked away down there? he asked. His eyes brightened behind his thick glasses, and he laughed. You carrying a concealed weapon?

I pushed his hand away. The bill dropped on the floor. He bent to pick it up, and I slipped out the door before he could try again.

As we drove away, I saw him standing at the window, watching.

For several Sundays I stayed away. I replayed the scene in memory, wondering what it could mean. Probably nothing, I thought—a joke I didn't quite get. Then I lost interest in that question. My mind kept coming back to the sight of that bill falling out of my pocket. I couldn't be sure, but I thought I'd glimpsed the face of Ben Franklin.

When I knocked on his door a few weeks later, he gave me a hug like nothing had ever happened.

I UNDERWENT TWO RITES of passage the year I turned 16: I earned my driver's license and undertook confirmation in the Catholic faith. Getting my license was easy. Beginning the confirmation process was not. I couldn't remember a time when I'd believed in God. I hadn't confessed this to anyone. My parents would've been scandalized by my lack of faith. In religious matters I had no choice but to pretend to agree with them, but I'd been instructed to pray to God so many times over the years, for so many things that never came to pass—rain for the crops, higher prices for the crops, a glut of converts to the Amway family—that I'd long since grown tired of the Lord's noncompliance with our needs. I found it more comforting to believe God didn't exist than to think He might actively wish to thwart us, or just didn't have time for us, so I'd become a secret atheist, convinced that all the stories we were told each Sunday were basically Grimm's fairy tales for adults, another phrase copped from a skeptical relative. I sat sullenly in the first pew, mouthed the hymns and prayers, and dreamed about the girls who'd reveal to me the mystery of pecker tracks once I became a basketball star with a clear complexion.

To undergo the confirmation process I first had to pick a mentor, someone who would lead me into an adult relationship with the Risen Lord Jesus Christ, and the thought made me sick with dread, all the hours of boring Bible study, the contorted poses of false piety. I considered my options for several weeks, but every plausible candidate was either too fervent a believer or too close a friend to my parents. I wanted a sponsor I could be myself around, someone who wouldn't make me put on a show of faith. If I knew anyone I could count on to be irreverent when reverence was called for, it was the old man. Even better, he'd probably give me money just for showing up.

When I told my parents, they made halfhearted protests about his age. They said I ought to choose someone younger, someone more involved in the activities of the church. I pointed out that he was the most generous donor to Immaculate Heart of Mary—the church treasurer handed out a booklet once a year, listing how much each family gave, to shame everyone into giving more—and he went to mass every Saturday evening with his wife. Since the whole process involved me becoming an adult in the eyes of God, and if they and God trusted me to take that step, why wouldn't they trust me to choose my own sponsor?

At our first meeting, the old man led me to the family room in his basement. We sat at a small table, and he handed me a stapled photocopy of the Baltimore Catechism. He said I should read it, and we'd talk about it when I came back the next week.

Do you really think I need to? I said. I'd rather talk about the Baltimore Orioles. I don't care about any of this. I'm only doing it to make my parents happy. I don't even believe in God. I never have.

Come on now, you have to believe in God, he said.

I shrugged.

Well, I have no idea what I'm doing, he said. That's the only thing I could think of.

He sat in silence for a moment.

If I ask you something, he said, will you promise it doesn't leave this room?

I nodded.

How would you like to have a beer?

We never again mentioned the Father, the Son, or the Holy Ghost. We didn't strategize about how I might squeeze my soul through the pearly gates into the garden of life everlasting. The only ritual we honored involved the lifting of our cans of beer in mutual salute before the first sip. I couldn't believe how lucky I'd been, choosing him as my sponsor—my sponsor in the Church of Old Milwaukee. I came up with that one, and he laughed so hard his wife must have wondered.

One night, after a few too many sacramental slugs of beer, I told him I'd finally found a girl who was interested in me. I'd met her at a friend's birthday party. Her older brother played varsity basketball, and she'd noticed me at a couple of games, playing on the JV squad. She lived in the town just east of Tracy. She enlisted a friend of hers to tell me that if I asked her to the Snow Dance that winter, her answer would be yes. We'd been going steady ever since. Her parents wouldn't let me take her out on a real date until she turned fifteen, so we watched movies on the Betamax at her house and counted down the weeks.

The old man wanted to know if she'd given me a blow job. I told him that was between me and her. He gave me a nudge with his elbow and said, Come on, just between friends, but I stayed mum. I felt very protective toward her. She was the second girl I'd ever kissed, and that was still as far as we'd gone.

He said, You know, I'm 67 years old and I've never stuck my pecker in a woman's mouth. My wife wouldn't let me. Not that I didn't try. Jesus, I tried. You know something else? We haven't had sex in eight years. I doubt we'll ever have sex again. I envy you, buddy. You've got all the good stuff ahead of you.

I drained my beer in one long gulp and went to the fridge for another. I'd never heard an adult talk this way. Sex was a subject utterly off-limits in our house. My mother had knocked on my bedroom door the previous year, thrust a pamphlet into my hand, and said, You should read this. It was called "A Christian Guide to Sexuality," and after scanning it for the dirty parts and finding none, I tossed it in the back of my closet.

I felt bad for the old man. It hadn't occurred to me that anyone over the age of about 40 still felt sexual desire. Trying to picture him acting on it made me think of some freak carnival act.

Every Wednesday night I tried to steer the conversation to other subjects, things we'd talked about before—the budding greatness of Minnesota's favorite athlete, Kirby Puckett; the old man's memories of World War II; the oratorical genius of Ronald Reagan—but he mainly wanted to talk about my girlfriend's tight little virgin pussy. He wanted to know whether I'd licked it. He wanted to know how it tasted, how it smelled, how many fingers I could fit inside of it.

Another thing I'm curious about, he said, after a couple of beers. The size of that pecker of yours.

He reached for my crotch. This was the first time a hand not my own had gone there since I'd been in diapers. Not even my girlfriend had been so bold, not yet.

Feels like you've got a nice package, he said. What, seven inches? Eight? Oh, come on, every guy has measured it. Anyone who says he hasn't is a liar.

I was horrified to think he knew I'd measured my own cock. After a few seconds of dumbfounded silence, the words blurted out of me: It's nine inches, if you want to know. A lot bigger than what you've got, I'm sure.

His eyelids quivered weirdly. Nine? he said. You're shitting me.

Of course I was, but I finished my beer as if I hadn't heard him, crushed the empty in my hands. He followed me up the basement steps.

I'm sorry, he said. That was wrong of me.

He was whispering so his wife wouldn't hear. He fumbled for his wallet and pulled out a bill.

Keep your money, I said.

I tried to knock his hand away, but he thrust it into my coat pocket.

I know you need it, he said. I want to help. We're buddies. Buddies help each other, right?

Sure, I said. Buddies help each other.

It was an easy thing to say with a hundred-dollar bill in my pocket.

The next week we resumed our worship at the Church of Old Milwaukee. He kept his hands to himself, but he still wanted to talk about sex. He began by asking if I liked to masturbate. When I didn't answer, he started reciting all the euphemisms he knew: choking the chicken, spanking the wanker, pounding the flounder, tickling the pickle, tweaking the Twinkie, wiggling the walrus, petting the pink pony. Most of these I'd never heard. He got me laughing so hard I nearly cried.

He said, I remember being your age, having blue balls like you wouldn't believe. I wanted to stick my pecker in anything that moved. The girls were different back then. They wouldn't let you go so far so fast.

He said I was lucky to be born when I was, after the creation of the pill and the heyday of the women's libbers.

He was more subtle the next time he put his hand on me. I had told him a joke or a funny story, and we were both laughing. He gave my thigh a squeeze like he had in years past, when we'd sat on his lawn together, him drinking beer, me drinking Coke. I let it set there; it seemed unthreatening enough, until it began to slide toward my groin.

How many inches is that pecker of yours again? he asked.

Ten, I said.

I thought you said nine.

I told him I'd remeasured it, just to be sure, and I found it had grown. He surely knew I was bullshitting, but he didn't call me on it. I felt a tremendous power in the lie, as if, under circumstances in which he thought he could get away with anything, I could too. I let his hand creep up until it crossed some imaginary line separating friendliness from creepiness. Then I pushed it away.

Each Wednesday night, as I drove the fifteen miles to the old man's house, I felt an adrenalized anticipation, not unlike the feeling I had when I drove to pick up my girlfriend for a date, thinking all the while of what we'd do in the backseat of my dad's car. We'd tell our parents we were going to dinner and a movie in a college town thirty miles away, but we'd pick up some food at McDonald's, go to the early show, and find a quiet place in the country to park and make out. Or we'd have dinner at the Happy Chef but skip the movie to leave enough time to park and make out. I felt an intoxicating power in our shared ability to deceive our parents, but I never knew how far she'd let me go. That decision was hers and hers alone, and I always felt ashamed when she told me to stop. I didn't want to stop.

With the old man, I knew the basic outlines too. I'd tell my parents we were making progress on my study of the ways of the Lord, but instead we'd drink a few beers, and I'd get a nice buzz. He'd ask about sex, maybe try to get his hands on me, and before I left he would give me some money—a twenty, a fifty, a hundred. The decision about how far he was allowed to go was mine and mine alone, and I sometimes wondered whether he felt ashamed when I told him to stop. I knew he didn't want to stop. I also knew I was stronger and could probably fend him off if I had to. With his wife just up the stairs, I figured he wouldn't try anything too crazy. I never thought of telling anyone. To have ratted him out, after all, would have meant giving up his money. And that was something I could not do.

THE RED OWL CLOSED when a new corporate grocery moved to Tracy, so I took a job at the town bakery, frying donuts and bagging bread in the middle of the night. With the money I was earning I bought a used car on payments, an '82 Buick Regal, maroon, two-door. My new wheels allowed me to go out on the weekends without asking permission for the family ride. I spent my weekends water-skiing with friends at the lake, taking my girlfriend out with my own money, drinking beer and vodka on the sly. Everything interesting going on in my life was going on without my parents having a clue about it. I wanted to keep it that way. It made me feel grown-up to have a secret life. What happened between me and the old man was just one more thing I filed under the heading of secrets, although of course it unsettled me in a way my other secrets did not. I wondered what kind of person aroused such feelings in an old man, what his attentions said about me. Had he judged me impure and corruptible? Had I given him reason to suspect I was game for whatever it was he had in mind?

During our last month of confirmation meetings, at a time when I was supposed to be drawing near to the numinous embrace of the Holy Trinity, he tried every time to grope me, and every time I swatted his hand away. It became as much a ritual as our three cans of Old Milwaukee apiece. During our last meeting, just before I was to be confirmed with my classmates in a ceremony before the whole church, he tried with particular insistence to cop a feel while simultaneously straining for a kiss in the manner of the French. It was a terrible thing to see, the purple, swollen tongue of an alcoholic old man; it made me ashamed to be human. I knocked him away with a punch to the chest, a punch as hard as I could throw. He slumped in a corner of the couch, wounded. There were tears in his eyes, whether from pain or thwarted longing I wasn't sure.

I bet you'd love it if I pulled out my cock and let you touch it, I said.

He looked at the floor and shook his head, one hand holding his chest.

Shit, I bet you'd even pay me if I let you suck it. How much would that be worth? A hundred? Two hundred?

He didn't look at me, didn't say a thing.

I climbed the basement stairs and listened in vain for him to follow with his wallet open.

My confirmation was complete.

THAT SUMMER, in addition to working nights at the bakery, I coached rec-league baseball for grade-school kids. Three afternoons a week we played in Tracy; two days a week we played next to the cemetery behind Immaculate Heart of Mary in Currie, where I still joined my family every Sunday for mass. No one ever came to watch—no one, that is, except the old man. Two of his grandkids sometimes played, but even if they didn't show up, the old man did. He parked his car under the big shade trees along the right field line. He never got out, just sat there staring through the lightly tinted windows of his Cadillac. When he'd watched me shoot hoops in the town park he'd made me feel important, but now I feared other people would notice his interest in me. I no longer felt important. I felt hunted.

When he called me over after the games to say hello, I kept the conversation short. The old man looked wistful every time I said goodbye. By the time I picked up the equipment and drove out of town, his Cadillac would be parked at the American Legion Club or the municipal bar, his usual afternoon haunts.

To be told never to drink again or risk death—and yet go right on drinking—seemed, to my adolescent mind, a gesture of heedless heroism; no matter what else he did, I respected him for that. My friends and I had entered into a pact by which we agreed to give our girlfriends only one night a weekend of our precious company. We spent the other in a hunt for beer or vodka or whiskey, peppermint schnapps or Mad Dog 20/20, whatever we could get our hands on. Our search for booze represented the most exciting and agonizing hours of the week. We couldn't be certain we'd meet with success, which only made the quest more tantalizing. A few old boozers we knew bought liquor for us if we sprang for their night's drink too, but we couldn't always track them down when we needed them.

Once, in desperation, I stopped by the old man's house and begged him for a case of Old Milwaukee. At first he refused.

I don't want to be responsible if you do something stupid, he said. You wreck your car and kill someone, I'll have that on my conscience forever. I could go to jail.

I pestered and pleaded, promised that my friends and I would choose a designated driver—a lie, of course, since all of us always drank—until the old man led me downstairs and opened his fridge. I tucked cans of beer in every pocket I had, inside my socks, under my armpits. His wife sat in her customary place in the living room, obliviously sucking on a Pall Mall.

I mean it now. You guys be careful. I'd hate myself if something happened to you. You're the best friend I've got left in the whole world.

He leaned in. I turned my cheek. He hugged me, nuzzling his stubbled jaw against the flesh beneath my ear, running one hand slowly south of my lower back. I closed my eyes and let him savor for a moment these affections, figuring they were a reasonable trade for the beer.

The guys are waiting, I said. We'll raise a toast to you at the lake.

Don't ever forget who's your old buddy, he said.

Two or three times after that, when we couldn't rustle up beer from our regular buyers, I dropped in on the old man. He was always reluctant, always gave in. He did his best to make me feel guilty for only stopping by when I needed beer. He wished I'd stay awhile, so we could sit around and drink a couple of cold ones like we used to.

Down at the bar, he said, it's the same conversation for the last twenty years.

M Y DREAMS OF BASKETBALL GLORY were dashed my junior year, when I underwent surgery on my left knee. Just as I was supposed to be coming into my own, a starter on the varsity, I was relegated to the end of the bench, where I moped in street clothes. My name wasn't appearing in the local paper, but that didn't hurt as much as the fact that my shot at a scholarship appeared to be slipping away. I couldn't think of another way out, couldn't think of what to become.

What I became, more by default than design, was a solitary drinker. Alcohol made the world glow again, for a little while. I'd steal some sloe gin from my grandparents' cupboard when we went to see them in Iowa, or I'd ask one of my buyers for a fifth of vodka. I'd sneak into the kitchen after dinner and smuggle some orange juice mixer back to my room while the rest of the family watched television. I'd listen to the latest in hair metal through my headphones—Cinderella, Whitesnake—and drink until the room began to spin, and after a few hours of sleep my alarm would ring to wake me for work at the bakery, where I was expected by 3 AM. Driving through the empty streets in the middle of the night, my tongue like sandpaper, my eyes bloodshot, I felt solitary and dangerous and more than likely doomed, capable of just about anything, a man without a future—an adolescent, in other words, with a really nasty hangover.

Once, just to see whether I could get away with it, I called the old man and told him a vague story about a friend of mine who was in a jam and needed $300 by the end of the week. The old man asked why my friend needed the money. I told him I couldn't say but assured him it was nothing illegal. He said to meet him at the bank, where he'd left his checkbook.

His office was on the second floor. A glass window made up one whole wall overlooking Mill Street. He sat behind a big oak desk. I sat in a small chair opposite. He clearly knew how to work power dynamics with office furniture. I was learning how to work them with sexual unavailability. The air in the room was electric with manipulation. We both knew the score, both knew what the other wanted, but only one of us was going to get it.

For a moment I had an eerie sensation of déjà vu, except I was reliving a scene not from my own life but from my father's, asking for a loan from a man who, with a few strokes of his pen, had the power to relieve anyone in the county of his money worries, for a little while anyway. Given that he'd been the one to put an end to our life on the farm, I can see how the old man may have pitied me on our first meeting. He'd pulled the plug on the only life my father had imagined for himself, the family calling for a century, and I doubt he felt very pleased about it. The bank of which he was president and chief loan officer had lost money on us, and my father had lost everything he'd ever cared about. Maybe those first $20 bills were the old man's way of saying, if not to me then perhaps to himself, *I'm sorry about what happened*—a guilt offering of sorts.

Then again, maybe knowing my family's finances from the inside out, he'd calculated that cash was the way to keep me coming back, again and again. I later wondered whether I was unique—whether his impulses were something he'd ever acted on when he was coaching boys' basketball all those years, or whether he'd kept it to himself, or even whether he'd had the impulse at all when he was younger and more of a man. I don't know. But I guess I find it hard to believe I was the only one.

He slid a check across the desk. I thanked him for it, told him my friend would pay him back, via me, as soon as he was able. Which, we both surely knew, was going to be never.

All these years, he said, and you've never come to see me here. I'm glad you finally did. There's something I want to give you.

The look on his face went from solemn to sassy in a heartbeat. He opened a drawer and produced a mass-market paperback with brittle yellow pages. A woman with heavy lavender eyeshadow and a lascivious, half-open mouth looked up from the cover. *Xaviera on The Best Part of a Man,* it said above the picture, and below it: Author of *The Happy Hooker.* The woman was the writer, the Dutch prostitute Xaviera Hollander.

An old friend gave that to me years ago, he said. It's the kind of book that ought to be shared. There's some pretty racy stuff in there. Even a stud like you might learn a few things.

I knew I'd appear ungrateful if I took the one thing—his money—and not the other, so I picked up the book and flipped the pages, trying to look interested.

I'll be curious to know what you think of it, he said.

I told him I'd let him know, though I had no intention of reading his kinky little book.

Out in my car I studied the check, giddy with greed. The memo line read: LOAN.

Curiosity eventually got the better of me, and I read that kinky little book straight through to the end. As the title indicated, it was a paean to the penis, and while certain parts of it aroused the best part of me, I would've preferred a book about the best part of a woman. The passage that turned me on more than any other involved an orgy during which half-set Jell-O was inserted into a woman's vagina with a turkey baster and then sucked out by three men with straws, producing, for the woman, a phenomenal orgasm. I petted the pink pony with the book open to those pages more times than I'd care to admit.

M Y SENIOR YEAR OF BASKETBALL, like so much else in my life at the time, turned out to be a disappointment. I never made good on the promise I'd shown when I was younger, although I had my moments. I'd spent thousands of hours honing the mechanics of my twenty-foot jumper until it was one fluid motion, as natural as walking or lifting food to my mouth. Left open for a couple of seconds, I was deadly from three-point range. There were games in which no one had any chance of stopping me. Then there were others in which I missed a few early shots, became frustrated, and flailed. I'd sat out an entire season. I was trying to make up for lost time. All my angst was forgotten during those moments when I seemed to float just above the action, able to see everything a fraction of a second before it happened. They were, in the end, too few.

My finest game came against our rivals from Balaton, the nearest neighboring school. I remember bursting out of the locker room for warm-ups, the smell of popcorn in the air, the gym overheated by the bodies of several hundred fans. As we ran through our opening drill, in which the team would sprint single-file and each player would leap and bounce the ball off the backboard at the moment of full extension, I happened to see, amid the faces in the crowd, the old man. He was leaning forward, elbows on his knees, watching me. I felt the old thrill of having an audience of one, and the adrenaline in my blood made my knees tremble. During the playing of the national anthem on the loudspeakers I closed my eyes and held my hand over my heart, trying to calm its thumping. When the song was over I opened my eyes and saw the old man staring at me. He raised his arm and clenched his fist in my direction.

From the moment of tip-off I was feeling it. The jumper was on, the X-ray vision intact. When crowded or double-teamed, I threaded the needle with fancy bounce passes, or spun away to tiptoe the baseline on quicksilver drives to the hoop, dishing or scoring at will. The game was close until late, when I went on one last scoring spree that sealed the deal, finishing one point shy of thirty.

After it was over and we'd slapped hands with our opponents, I saw the old man lingering in the bleachers. I couldn't help myself. I still wanted his approval. I walked toward his smile like a moth to a flame.

Jesus, buddy, that was something else, he said, clasping my hand.

You showed up for the right game, I said. And then, knowing it would please him, I added: This one was for you.

He wrapped me in a bear hug, kissed me on the cheek. I looked over his shoulder to see whether anyone was watching us, but no one seemed to notice.

FOR A WHILE I STAYED AWAY after the bit with the so-called loan, but I couldn't let that be the end. Like a junkie, I wanted my line of credit open; I was delusional enough to think he might even help me with college tuition when the time came. He'd hinted at the possibility more than once.

I stopped by his house one weekend unannounced, thinking he'd be happy to see me, thinking I'd score a bill. It was the middle of the afternoon, and the old man was drunk, reeking of brandy, slurring his words. His wife was away visiting her family in Iowa, so for the first and last time we sat in her domain, the living room. He said it was nice to have the place to himself. He could stay late at the bar if he wanted to, or drive up the road and visit one of his drinking buddies, a man his wife didn't like him to see. Drinking had become not only his primary diversion but the ordering principle of his days. He spent less and less time at the bank, having ceded control to others. His back and hip were failing him. He moved awkwardly, gingerly, like a man breaking in a new prosthetic leg. For years he'd laid off cigarettes, but he lit one now. I grabbed the pack and took one too without asking.

You must be excited to graduate, he said. This is it. Your time has come.

Excited to get the hell out of here, I said.

He ignored me and played the pity card, as he had so many other times. He often said he was an old man with nothing left to look forward to, nothing but his friendship with me. Now he said he wished he were me. He wished he were in my shoes. Everything good was still ahead of me. He was just an old man creeping up on death, drinking the days away.

I confess I didn't see the allure of my life. It felt like everything good was behind me, and I told him so. My basketball career was over. My girlfriend had dumped me, but not before we'd lost our virginity together. I was as heartbroken as only a recent novitiate in the joy of sex can be.

Forget about her, he said. You'll go to college and get more ass than you know what to do with.

Not to mention my back, I said. It's been killing me. I think it's all that lifting at the bakery.

Why don't you lie on the couch? he said. I'll give you a little rub. You'll feel a lot better.

I doubt I could have told you at the time why I let him do it, but from twenty-five years on the answer is as clear as day. This was one part of my life where I had the upper hand. In school and at home I was subject to rules devised by others. I thought I was an adult—the overnight job, the car—but no one treated me as one. So be it. The adult world was an elaborate sham anyway, a web of unspoken disappointments, outrageous hypocrisies, crooked desires of unaccountable origin. I wanted to punch a hole in that web, but if that wasn't possible I could at least feel righteous while punching an old man.

He wasted no time getting to it. He worked with a firm tenderness. His hands moved lower and lower. There was no doubt about where he was headed. He began to get pretty cozy with the contours of my gluteus maximus. I tried not to flinch as he pressed himself against me. I felt his breath on the back of my neck, his lips tickle my ear. He had me in a spot where he could have held me down if he wanted to, the sudden thought of which sent a charge through my limbs. I twisted my torso and boxed him upside the head rather viciously with my elbow. He slipped off the couch and let out a shrill cry as he landed on the floor. It took all my willpower not to kick him in the ribs while he lay there, whimpering.

Before I left I made sure to grab some beer for the road.

Our story should have ended there. Soon I would graduate. The old man would officially retire, settle in for a jaundiced decline in the company of drink. His world was closing in. Mine was opening up.

I almost didn't get out, though, and when I say almost I'm talking inches—literally twelve or fifteen inches from ending up dead or trapped in a long-term care facility, sucking watery Jell-O through a straw. A fairly simple story: a night of drinking with a friend, a twelve-pack apiece of Colt 45, a bank of fog, a telephone pole in a highway ditch, and just like that the money I'd sunk into my '82 Regal was gone. The body folded up like an accordion, the windshield splintered. I paid a salvage yard the towing fee to take it off my hands and I wasn't even done with the payments. I walked away with a sprained ankle and a few cuts on my forehead; the next morning I woke to a parental silence so arctic in its fury it made me wish I'd died. The mother of my drinking buddy happened to work for the county attorney, and feeling guilty that I'd dropped off her son at midnight and continued on my drunken way home, she finagled the charge down to reckless driving, alcohol-related, which saved me the money and trouble of a DWI.

Despite the many hours I'd spent admiring college catalogs from Tucson, Seattle, and Boulder, I experienced a failure of nerve in the end. I'd made a visit to a fancy Catholic college in St. Paul, where the Mercedes and BMWs of rich suburban kids gleamed in the dormitory parking lots, and was instantly transfixed by the limestone buildings honey-colored in the afternoon light, the ivied walls of the football stadium, coeds strolling with books in their arms across the fastidious lawns. I'd never seen so many girls in one place. The whole scene was like the previously missing, wide-angle prelude shot to the porno film I'd been writing, directing, and starring in every time I thought of what my college years would be. Even deeper in my reptilian brain I sensed a chance to learn how to be rich by living in proximity to rich kids, the old dream not yet dead. Here I could finally begin the process of reinventing myself as a man of debonair tastes and urbane manners, a prairie sophisticate with a fancy car. I learned that through a University of St. Thomas scholarship fund I stood to earn $3,500 per year for my high school GPA, class rank, and ACT score. This seemed a phenomenal sum, the equivalent of nearly six months of work at the mom-and-pop bakery where I was then making $3.80 an hour. If the sight of pretty girls and shiny cars had been the initial seduction, the promise of free cash clinched the deal. I didn't for a moment acknowledge the fact that I was merely getting a discount on a very expensive product. Nor did I bother to imagine, given that my parents were in no position to help, where I'd come up with the remainder of the $15,000 per year I'd be charged for tuition, room, and board.

Needless to say, I was not the prototypical Tommy. I drove a 1970 Ford pickup of a pale green hue that earned it the nickname Phlegm. I arrived with $2,000 in savings from my job at the bakery, which bought me six heady weeks of Coors Light party balls and Mexican ditch weed. Over the next few years I borrowed exorbitantly while working all sorts of stupid jobs: painting houses, unloading package trailers at a UPS hub, frying donuts for a little shop in the suburbs. It was the same work I'd performed since I was 15, and I came to loathe the stupefying repetition of it, eight at night till three in the morning, five days a week, the clicking handle of the donut dropper, the pox-like burns on my hands from the splash of fryer oil. The way I smelled like a jelly-filled bismarck even after I'd showered.

○   ○   ○

I DROPPED OUT for lack of cash, worked three jobs, returned to school for a couple of years, dropped out broke again. When the friends I'd met as a freshman graduated to begin their careers in corporate finance and accounting, and my girlfriend left for a magazine job in New York, I mostly sat around drinking wine alone in the afternoons. I was as confused as I'd ever been, which is saying something. I'd sunk tens of thousands of dollars—much of it borrowed, some of it earned by my own labor, some of it a gift from my grandfather—into a journalism education, but my scholarship had been revoked when I didn't finish my degree in four years. Internships at the *Fargo Forum* and *Kiplinger's Personal Finance Magazine* had left me sour on the strictures of deadline hackery and service-mag pap. I didn't want to be a cops and courts reporter; I didn't want to be a mutual-fund guru, a blue-chip stock watcher. I wanted to be a novelist. Unfortunately, I didn't know the first thing about writing a novel, and it was clear that even if I started tomorrow I'd be a long time in earning a dime from writing novels. I did what many before me have done in such circumstances: I became a bartender. This offered all the intellectual stimulation you'd imagine, which is to say none. The pleasures were other. I met party people. I drank on the job.

One night my telephone rang. It was the old man, of all people. He'd tracked down my home number. I never did learn how. The number was unconnected with my name, since I was living with my girlfriend's gay uncle Charlie, who'd offered to put me up rent-free so I'd have time to write the great American novel, in compensation for which he merely asked that he appear, lightly fictionalized but still identifiable, as a demon lover with a giant cock in my great American novel. I'd overcome the residual homophobia of my Catholic boyhood by then, thanks in no small part to Charlie, whom I'm very happy to describe for posterity as one of the most generous people I've ever known, as well as a demon lover with an enormous and stunningly beautiful cock.

Anyway, the phone rang. I let the answering machine answer it. A familiar voice began speaking, haltingly. I knew right away he was drunk.

I picked up the phone.

Old buddy, he slurred. It's been so long, so long I can hardly believe. I miss you.

Yeah, I said.

We used to be so close.

Sure, I said.

There's no one around I like as much as you. I wish you'd call sometime. We could shoot the breeze like in the old days.

Right, I said.

Why don't you call? I feel like you've abandoned me. Like you've turned your back on your old buddy—

I don't care what you feel like. You know why I don't call.

There was a pause on his end. Everything would have turned out differently if he'd made the right move at the end of that pause.

He did not make the right move.

He said he didn't know what I was talking about. I offered some reminders. He said it was nothing but a lark, some innocent horseplay among friends. I told him I didn't think it was innocent. He said I was a smart kid, mature for my age, I knew all along what was happening. I told him I knew exactly what had happened, he'd worked overtime on getting me to take his dirty dick in my mouth. He said he went to confession and told the priest everything, he was very sorry if he hurt me in any way, we were such good friends and he never meant to harm our friendship. I told him he wasn't my friend, he was a creepy old man with a thing for underage boys. He said I was the one who'd led him on, if anyone was to blame it was me, and besides no one would believe my word against his.

That was another mistake.

Until the moment of that call, whenever I remembered the old man, I found myself tempted by the thought that we could have been friends, real friends, although we probably never were. I'm pretty sure we never were. I'm pretty sure he was plotting and scheming most of the time he knew me, plotting to get into my pants, until I finally caught on, after which it was me plotting to get into his wallet, as deep as I could get without breaking down and becoming his boy toy. It's totally fucked, I know, but I nonetheless kept alive the thought that maybe we could have found a way to get beyond all that. I see now I was being willfully naive, perhaps even fetishizing the power of forgiveness, that cornerstone of the Catholic faith, along with its partner confession. I had needed an alternate narrative to the way things turned out; the other, more plausible alternative, the one in which I became his boy toy, was too much to contemplate. I had managed to convince myself that he'd taught me a lot of things a person ought to know—about the persistence of desire, the allure of youth, the heartbreaking frailty and mind-boggling confusion of human relations, priceless lessons really, unintentional though they may have been. I hadn't had to spend years in therapy. I never tried to kill myself for the shame. Countless Catholic kids had it far worse than me, unspeakably worse, in the realm of predatory sex. The newspapers were beginning to tell their stories, and they were awful beyond imagining, the ritual acts of sadism, the damaged lives. Mine was the world's sweetest love story by comparison.

In practical terms, his example—the first such of my life—made me reluctant to pursue my sexual attractions with any gusto, which prevented my college years from becoming the sexual smorgasbord they were for a lot of my contemporaries. I had seen a man's face contorted by lust unconsummated—I'm talking up close and personal—and it was not a pretty sight. A smoldering passivity became my style, and a tendency toward long-term serial monogamy with women who made the first move. Which, when I thought about it later, may have been a blessing, considering the kind of woman with whom this involved me, typically horny and radiant with self-confidence, the kind of woman you want to remain a friend even after you split.

Once he blamed me, though, all bets were off. It was time at long last to make him pay—really pay, this time in the currency of fear.

If I could be said to have accomplished one momentous thing in my abortive undergraduate career—and it's a bit of a stretch to say any such thing—it was to have unearthed, as editor of the campus newspaper, the existence of a lawsuit against the recently retired dean of students, who was accused of initiating unwanted intimacies with a male undergrad he'd counseled decades earlier. This was news, no doubt about it—the school paying the ex-dean's legal fees, the presence of a high-profile lawyer for the plaintiff—a story altogether more consequential than the paper's typical offering, which plumbed the tension between hard-partying undergrads and neighborhood residents whose lawns were watered with urine most weekend nights. By the end of my reporting I'd come to have doubts about the validity of the charges—the alleged crime was almost three decades old, a "recovered memory," and the plaintiff seemed a sad sack on a fishing expedition—but the story proved useful to me now.

I picked up a copy of the paper, a whole semester's worth of which was neatly stacked in a cardboard box close at hand, and began to read from the story in question. The lead was classic inverted-pyramid newspaper style, sober and precise, the who-what-why-when-where up front:

Former Dean of Students William Malevich is accused of sexually exploiting and abusing a student he counseled from 1966 to 1967, according to a civil lawsuit filed in Ramsay County District Court.

I told the old man that, insofar as our situation was concerned, the dean's guilt or innocence was beside the point. The point was, I still had a copy of the lawsuit. It was all just boilerplate. It would be so easy to swap my name for the accuser's, his name for the accused. I asked him if the name Jeff Anderson rang a bell. No? He was the plaintiff's lawyer and he knew what he was doing. Case by case he was revealing the Catholic Church to be one big pedophile protection racket. Maybe the name James Porter was familiar. Yeah? The priest who was taken to the tune of $5 million for abusing young boys? Good. Now we were getting somewhere. Jeff Anderson was the lawyer who'd gone after him. He'd brought hundreds of cases against the Catholic Church and he usually won. He won, in fact, about 85 percent of the time. I had his phone number. It would be the easiest thing in the world for me to call him up. We could have the papers filed so quickly it would make his head spin. How would he like to see his name on the front page of the local paper? I could see the lead already: *Former bank president J. P. Hansen is accused of sexually exploiting and abusing a boy he counseled in the late 1980s, according to a civil lawsuit filed in Murray County District Court . . .*

He said he couldn't take this, couldn't live with this, he'd rather die than see a story like that published. He said he'd be forced to kill himself if I was serious. He said he was going to get his gun and shoot himself and put an end to it all right now.

I told him he was a liar; I knew he didn't own a gun.

He said, What is it you want from me?

I told him I didn't want anything *from* him. I wanted things *for* him. I wanted him to see his name on the front page of the local paper, wanted to see him seated in court, wanted to watch him squirm while I told the world what he'd done.

He said he knew me well enough to know that I'd never go through with a court case. He said, Just tell me what it is you want, and I'll do it.

I told him he didn't know me at all, but he'd raised a good question. What did I want? I wasn't sure. Maybe I wanted to put it all behind me. But I wasn't sure how to do that. I wasn't sure if a trial was the best way to do that but I thought it could be just the thing.

He said, Please, whatever you want, I'll do it.

He said, Please, just keep this between us.

I told him the going rate on one of Anderson's cases was fifty to a hundred grand in damages per victim. I couldn't even remember if that was true but it sounded good.

He said, Is it money you want, is that it? He said all his money was tied up in the bank. He'd have to sell the bank if it came to that. He'd send me a little if that's what I wanted. He'd send it right away, a few hundred.

I told him not to insult me, although my antennae were buzzing, as he must have hoped.

He said he had maybe five grand he could access right now but he needed some of it for Christmas gifts for his wife and kids, his grandkids.

I told him OK, send me the five grand and we'll call it even.

He said he couldn't send me the whole five grand, he really needed some of it for Christmas, he could maybe spare a grand, a grand and a half at the most.

I told him five grand was our number, he could send half now and half later, let's say March 1. I'd give him my account number so he could wire the dough, pronto.

He said he could send $1,500, no more, and he'd have to write a check so he had a record of my signing and cashing it, and he'd need a letter from me, acknowledging receipt of the check and spelling out how much more to send and when to send it.

I told him no dice on the official correspondence, but nice try anyway—no, really, great effort, much appreciated. Half now, half by the end of February, and if he wanted to write a check that was cool, but it had better arrive in my mailbox by the end of the week or he'd be sorry. Then I hung up.

Two days later a check arrived in the mail, in the amount of $2,500.

The memo line read: LOAN.

I promptly cashed the check and booked a plane ticket to Amsterdam for the holidays. Out of the country for the first time in my life, loose on the Continent with a Eurail pass, I spent every dime of that dirty money as frivolously as I could—champagne in Paris, dope in Amsterdam, ephemeral pleasures of one sort or another from London to Venice—shadowed the whole time by a mixture of exhilaration and shame, that familiar cocktail of emotion in all my dealings with the old man, almost from the beginning: the exhilaration of having got away with something, the shame of having let him off the hook for one more gift of cash.

He had at last made of me an American hustler, just not the kind he'd hoped.

I HAVE TWO DOCUMENTS that serve as tangible traces of the man, aside from the account I immediately wrote in my diary after our telephone confab. One is a letter he sent after I returned from Europe. I'd been in touch by phone to let him know I'd transferred to the University of Montana, and, more important, to give him my address in Missoula, so he'd know where to send the balance on the—what to call it, exactly? Hush money? Blackmail? Some unholy amalgam of both? This letter would be the only one of its kind. I didn't reply to it, and he never wrote again. In its mixture of affection, evasion, bluster, and strained jocularity, it strikes me now as a pretty good encapsulation of the man. It mentioned, in his impeccable cursive handwriting, that one of his daughters had attended the University of Montana in Missoula, where he had visited for a week many years earlier, and that he therefore knew the precise part of town where I lived; and although he went on to add that he was still involved in the work of making sure the bank was in compliance with regulatory examiners and, almost parenthetically, that his older brother had recently passed away, he eventually got around to the business at hand:

> Phil, according to my atty, because of your court records back here, a judge would have a hard time to believe your stories about me.* So lets get back to our friendship and caring about each other, and I will help you out like I always said I would do if you need it.
>
> I am short of cash now, but should have 4 or 5 hundred by the 1st of the month.
>
> Let me know if you need some now and for a few more months while at school out there?
>
> P.S. Call me collect at home if you want to. Hope to hear right back from you. Still love you, you big stiff.

o o o

---

* A reference, apparently, to my car crash and the charge of "reckless driving, alcohol-related."

If he'd been more diplomatic, perhaps I'd have let him off the hook. I couldn't believe the chutzpah. "My atty"? I knew he hadn't said boo to a soul. I figured I'd outfox him, though. I would keep quiet; nothing to gain from writing him back in anger. He could send more money or not, it didn't really matter. It hadn't been about the money, disingenuous as that no doubt sounds. What mattered was keeping him scared. What mattered was the final and decisive shift in the balance of power. Besides, I'd see him eventually; I'd open my palm, and he'd do as I said. In the meantime I wanted him paranoid, muttering helplessly to himself in the night.

That summer, home for a funeral, I drove to his house and knocked on his door.

Old buddy, he said when he answered. I can't believe it's you.

Believe it, I said.

Why don't you come in? he said.

I don't want to come in, I said. You know why I'm here.

All right, he said, trying to remain friendly. How about we go have a drink downtown. My checkbook is at the bank. I'll pick it up on the way.

How about I meet you at the bank, I said. We can skip the drink.

Ten minutes later I had a check in my hand for $1,000.

I never saw him again.

THE OTHER DOCUMENT is the obituary my mother sent me in the mail, clipped from our hometown paper, the *Tracy Headlight-Herald*, in the fall of 1999. "Thought you'd like to know," she'd written on a Post-it note, assuming, correctly, that I'd be curious about this final news of my mentor in the Catholic faith, although she didn't know the half of it. No one on earth had known a thing of our entanglement; it had always remained just between us, my way of perpetually honoring the first request he ever made of me, that his generosity with money remain a secret—our secret.

The obituary said he was born on October 3, 1920, on a farm in southwest Minnesota. I'd forgotten our birthdays were just a few days apart, our boyhoods so similar; he rarely spoke of his. It said he and his wife had celebrated their fiftieth wedding anniversary in June. I couldn't imagine them feeling celebratory. It said that after college he moved to Southern California and joined the Marines, served a tour of duty, and was there for the invasion of Iwo Jima. I remembered the stories he'd told me about the war and the way his eyes got real spooky when he thought of his buddies blown apart in the mud, crying like little girls. It said one of his proudest accomplishments was building a new bank facility as president and chairman of the board of Currie State Bank, and it noted that he was a lifelong member of Immaculate Heart of Mary church, had served on the church council, was the first president of the Town and Country Club, had been the city treasurer, and belonged to the local American Legion, the county bankers' association, and the Minnesota Bankers Association, where he was a member of the Pioneer Club, signifying fifty years with the organization.

It said, in the obligatory sentence offering a hint of his personal life, that he enjoyed sports, crossword puzzles, his career in banking, and spending time with people.

I couldn't suppress a laugh at the phrase "spending time with people." +

ENRIQUE MARTÍNEZ CELAYA, *THE FORGOTTEN*. 2013, OIL AND WAX ON CANVAS, 100 × 75".
COURTESY OF LA LOUVER, VENICE, CALIFORNIA.

TWO STORIES

Christine Smallwood

STEWARDS

In the beginning it was an in-ground swimming pool Ruth wanted, but she got over that idea pretty quick—too expensive, all the upkeep. She first mentioned koi on her birthday, about two months after Ken got the job at Hofstra and they moved to Freeport.

She had always liked koi, she explained—their unreflecting googly eyes, their fussy barbels. Their toothless mouths like open sucking nostrils. It was impossible for a koi to smile, Ruth said. This stayed with Ken, because she herself was smiling when she said it, like it brought her true joy, this other creature's fixed expression of stalking hunger. He was struck by her insistent preference for white longfins splashed and ringed with orange flames. She, usually so silly and loose, became specific and grave over the matter of the orange flames. She knew about them. She was reading things when Ken wasn't around, or maybe right under his nose, clandestinely.

All of which is to say that Ken knew that Ruth wanted koi but also that she liked talking about things more than doing them, which suited him fine. She threw out the idea now and again, and for two years Ken never denied that they had the perfect setting: a hi-ranch at the end of a cul-de-sac, a half acre of fenced-in yard flanked by shrubbery and shaded by the neighbors' trees. A stone patio jutted out from the back door, providing what the real estate agent called a "transition." Their old house had been a Trinity with plush aquamarine wall-to-wall and a poured-concrete outdoor space; it had soft insides and hard outsides. This new one was the opposite, and Ruth was surprised at how often she missed sitting cross-legged in comfort, and burying her face in carpet as comedic protest when Ken said something she didn't like.

It wasn't clear, when Jeff and Terri announced that they had built a koi pond, whether they had known that Ruth had been so long suffering for one. The two couples were sitting in Jeff and Terri's living room on a stiff modern sofa that lacked arms. They never stayed at Jeff and Terri's long enough to relax, mostly because it was horrible sitting there. Terri worked on visual culture and talked a lot about "clean lines" and the "provenance" of this or that object—a planter, a frame. There were other rooms in the house, rooms that were habitable or looked to be in passing, but Terri always shepherded guests to this room, which she repainted every two years a different shade of neutral. The current color was Butter Cookie, a name whose associations did not at all capture the feeling of being in the room. Ruth preferred it to Oklahoma Wheat, which had been insincere, but was looking forward to Lemon Sorbet, which promised to be cleaner, more open to the future.

"Lemon Sorbet is the color of the year," Terri said, and Ruth imagined Terri fingering the paint strips, holding them up to the window, examining them against her skin, licking them in surreptitious delight.

Jeff and Ken and Terri taught in the same department; that's how they all knew one another. Ruth had recently acquired a real estate license but she didn't define herself by her work.

Jeff and Terri were much better looking, in a conventional American way, than most professors: lean, elegant, small tactful features. This fact was starting to bother Ruth less, but it had been a problem, historically, in the foursome. Things work better when everyone is about the same degree of good-looking, and in the same way. People have known that for centuries.

It seemed like Terri was going to say they were having a baby. She acted just like women act when they announce they're having babies. She smoothed her stretchy black pants and she looked sideways at Jeff and twisted her wedding ring and grinned ear to ear like the cat that et cetera. When she said, "We built a koi pond!" Ken asked her to repeat it, because he had been busy preparing his baby face and thought he must have misheard.

Ken put a hand on Ruth's knee, steady unlike his own, which was bobbing and broadcasting nerves—typical Ken behavior. His body had been built for the tarmac, one jolt from takeoff, always about to be somewhere else. Ruth was radiating serenity, her face painted with a sweet smile like she was also the cat that et cetera. Ken felt his mouth twisting dementedly into a smirk. They followed their hosts through the sleek glass door that slid open soundlessly, and under the full flush of a golden sunset sky they loudly admired the pond. Ruth nodded as Terri pointed out this or that feature, and playfully refereed the debate over the dollhouse-size pagoda. (Jeff wanted a lacquered black one, Terri rustic white.) Ken could not understand how Ruth could be smiling and nodding and never saying a word that betrayed her expertise. He tried to remember why they hadn't built their pond already. He guessed that it had seemed like there would always be more time.

This pond, the pond that had been built already, was elaborate and it looked good: there was no doubt about that. A triple shelf of askew slate-colored rocks formed a waterfall. It was no trickle, either, but full curtains splashing down. Plants, ferns, and mosses bordered the pond on three sides. The water was a natural-looking brownish-green. Three dozen pea-green lily pads clustered together, trembling since the group's arrival, when a frog had plunged into the water to escape. Jeff sprinkled some fish food from a metal bucket that stood at the pond's edge, and a dozen koi snaked to the surface, mouthing the air, thrashing. They were white, streaked and blotched with red and gold. A gentle breeze rustled the grasses.

"I never thought that Terri would clutter up her yard with any landscaping," Ruth said in the car, innocently. Ken wasn't in the mood for pretending not to be in a mood, but Ruth plowed into the silence. "I guess she figures it's Japanese, so it's elegant." Ken reminded her that Terri had studied in Kyoto in the '90s, and that was all anybody said until a cat leaped into the street and Ruth slammed her leather moccasin on the brake pedal and screamed something foul at the windshield.

THEY WERE OFF-SCRIPT NOW. This was a contingency Ken had not foreseen. He worried, as he lay curled and counting backward from 100 *en español*, trying to bore himself to sleep, that Ruth would want to sever or otherwise diminish their contact with Jeff and Terri. They were his colleagues, and the only ones he and Ruth socialized with outside of the command performance of the end-of-the-year department party. He feared isolation.

By the time his phone broke into arpeggios, the alarm steadily increasing in volume, Ruth was handing him a cup of coffee and a Cheshire grin, a smile without a face. She seemed to have been up for hours.

"A pond, a pond!" she sang. "I'll call the man today."

In the early 2000s, at one of the first Christmases Ken spent with Ruth's family, she received from both her mother and her sister vegetarian cookbooks. (Different chefs.) She was so angry at this double lack of originality, a twin nullity, that she refused to pose for any pictures around the tree, and two months later Ken found both books in a bag for Goodwill. *That* was the scene Ken was expecting. A fight. Yelling. Frozen silence. Complaints, more curses directed at windows or doors or animals. A finale of total renunciation of ponds, perhaps a rejection of landscape architecture altogether. He had expected dismissal, not pursuit.

"Did it seem to you," he asked, hoisting himself to a seated position, "did it seem to you like Terri was going to say she was pregnant?"

Ruth scoffed. "Terri doesn't want children," she said. "Everyone knows that."

Terri didn't want children and Ruth wanted a pond. Now more than ever.

"I wanted that pond first," she said.

Ken pointed out the potentially devastating effects on their friendship. Ruth shook her head from side to side. "No, no, no," she said. "It's not like they're the only people with a pond. Lots of people have ponds."

"The balance of pond power is shifting!" Ken said, and dribbled coffee on his chin and chest hair. He wiped it with the sheet. Ruth took his cup and drank from it. She seemed very caffeinated already. She hadn't slept well since they moved to Freeport, but she didn't complain. She didn't make it worse for him. Ken asked if he should mention her plans to Jeff.

"That's up to you," Ruth said. Ken had to admit that he found Ruth very sexy in her newfound greediness and impatience, and he lost a nice ten minutes of his afternoon imagining her naked and with her mouth on various parts of his and other people's bodies. Some of these fantasies also involved Terri, which is normal, he counseled himself as he washed his hands in the single-occupancy unisex bathroom, which had no mirror above the sink.

WATERFALLS, GROTTOS, waterfalls overhanging grottos. Bowers. Stone walls, hanging plants, saltwater, freshwater, filtered water, springs, fountains. Docks. Pumps, sealants, tubes, rocks, plastic rocks, fiberglass rocks, rock lids, drains, cleaners, diverters, skimmers. The *Watergarden World* catalog, world inside a world. Ruth pointed to a page in the floppy book, a shelf of askew slate-colored rocks that formed curtains of water that dropped into a greenish-brown basin. Plants, ferns, and mosses formed a border on three sides. Three dozen pea-green lily pads clustered together. A metal bucket leaned against the foot of the flat stones that formed the hidden stairway.

"That's the one Jeff and Terri have," Ken said.

He took the opportunity to say that Jeff and Terri's pond was very busy, with many kinds of plants and rocks, and that if they were also going to have a pond it would be best if it were simple. They should reduce the pond to its elements: water, grasses, orange flames.

"No one likes a copycat," he said. "Our pond has to be different."

Ruth did not understand how building the most elemental and quintessential koi pond would be a way of making their pond different—it seemed to her that it would be a way of making their pond the same as every pond—but she didn't argue. Eyes on the prize.

IT TAKES VERY LITTLE TIME to build a pond. After so many years of pushing it off, the project had come to seem stupidly Herculean, like rock climbing or running a marathon, and Ken had expected to have men in their yard for weeks, many men, with many loud machines. But the entire affair took one weekend. Ken and Ruth watched from inside the house as the men dug, lined, filled, filtered, planted, and arranged.

"See," Ken said to Ruth. "It's taking less time because we're making ours so simple. That's another advantage."

Ruth had her way on two points. She insisted the pond be installed directly off the patio, so that even with their faux-wood alfresco dining chairs tilted into a semi-recline, they could hear the water lapping and, through half-slit eyes, admire the grasses and, when the orange-licked white longfin koi arrived from Tri-State House of Koi, be soothed by the hypnotic swimming circles of their submarine forms. They ate outside that night, cradled in the chairs' granny-apple-colored cushions, and the white of the pagoda glowed like a fallen moon caught in the light of the citronella candle. The pagoda was the second point she had carried.

They could not hear each other talk over the din of the cicadas. Ken was not used to crickets, let alone cicadas, and had transferred all his citified loathing of cockroaches to whatever thrumming he heard coming from the woods, which he imagined as the noise of an army gathering strength on its long march to victory.

It was Ruth and Ken's turn to host, and Terri and Jeff arrived punctually bearing a bouquet of bare twigs that Ruth made a point of arranging in her favorite terra-cotta vase.

"I have no idea where I got this vase!" she said. While Terri helped to set the table, Jeff yanked on the sticky sliding door and wedged himself outside. Ken was fiddling with the grill.

"Hey!" Jeff said. He pointed, past the alfresco dining set, to the clumps of grasses bent crookedly like paper cranes. "You built a pond."

Ken put on his casual voice. "We always wanted one. I guess you inspired us!"

Jeff inspected it closely. "You didn't tell me you were doing this," he said. He crouched down and whispered to the fish. "Puh-puh-puh-puh-puh," he said to them. "Where do you keep their food? They look hungry."

Ken used the underside of the spatula to press down on the steaks so that juice dribbled out. He would have to clean the grill later. "I don't know," he said. "Ruth handles all that." He jumped back. Jeff was under his legs, pulling beers from the red and white cooler that leaned against the white vinyl siding of the house's backside. He handed one to Ken. They were slick with sheen, the men and their bottles.

"I like longfins," Jeff said. "We talked about getting those, but we decided not to. They don't live as long as true *nishikigoi*." He paused and shrugged, a tiny and enclosed movement, a gesture for himself and not for Ken. "Of course, they're beautiful."

"I thought the koi were Terri's thing," Ken said. "Because she's been to Japan?"

Jeff never liked talking about things Terri had done before he met her. "Her thing, my thing—they're our thing," he said. "We're a team. That's our theory of marriage."

There was nothing to do out here except circle about the pond, balancing on the jagged shale of false starts.

Jeff went back inside. "Terri will want to see this," he said. His emphasis was on the word *this*; Ken thought it should have been on the word *Terri*. Since they were a team.

He was alone with the steaks and the fish. Ken carried his beer to the water's edge and knelt down to try out the "puh-puh-puh" that he had heard Jeff whisper. The koi ignored him. He worried that longfins were fated to brief life. How brief would it be? He had no idea what a brief life span was, for a koi. And should he water the grasses, or did being in the pond make them wet enough?

Ken's office was so full of books that they called it the storehouse. Ruth had named it that. She had never been there, but the shelves were visible behind him in his picture on the department website. The books were organized by color, a system Ken had deplored until he tried it and discovered its analgesic effects. A framed poster of an exhibition from the Philadelphia Museum of Art reclined against a file cabinet. It was an office-warming present from Ruth. He liked it, but when he looked into his soul he knew that he would never hang that poster on the wall.

"I'm sorry for bothering you at work," Ruth asked when he picked up his desk phone. Her voice was low and morbid and her own.

"The koi are gone," she said.

She had noticed, she said now, that there seemed to be fewer koi several days ago, but hadn't said anything about it. She wasn't sure; didn't want to jinx it. She thought—it sounded loony, but it had to be said—that maybe they were hanging out near the bottom of the pond, where the water was warmer. Maybe they had been cold; it had been a mild spring. Then today, while working at the kitchen table, she saw, through the window, an egret swoop in and carry one away. Ken googled "egret eating koi" and clicked on a YouTube video with that name.

"I'm watching it on YouTube," he interrupted and described what he was seeing. The YouTube egret had chosen an exceptionally large koi, and juggled it in his beak several times before choking it down his gullet. You could see it, koi-shaped, cartoonishly descending. It was appalling.

Ruth asked what the video was called and pulled it up on her own screen. "No," she said. "Our koi are smaller. He swallowed them midflight."

Ruth had run outside, smacking wooden spoon on pot, but she was too late. The bird was gone. The pond was empty.

"Let's watch it again," Ken said, but Ruth didn't feel like it.

IN 1977, A KOI NAMED HANAKO died in Japan. Hanako was 226 years old. What Ken found most interesting about Hanako, when he started looking into the matter of life span, was that Hanako was said to recognize the sound of her own name. Dr. Komei Koshihara, the women's-college president who served as Hanako's last caretaker, said that he would call her from the edge of the water, saying, "Hanako! Hanako!" and she would glide directly to where Dr. Koshihara stood. Sometimes, he said, he would take the elderly fish out of the water and hold her in his arms.

Ken found this story hard to believe. It wasn't Hanako's age. There's plenty of reason to hang around underwater, Ken thought, if there were no predators to interfere; everything was provided for, like being 226 years old in utero. And it wasn't the facts that got to him, either: the problem of how-could-a-fish-breathe-out-of-water, the problem of a-fish's-slippery-body-that-would-slide-from-human-arms, the problem, the admittedly glaring problem, of a-scholar-who-should-know-better-willingly-exposing-himself-to-aquatic-bacteria. It was that Ken could not imagine having Dr. Koshihara's *relationship with a fish*, that *experience* of affection or comfort or needs mutually proffered and satisfied. He could not imagine a koi coming when called.

The night that the egret cleared the pond, Ruth was distracted. She kept talking about "Jackie" and "Lily" and "Pete"—it went on, the names she had given them. He hadn't known.

Ken recalled Hanako's longevity and felt failure spasm in him like a muscle he had forgotten to stretch: Hanako had been protected. Ken tried to push from his mind the thought that they had asked for this defeat, by rushing into koi before doing the proper research. Who did they think they were, that they could just go out and buy koi and they would thrive. They weren't experts at all. They were barely amateurs.

"I can't believe they have koi and we don't," Ruth said. Her emphasis was on the word *they*; Ken thought it should have been on the word *we*. Since they were a team.

She flipped through the channels and found a cooking show that she hated. A famous white chef was eating squid from a Styrofoam cup at a stall in an alley somewhere in China. "If they were going to die we could have at least eaten them," she said. "I bet Terri knows a great recipe." And then, with real passion, "Those assholes!"

"Come on," Ken said. "Terri and Jeff are our friends. And we don't eat fish," he added.

"Are they?" Ruth said. The famous white chef was now slapping the backs of the Chinese men who had prepared and sold him the squid. Ken wished a stomach virus on him. Nothing deadly. Just to teach him a lesson. "Are they really our friends?" she asked.

Ken didn't appreciate the challenge, so he raised it. "If we asked them, they would give us their koi," he said.

She searched his eyes, black and blue, twitching in the corners. The lines between his brows broke his face into two pieces like scores in a round loaf. If you had asked her, she could not have said what he would do next. "OK," she said. "Call them. Call them now."

This was definitely not what Ken wanted. Not this bowing and scraping and generally losing face. Not this asking for help and a handout, assuming the role of a student peddling excuses, angling for exceptions, exposing everything he had not learned in time. He, who had planned a pond perfect in its simplicity and totally self-sufficient in its essence. But Ruth. She was waiting. "Call him now," she said. It was a test.

Jeff was large and gracious on the phone and more than proved Ken right. He was a friend, acting like friends do. "This happens to everyone," he told Ken. It had not happened to them, but that was because they had read the horror stories and had strung fishing wire across their pond. To deter aerial attack. The threat to koi comes in all forms, Jeff added in the voice he used for lecturing and faculty meetings: egrets, herons, hawks, raccoons, foxes—even bears.

"There are bears here?" Ken said.

"Of course not," Jeff said. "But in other places."

There was relief in Jeff's voice, relief that there was a favor that Ruth and Ken needed. It put him at ease to know that their ponds were connected in this way. They would be caretakers of the same family; it was like they were in-laws! Both couples passed the phone back and forth and everyone talked to everyone. "Lily!" Terri exclaimed. "I named one of ours Pat!"

The next day Jeff and Terri brought two koi over in an old fish tank that Terri had borrowed from a neighbor. (This detail delighted Jeff: the giving trail went on forever.) They toasted glasses of wine and watched the koi find the perimeters of their new home. Ruth swore she would put up the fishing line immediately.

"Get busy, guys!" Ken said to the pond. He was having a hard time feeling anything for these new and un-homesick fish. Their prehistoric suction cups mouthed the air with what looked like despondency and what he knew in his disappointment to be only dumb instinct.

THERE WAS NO REASON to be on campus in the mornings so Ken sometimes lingered, drinking coffee in the kitchen. Ruth, who worked from home, ignored him. Today she was going to install the fishing line—just as soon as she went to the store and bought it.

Ken was rinsing his mug when he saw it happen. He ran to the sliding door and pulled but it was locked and in his confusion and haste the moment came to him as a choice between watching and unlocking. He watched.

Egrets are sky giraffes erased to blankness, plump and balanced on emaciated legs; their boneless necks curve like the Big Dipper. Very tall. This one was picking its way over gray chalkboard rocks, and it plunged into the water. Wings extended, it skimmed the surface in circles. One, three, four times, the feathered arms cocked wide and dangled, as if broken. But they were very strong. The bird hopped out with the koi in its beak, and bobbed its head up and down, pacing at the edge of the pond. It flapped its wings and bobbled its neck. Ken thought about the times he had eaten a slice of pizza while walking down South Street. This was what the egret was doing, or seemed to be doing, until Ken realized that he had stopped mouthing the koi and was beating its long, thick body against the patio. Now Jeff's ivory-white and golden-flecked *nishikigoi* was sagging and dead, and as the egret choked it down whole, out of the sky another bird dove, skimmed, nabbed, and pecked at the second fish, the mate. It flew off, the lifeless koi pinned in its banana-colored bill. The first egret left the way it had come, walk-hopping over the rocks and taking a long low running start over the yard and back up to the sky.

Ruth looked up from her computer. "Why are you standing like that in front of the door?" she asked.

"It happened again," Ken said. "The koi." If only he had left for work on time, he thought, he would not be responsible, he would not have met the depths of his own impotent inaction so early in the day.

"Why didn't you stop him?" she asked, her tone flinty. Ken, fundamentally a soft man, deflated under the accusation. He seemed to be leaking mass. If he stood there all day, by dinnertime he would be a thin man. It was his poor posture, of course, that accounted for this. Ruth knew that.

"If only you wanted a bird sanctuary instead of a koi pond," he said. "Then everything would be perfect."

It had taken all his energy to make this one bit of weak wit. Ruth did not like to see Ken puddling and losing shape in front of her. She laid her head in her lap and ground the heels of her hands into her eye sockets and did not move until he was gone. He did not try to kiss or touch her when he passed by on his way to the garage.

That evening Ruth told Ken that she was sorry for acting out and was fine now. She had decided they didn't need any more koi. She liked them but they were a lot of trouble, and having the pond was perfectly good on its own. What mattered to her was that Ken had agreed that they could try to have them. Now she knew what it was to be a person who had koi.

"You also know what it's like to be a person whose koi get eaten by an egret," Ken said.

"Exactly," Ruth said. "You really get me."

A FEW WEEKS PASSED, filled with things that had nothing to do with ponds or koi or the outdoors. They caught up on a popular television show about a child murderer, and talked about the criminal justice system. Ruth bought a rug so she had something to sit on when she wanted to sit on the floor. It had a black-and-white checkerboard pattern. It was large and expensive and soft, and little tassels hung off its edges that she intended to comb straight on a regular basis. "I can't believe I didn't do this right away," she said, stretching out on her back and flexing and wriggling her feet. "I love it down here." She jumped forward into a yoga pose whose name Ken didn't know, buried her palms and fingers in the plushness, and pushed her backside into the air. Her shirt fell over her face and exposed her bare breasts. Each of her toenails was painted a different color of the rainbow. Ken was very attracted to her. Then one evening he came in slumping and stooping and shuffling and slow.

"Were the students bad today?" Ruth asked.

"Yes," Ken said, his face all folds, the skin turning in on itself like it was running away. "But no."

It turned out that Jeff had called him to say that it was a silly situation, one of life's ironies, but now all of *their* koi were gone. He had emphasized it. "Now all of *our* koi are gone," Jeff had said. "I don't see how it could have happened, because of the fishing wire. But I guess our bird is really smart."

Ruth laughed and all her teeth showed. "He said that? He said *his* bird is really smart?"

Ken wasn't laughing and so Ruth made her face serious and empathetic. "Of course our bird is smart," she said.

It turned out that then Jeff had asked Ken for the koi back, so they could repopulate his pond. "I hope those two like each other," he had said, "because we need them to get busy!" Ken was especially stuck on this joke, which he had made first, and which now tortured him with its crass anthropomorphism. Hanako did not know the sound of her name and no koi was capable of "liking" any other.

"Jeff is a philistine," Ken said. "He gets his ideas about nature from Disney movies."

Ruth disagreed—didn't Jeff have experience? Didn't he know about the fishing line?—but nodded in appeasement. She had wished death on Jeff's koi and now they were dead. She felt no more regret than the egret did. Nature was on her side.

"You told him that the koi are gone, right?" she asked.

Ken had his head in the refrigerator and Ruth couldn't hear what he was saying.

"What?" she said.

He turned around and yelled. "I told him no!"

It was some work to make her understand the sequence of events, but in the end it was clear. Jeff had asked for his koi back and Ken had said, "I don't think so," and then, quickly, "I have to go, I'm at work." That was it. That was how it ended.

With exaggerated tenderness and guilelessness, offensively gentle, his wife asked why Ken hadn't told their friend that the koi he had given them were dead.

Ken drank from his beer and put it down on the table. "I didn't want him to think I was a bad steward," he said.

Ruth placed a coaster under the bottle. "A bad steward?" she repeated. "Now he thinks you're an asshole." It occurred to her that maybe Ken was an asshole, and she had never known it. Her anger popped like a balloon. He still had surprises, her husband—she had not reached the end of him yet.

"Or crazy!" Ken said. He could relax now that Ruth was laughing. He got into the spirit of the moment and circled a finger near his ear in a "crazy" gesture. Ruth loved this gesture. She grabbed the finger and nibbled on it. Afterward, as she rolled away from him, wrapping herself in a cocoon of stolen blanket, she said, cheerfully mannish, "G'night, steward," and gave him a pert two-fingered salute. She emphasized that word, steward, that she had never before spoken out loud. It kept Ken awake for hours; he sat in the kitchen snacking and stewing. In the morning she greeted him with it, "G'morning, steward," and another little salute, and that was when he asked her to please stop.

"But it's funny," she said.

"It's not funny," he said. Ruth didn't believe him. He's proud, she told herself, and went downstairs to put the coffee on. Harsh light was filling the kitchen unpleasantly. She was wearing a black kimono that Ken had purchased for her many years ago. She started most mornings in it and she never washed it because she was afraid it would shrink. As she drew shut the curtains, red and seeded with knots like strawberries, she thought that today she would order another shipment from the Tri-State House of Koi. They would be a gift for Ken.

HAND JOBS

It was my birthday and we were drinking white wine and waiting for the palm reading to start. We were at Henry's apartment. Henry was a friend of Carla's, and a scholar of illuminated manuscripts. He lived in a converted firehouse with his boyfriend, a fund manager, and he liked hosting parties, because it made use of the space. There were no closets. All their worldly possessions were displayed on modular shelves or hanging off horseshoe-shaped hooks. The palm reading had been Henry's idea. The palm reader had been recommended to him by a friend of a friend, and he kept saying she was the best, like he could tell the difference.

The palm reader, when she arrived, moved in a way that suggested she was not in too much of a hurry to arrive in the future. She was like some piece of human clutter purchased to give the room more character. Ceramic roses were clipped to her earlobes and beneath her black crocheted dress her breasts strained to get away from each other. On her left hand was a diamond the size of a Brussels sprout. She was between 40 and 65 years old. I was the guest of honor and I got to go first. She led me away from the drinks and the stereo and the cheese to the corner under the skylight, and sat me on an egg-shaped orange chair. The palm reader sat herself on a low wooden bench, a Shaker pew that had been bought at auction.

She smelled like lemongrass. The first thing she said was that I would change jobs many times, a statement that had the advantage of being already true. I had had all the jobs a young person has. I had been a telemarketer, taco maker, babysitter, barista, waitress, and tutor, and I had modeled for a life-drawing class, even though the money wasn't very good. I liked variety; I lived like a gatherer. At that time I believed that if you string enough moments together life becomes a collection, something worth talking about. Like that movie I saw at the repertory theater, *La Collectionneuse*, at the sea with the people talking on telephones. *Collectionneuse* is a word that feels good in your mouth, especially if you don't speak French. It's hard to believe now, but there was once a time when it really mattered if you spoke French or not.

The palm reader asked me to quiet my mind so she could concentrate. She told me that I had extra vitality. Then she told me that, vitality notwithstanding, I was strongly controlled by fate. I asked to see her palm for comparison, but she refused.

"That's against my policy," she said in her voice that was gravel crunching.

"You know," she said, "in a way, none of us are self-made."

I assured the palm reader that she did not have to persuade me that destiny was a good thing.

"What's *personal responsibility* anyway?" I said, mistaking our conversation for a dialogue.

"Why do you clean houses?" she asked. I looked at my hands. If it was a guess, it was a good one. There are lots of ways to ruin your hands.

"I need the money," I said.

When the palm reader opened her eyes, nothing else on her face moved. She leaned in until our foreheads were a hair from touching.

"Maybe," she said. "You also want something else. But it's not what you're going to get. Also"—here she pulled away—"I don't think your relationship is going to last."

"It already ended," I said.

"The next one won't last, either," she said.

T HE NEXT MORNING at eleven o'clock I was sitting on a bench under a tree whose name I didn't know waking up with a large sweet coffee and reading my own palm. The park was laid out like the spokes of a wheel. It was warm for October—it might have been the warmest October on record. The basics were easy. Every hand has a heart line, a head line, and a life line, but not every hand has a fate line. Having a fate line is special. For some people life is just one thing after another. Having a fate line means you have a purpose, and your job is to discover it.

I didn't have any jobs lined up that day so I finished my coffee and went downtown to see *Diary of a Chambermaid*. It gave me ideas. It also showed me the limitations of my own situation. In *Diary of a Chambermaid* Jeanne Moreau triumphs because life presents obstacles to be overcome; also, a little girl is raped, and dies. Perhaps cleaning houses on a drop-in basis wasn't going to give me enough material; perhaps I needed to become a live-in housekeeper. From reality would greatness issue. Living together presents a different kind of interest. Whatever was happening could not yet be fate.

Carla had said she would meet me at the movie, but something or someone came up and so she came over that night for TV instead. We both liked shows about sex crimes. Before she arrived I noticed a spider of hair behind the bathroom door and picked it up with my fingers and threw it away. I dragged a piece of toilet paper over the lid of the toilet bowl and took a paper towel and picked up the dust bunnies that had gathered along the living room moldings and near the front door, but I didn't have the energy to disturb the untidy stacks of papers and books and the piles of clothes. Uncompensated labor had started to seem like a phase of life I had grown out of.

We got high and watched four episodes of SVU. Somehow or another we started talking about greatness. Carla said that greatness resides in the pursuit of greatness, in simply making the attempt; Carla is the child of artists, and she has a tendency to go easy on herself. But at least she thinks greatness is *something*. Most people I know don't believe in it at all. Of course, when these people talk about greatness, they are not meaning the same thing that I do. I don't care about *prizes*. I only care about recognition.

She left and I ate more pizza and looked at the dishes piled in and around the sink and worried: What if a high professional standard inevitably meant that you slipped up at home? Did I care too much about getting paid? I stripped and got into bed. *What's the most important thing in life?* I wrote in my journal, longhand. *Food-shelter-water. But how do you get food-shelter-water? By being good at your job. What else separates us from the animals?*

MOST OF THE CLIENTS were one-offs—people hiring to impress a dinner party, or for a visit with family. People who would never hire a cleaner *regularly* but justified it for a special occasion. Like how maybe you do cocaine at parties, but you wouldn't buy it yourself.

Not everyone was awful. Once a cool dad was there, watching his daughter, and he was making a kale-celery-lemon cold-pressed juice in a German juice machine, and he offered me one, too. He ran out of kale so he gave me the good juice and he drank the celery-water. This showed his character. Once a middle-aged man hired me to clean his mother's apartment on the Upper West Side. The mother was a hoarder. I filled twenty trash bags with takeout containers and the man sat in the corner and held his mother while she cried. Once a skinny brunette followed me through the apartment apologizing for the mess and picking at her arms. The place was so clean that I stopped pretending and followed the brunette, assuring her that she had done a terrific job. But every time I told her it was great, she kept saying, "It's not *professional* quality."

Once I was in the big dining room of a posh townhouse on the east side, polishing silver, when a tax lawyer who worked from home called down that he needed help with a "big job" upstairs. It was annoying to be interrupted. I liked polishing. It made me feel noble and useful and a bit tragic, like I was Stevens in *The Remains of the Day*. I liked all the parts of the job that felt old-timey, like dusting. I usually got high before work, so it was easy to get into a good rhythm with it, to really get in there and make it gleam. Polishing also cost extra.

"Coming!" I called, nicely.

Up the plush stairs, steeling myself for the nasty hairball, silently pumping myself up with mantras, like *It's just dirty hair*, and *If you do it once you never have to do it again.* I held a red plastic plumber's snake in one hand. It had jagged teeth to catch the hair and draw it up to the light. Last time I had plunged a drain, the sight of the hair slick with dirt had made me gag—but I held it in.

Up the plush stairs, through the French doors of the master bedroom, sinking in the sea-blue carpet, looking through the open bathroom door. Months of weekly business magazines were stacked on a stool that was imitating something but I didn't know what, maybe one of the Louis, like Louis XIV. The oval mirror was wreathed with painted gold leaves. The lawyer was naked and holding his dick in his hand. His chest and stomach, round like a loaf of new-risen bread, were matted with glistening wiry black hair. His hand was moving furiously.

The lawyer was looking just to the left of my head.

"Do you want to touch it?" he asked and held it up, like he was willing to share.

The entire region had been rendered optimistically hairless. Keeping my eyes on the potato of the lawyer's round vacant face, I unbuttoned the top two buttons of my sky-blue uniform—not enough to see anything, but enough to suggest that seeing something wasn't so far behind. His eyes tracked down and hovered at the tit area.

"How much?" I said.

"A hundred dollars," he said.

"For what?" I said.

"*You know,*" he said, but neither of us did.

Sometimes sex is a thing we do for those in need out of compassion, or for ourselves, out of curiosity. I unbuttoned another button. The lawyer, who in all this time had not stopped handling himself, took a step back and collided with the sink. I pulled one bra cup down and lifted out a single breast. The executive shuddered. It was finished.

He wiped his hand on a washcloth and turned away from me to pick his pants off the closed toilet bowl and rummage for his wallet. He counted out five twenties and handed them to me without turning around. I made sure to finish polishing and put away the silver before I let myself out and locked the door behind me. I thought that was just what Stevens would have done. On balance, it had gone pretty well. I had been efficient and sensitive. I had not had to touch anything.

At home that night I turned on the kitchen light and something scuttled into the corner with the trash—a rebuke for leaving my professional zeal at the door. I took my computer to bed and stared at the white screen and tried out first sentences. *Dick* was better than *cock*, for this situation. It left more dangling. I texted *Lawyer = Flasher!* to Carla and spent some time in front of the mirror lifting one breast and then the other out of my shirt. They both had advantages. The next day Carla brought over a picture she had drawn of a fat man jerking himself off. His face was pockmarked and punctuated with a bread-roll nose. We hung the picture on my refrigerator. The money, we agreed, was a problem. What does $100 buy you?

This was a problem I had faced before. In college I babysat for a philosophy professor named Talia who had adopted a little girl from China. She needed a regular babysitter because most weekends her dog traveled to compete in obstacle courses against other dogs. The dog was an excellent competitor and the dining room was filled with trophies and ribbons and medals. When I graduated Talia gave me a $100 gift card to the local liquor store. I went in alone and asked the first person I saw to show me a $100 bottle of white wine. The person suggested a nice Chablis, but at the register it rang up for $20. I lowered my voice to explain to the cashier that there had been a mistake.

"She wants the $100 bottle!" the cashier yelled across the store.

That night I drank the whole bottle myself and had no hangover the following morning, because that's what you're paying for with a $100 bottle. One thing I learned from that experience that I hadn't known before was that there is a $100 version of everything, even Chablis, which I had only associated with church ladies and Tennessee, because I once heard about it in a country song.

Carla, who knew this story, proposed that I use the lawyer's money to buy another nice wine, but I wanted to feel like I was growing.

THE AIR HAD THAT very clean taste, like breathable ice. I felt healthy in it, new. It was Saturday afternoon and to kill time while we waited for a brunch table we went to the park to enjoy the leaves, and in the park we saw Henry, walking with his boyfriend and his boyfriend's dog. The dog was tan and tall and had four skinny legs. We said hello and tried to pet the dog, but the dog was pulling on the leash, so the boyfriend gave up the slack. We all silently watched the dog scurry on its twiggy legs up to the top of a nearby pile of wood chips and tremblingly squeeze out a pale log of excrement. Henry's boyfriend groaned and scrambled after the turd and rejoined us holding a lumpen plastic bag a ways out from his body.

"Your dog is the king of that pile of wood chips," I said.

"He thinks so," he said.

Henry was reminded of a research librarian he had seen in a rare-books room some years ago who had the most fastidious manner of handing him extraordinary objects from the special collection and a way of presenting and opening the materials as if the two of them were joint explorers on a sacred mission.

"I felt that I loved him," Henry said, "in the way that you love someone for only an instant. I loved that he was opening this world to me."

Henry's boyfriend made a joke about opening "something else" and everyone laughed too heartily and then Henry went on.

"But later in the afternoon," Henry said, "we were next to each other at the urinals. After the librarian zipped up, he left without washing his hands."

"What does this have to do with the dog?" his boyfriend asked. "She doesn't have hands."

Henry and his boyfriend often had these breakdowns in communication. The boyfriend just didn't have a poetic imagination.

"I taught myself how to read palms," I said. "After the palm reading at my birthday."

"What?" Carla said. "You didn't tell me that."

"Will you read my palm?" the boyfriend asked.

"Twenty dollars," I said, and he laughed and stopped laughing when I didn't start.

"I have my future to consider," I said. "If I start giving it away now, where will it end?"

Henry's boyfriend gave Henry the plastic bag to hold and opened his wallet.

"I only have a five," he said. I took the bill and examined his hand, twisting it this way and that in the shadowless light. No matter what I did, his great love would die terribly young. Whether this was Henry or not, though, I had no way of knowing.

"You have a fire-shaped hand," I said. "That means you're bold."

He was pleased, and asked me to go on.

"You are very healthy," I said, stalling.

The boyfriend didn't care about getting his money's worth. The dog started pulling and straining on the leash, and they lifted a hand to wave good-bye. After they were gone I told Carla what I had learned about the young death of his great love.

"Maybe he is going to leave Henry and date someone else, someone young, and that person is going to die," Carla said. "Or maybe Henry is going to die. Are we still young?"

I felt uneasy that I hadn't told the full truth to a paying customer.

"It wasn't ethical," I said. "It wasn't professional."

Carla shrugged. She's a good person, but it's hard to interest her in questions like this.

That Monday I got my schedule for the week and saw that the lawyer had left me an online review: five stars for professionalism and four stars for satisfaction. I had not realized he had such a keen sense of humor. Still, I was proud. Is that so wrong? I had comported myself admirably in a difficult moment. It was like those five golden stars all colored in in a row were five golden hands tipping five golden hats, saying, *I see you.*

I knew that the best moment of my house-cleaning career was behind me. I would have to work another year at least to have an encounter like that. I was done with research. I logged on and deleted my account with the agency. Instantly I received an email asking me to rate my experience as an employee. Instead, I set up a user account with a different email address and scheduled a cleaning for my apartment. The woman they sent was named Yasmin. She was 50 years old and wore a diamond crucifix and a hairnet and talked about her very intelligent grandchildren. She was there for one hour. She cost $60 and I gave her a $45 tip. Problem solved.

My tenure as a maid had lasted forty days. To celebrate my freedom, Carla took me to a dark bar where we toasted our past and future selves. Carla said she would let me read her palm and I promised to tell her the truth.

"Even if someone is going to die," I said. "I'll tell you."

It was hard to make out the lines by candlelight. I held her hand close to my face and touched the inside of her palm. She giggled. Carla has always been ticklish. Once I saw her kick a Korean lady in the face during a pedicure. She didn't mean to do it, but when the lady started scrubbing the sole her leg jerked out and she made contact. The Korean lady was a real professional. She wiped off her glasses and finished the job. We never showed our feet in that nail salon again.

On Carla's hand I saw vitality and creativity and success. Then I showed her how her health line branched out from the life line.

"Your life will be threatened in old age," I told her.

"That's what the palm reader said on your birthday," she said. "But everybody's life is threatened in old age."

"Not like this," I said. "It looks like something violent."

Carla was pleased. Everyone wants to meet a dramatic end.

We got drunk and talked about Henry and how long he had to live; and if he died, how he would die; and when he died, would I tell everyone that I had known all along? Because what was the truth? There are some things you can know about yourself, and there are some things only someone else can know. There are things you can't tell now that you find out later you knew all along. +

ENRIQUE MARTÍNEZ CELAYA, *THE TRANSIT*. 2012, OIL AND WAX ON CANVAS, 108 × 120".
COURTESY OF LA LOUVER, VENICE, CALIFORNIA.

DISPATCHES FROM GUERRERO
Alejandro Almazán

On September 26, 2014, forty-three normalistas *(student teachers) from a school in Ayotzinapa, Guerrero, Mexico, were kidnapped in the town of Iguala and allegedly murdered by a drug gang with the cooperation of the mayor and local police. Originally published in the December 2014 issue of the Mexican magazine* Gatopardo, *Alejandro Almazán's reportage explores the larger catastrophe of the drug war in the state where the kidnapping took place.*

> To lose your hair, to lose control,
> You know, to lose valuable time,
> ....
> To lose blood, your father and mother,
> The heart you lost in Heidelberg,
> ....
> To lose, again and again to lose,
> Even illusions lost a long time ago.
>
> —Hans Magnus Enzensberger, *The Sinking of the Titanic*

I ASKED HIM TO TELL ME about the poppies overrunning his district, but Mario Chávez, the young mayor of Tlacotepec, seemed as if he came from a different country: he told me that there were no poppies in his district, that it was just a rumor, nothing more, and then he started to tell me about a man with wings (though others insisted it was a dragon) who for many nights now had been flying through his town.

"Tomorrow the bishop will go to bless the sky for us from a helicopter that we chartered for him," the mayor told me, as if this were their only salvation. I should have gone to Tlacotepec to see how the story ended, but outside the restaurant where we were chatting was the rest of Guerrero, and somewhere in it our dead, our disappeared.

FIFTY PERCENT OF COMMERCE in Chilpancingo has shut down indefinitely. Seventy percent of the still-existing businesses are shuttered by seven at night. A dozen money-exchange establishments have been shut down; they'd been laundering narcodollars for two or three years. Two hundred and fifty taxi licenses were given out to the narcos via the state government. One hundred and twenty garbage trucks are owned by narcos. Ten percent of the cost of each building project is the cut that politicians and narcos demand from the construction companies. Three hundred wealthy families have fled the city. Three hundred homes are on the market; only two have sold. Three thousand five hundred pesos is the amount bar owners remit as their weekly quota. Five thousand pesos are coughed up weekly by hardware store owners so that they aren't kidnapped and are able to stay open and do good business. Fifty pesos is what the narcos charge for every pig the butchers buy from the slaughterhouse. Every taxi driver gives up twenty-five pesos daily as his contribution. In Iguala, a jeweler might be asked to hand over twenty thousand pesos a month if he doesn't want to be bothered. Twenty thousand. Fifty percent is what the narco takes from a campesino when he receives benefits from social programs or the profits of his harvest. The narcos charge two pesos for every chicken sold in the *pollerías*, and fifty cents for the guts.

I wrote down each figure I heard from Jaime Nava, the president of the Coparmex (Mexican Employers' Association) in Chilpancingo, but two trends say it all: among the few businesses that have prospered since the violence in Guerrero intensified are the private security industry and the speculators. The former owe their success to the kidnappings, extortions, and robberies. The latter live off the consequences: the people who go into debt to pay a ransom, to pay the weekly quota, or to escape from the city.

"Even just two years ago there were only five pawn shops in Chilpancingo, and now there are more than sixty," complains Nava. Seconds later, he tells me that he owns a printing business and that, in fifteen years of business, the demand for signs—FOR SALE, FOR RENT, or WE'VE CHANGED LOCATIONS—has never been higher.

"The funeral homes must do well too," I said.

"They've always done well, which is why I didn't even bother mentioning them."

In the past ten years, according to the figures published by the National System of Public Security, Guerrero has been a death machine: 14,118 people have been murdered in the state.

Later I called I-Tec, a security-systems business in the center of Chilpancingo. The employee who took my call told me that the basic package—four cameras, one video recorder, and the installation—costs seven thousand pesos, that this was the most popular package, that they have cameras as expensive as eighty thousand pesos, that they're ordered more often than you would think, and, as if it were a publicity slogan, that it was true, businesses like I-Tec succeed because of fear.

I MET JAVIER MONROY in 2010, and back then the vultures were circling low over his head: gunmen were stalking his house on the outskirts of Chilpancingo. But a few months ago, the Templarios (Knights Templar)—the cartel from Michoacán that moves drugs in Guerrero as easily as if they were exporting fruit—picked him up and took him to see one of their bosses.

"He wanted me to help him clean up his image," Javier told me. "Imagine that!"

Javier is an activist: for twenty years he's led Tadeco (the Community Development Workshop), a collective that over time turned into an itinerant help desk that took on the cases of Guerrero's disappeared, kidnapped, and murdered. They started investigating cases in March 2007, after one of their own comrades, Gabriel Cerón, was taken away. At the time of his disappearance, Gabo was an architect and about to be married. To earn extra money for the wedding, he drafted some blueprints for Francisco Cortés, a protected witness who had never actually cut his ties with the narcos. When Gabo went to turn in his work to Cortés, cops showed up and took the two men away, never to be seen again. Since then, Tadeco has had a small tent set up in the main square of Chilpancingo, where hundreds of people, from every district, have come to tell Javier their horrible stories. Since then, threats have been coming in too.

On December 25, 2009, for example, Javier and other members of the collective received a host of grammatically inscrutable text messages after another Tadeco member had his cell phone stolen:

> We're going to get to you by going after the person that would hurt you the most and we are referring to the woman in the center.

> One of these days your going to be part of the mural of the disappeared. sincerely the family ok.

> So easy it would be for us to took the girl in the black pant and brown sweater that's under the tent

"One day they called to tell me that I should start shopping for my coffin," Javier told me.

"And who do you think it was?"

"Tadeco is inconvenient for the authorities of Guerrero, for the army, for the caciques, and for the narcos. It could have been any of them. We've accused each of them of carrying out forced disappearances."

The Committee for the Disappeared of Guerrero has reported that between 2005 and December 2013, more than 6,500 people were victims of forced disappearance or murder. Tadeco has received only six hundred cases over more or less the same period. The reason for the discrepancy is that Tadeco only receives cases in which a preliminary inquiry has already been made—something that happens rarely, since people either fail to bring their cases to the police or find themselves threatened when they do.

WHILE WE CLIMBED one of the hills that hug Iguala—poor Iguala, which was once the "Cradle of the Independence and the Flag" and no longer lives up to any such renown—I asked a veteran campesino when exactly he thought Guerrero had gone to shit. "You're getting to the scene pretty late," he said. He said it without any resentment, but still I apologized. He was right: we'd all gotten here late. Only the narcos—*El Crimen*—had gotten here on time.

You could say El Crimen made its appearance in Guerrero as far back as the '70s, when the Cuban trafficker Alberto Sicilia Falcón colluded with army leadership to oversee the farming of marijuana and poppies; today 60 percent of the opium poppy grown in the country is concentrated in the state of Guerrero. Or El Crimen may have come to town with the politicians who thought that the state was their personal plantation, like the Figueroas, the family that has governed Guerrero multiple times and today controls all the fertilizer in the region.* Or maybe it came in 2001, when the Torres and Arizmendi clans, two groups who ran a large part of the drug trade in Guerrero, slaughtered each other in the town Kilómetro 30, near Acapulco. Since then the cartels have flourished in proportion to the corruption of the government.

Maybe El Crimen came in November 2009, when Comandante Ramiro, of the ERPI,† was murdered by paramilitaries in the service of the army and the federal government. Ramiro was known for organizing villages, doing community work, and confronting the narcos. Or maybe it came a month later, in December, when the navy killed Arturo Beltrán Leyva, and his family business—the dominant cartel in Guerrero—split up into what are today the Rojos and Guerreros Unidos.

Maybe El Crimen came when the political parties started handpicking candidates on the basis of whether they could fund their own campaigns; the *perredista* (PRD party candidate) José Luis Abarca, the former mayor of Iguala and the one allegedly responsible for the disappearance of the forty-three students from Ayotzinapa, wasn't the first such candidate, nor will he be the last. El Crimen could also have come when the drug traffickers started to co-opt the local police forces; in Iguala, for example, Mayor Abarca's brothers-in-law, the turf leaders of the Guerreros Unidos mini-cartel, controlled the police and even formed their own anti-kidnapping unit called Los Bélicos (the Bellicose). Or maybe El Crimen came when the public offices filled up with crooks. The former state secretary general Jesús Martínez Garnelo, to cite one

---

* Both Rubén Figueroa Sr. and Rubén Figueroa Jr. presided over despicable human rights violations during their terms as governor of Guerrero. The former's government targeted activists, campesinos, and students as part of the larger Mexican Dirty War campaign against progressives during the 1970s, and the latter had to step down after the Aguas Blancas massacre of 1995, when seventeen activist campesinos were slaughtered during a political rally.

† The Insurgent People's Revolutionary Army, a leftist rebel group local to Guerrero.

case, was fingered in 2001 as the judge responsible for freeing one of the most violent and notorious kidnappers in the region, Pedro Barragán. Martínez was disbarred for doing so—but for only two years. Afterward, his license was restored indefinitely, until it came to light that he had ties to Mayor Abarca and took a call from him in the hours following the kidnapping of the forty-three students, and he finally resigned.

El Crimen could have come at any of these moments, and regardless I would have been late. "Forgive me," I told the veteran campesino, and we kept walking.

IN CHILPANCINGO, a garbage scavenger told me the narcos took his 12-year-old son two months ago and now force him to work as their *halcón* (hawk), or in other words as a lookout for their crime syndicate; a reporter colleague told me they kidnapped his brother in 2012; and a young businessman mentioned to me that he hadn't taken his luxury SUV out of the garage since he bought it six months ago. In Zumpango, a lady told me that it was common to see pickup trucks passing by filled to the brim with dead bodies. At the Mezcala Bridge, a man from the area told me how all day Rojos and Guerreros Unidos alike throw their dead over the side. And in Iguala, I saw the army, the federal police, and the city cops pretending that they had control over the city.

I reached a point at which I wondered whether there was any hope left amid all the barbarity, and so I went to seek out the people from the Union of Villages and Organizations of the State of Guerrero (UPOEG). They arrived in Iguala at the beginning of October. There are three hundred of them, and they came to search for the forty-three normalistas who (the official story holds) were disappeared by the police and the hitmen of the Guerreros Unidos this past September 26.

The UPOEG formed as a splinter group of the Regional Coordinator of Communitarian Authorities (CRAC), an indigenous organization that emerged in 1999 in order to protect villages from the narcos, the soldiers, the police, and paramilitary organizations. People affiliated with CRAC insist that the UPOEG actually started as an armed organization backed by the government, and that one of its leaders, Plácido Valerio, has ties with ex-governor Ángel Aguirre. "From the government we've accepted weapons, radios, trucks, and uniforms, but we're not their strongmen," I was told by Don Crisóforo García, another of the leaders of the UPOEG. "In Ayutla a lot of shit was going down: the authorities were protecting the bad guys, the bad guys were taking our women and our daughters, the military and the police were disappearing people, and folks were getting their lands taken away for the poppy crops. A lot of shit. And the same thing was happening in Tierra Colorada, in Tecoanapa, and in Valle del Ocotito. The town got organized quickly, we brought the experience of the CRAC, and we started to take care of each other. Our organization was born on January 4, 2013. In Ayutla, just about two months after coming together, we had already rounded up fifty-three criminals; thirty-six of them were *descuartizadores* [roughly, people who dismember] and gunmen. We handed all of them over to the district attorney's office, and they let all of them go. That's why, now when we catch a bad guy, we rehabilitate him ourselves: we sentence them to between six months and five years of community service. Many of the rehabilitated have stayed on to live in our villages: they've become good people. Think about this: one kid turned himself in all on his own, he told us that he'd already killed people and the council of elders spoke to him; and today he's still among us, helping people. We also had a descuartizadora, but she just completed her sentence and left. The word on the street is that they've killed her."

After the normalistas disappeared, members of the UPOEG went up into the Cerro del Zapatero mountainside. They found six graves, two of them empty but freshly dug and ready for use. They were willing to start digging, but they only had one shovel among them. "This fucking government, if they wanted to find the boys they would give us a hand, but they won't even lend us shovels," said Don Crisóforo.

At that point an old man showed up with another shovel and a crowbar: "My son was killed by the Iguala police, they just shot him for no reason, when he was walking out of the middle school, but on the death certificate they put down that he was a cartel hitman and had died in a shootout; at the district attorney's they told me not to stir up trouble; that's why I'm here, because in my mind I believe that if I help to find the normalistas, I'll bring justice for something at least." The guy immediately went to work digging.

By the end, the UPOEG had dug up three out of the four mass graves. They found sandals, a glove, and something that Don Crisóforo said was a finger. I can't describe the smell, but I know that the whole day I carried it on my clothes and in my hair.

○ ○ ○

WHEN I WENT TO SEE the businessman Pioquinto Damián, he hadn't left his apartment in 275 days.

Two guards patrol the entrance to the building, all of which is owned by Pioquinto. The doors are bulletproof, and there is a panic room in the event that things really go sour. He rarely looks out the window, and his wife and kids never leave the house without bodyguards. In his apartment I saw a bar stocked with good whiskey; I saw a dining room full of shining crystal and big enough for ten people; I saw a kitchen that would be a joy to cook in. It was all so clean that I suspected even Pioquinto's two tiny dogs ate with a fork and knife.

"And you don't miss the city?" I asked him at one point.

"You know, I feel fucking great here," he answered me and tossed back the second coffee he had had in the half hour I had been there.

Pioquinto was once a congressional representative for the PRI (the Insitutional Revolutionary Party), but that isn't why he doesn't leave his house. His problem is with the current mayor of Chilpancingo, Mario Moreno.

As president of the local chamber of commerce, Pioquinto used to complain to Moreno that the police were working for the narcos. "I went to see the asshole eight times to demand security, and every time he played dumb." On August 3 of last year, after meeting again with Moreno, Pioquinto received a call: a group of gunmen had tried to kidnap one of his sons. In the months that followed, Pioquinto barely left his house. He met with a capo so that they would leave his kids in peace, and he held a few press conferences in which he openly condemned Moreno, saying that he had given out permits for flea markets managed by organized crime, that he had given the narcos the license for the town fairgrounds, and that he was working for the mafia.

Then came January 28. On that day, Pioquinto was invited to a meeting with the *policía comunitaria*, or unofficial community police, of Mazatlán, an hour away from Chilpancingo. Plácido Valerio, one of the leaders of the UPOEG, had taken it upon himself to persuade him to go. "*Cabrón*, you know I don't like to go out," Pioquinto said, refusing the invitation. "We want to recognize you for all the help you've given the UPOEG," insisted Plácido.

"As soon as we left the house I was nervous," Pioquinto told me. "When we got to Mazatlán, and I saw that Plácido wasn't there, I got really pissed. I had gotten myself out of the house for him, and the asshole had gone to a different event. I talked with the comrades at the UPOEG, and I started heading back in a caravan of something like twenty trucks. At an intersection, I told my son to go a different way and gun it for Ocotito, where I'd been told Plácido was. We lost the rest of the caravan. Once in Ocotito, I saw that Mario, the mayor, was there, speaking at a popular assembly. I tried to stay at the back to listen, but the crowd pushed me to the front and onto the fucking stage, which was the plaza bandstand, and then I found myself onstage, accusing Mario of being a narco. Anyway, you can watch it for yourself," and Pioquinto gives me his cell phone so I can watch the video that someone posted to YouTube.

In the video, to the left of the frame, there is a man in a pink shirt with a face that looks like it was molded by machete blows; this is the mayor. The one in the striped shirt and dark pants, with the slicked-back hair, the one who is talking, is Pioquinto. Plácido Valerio is the short one who has his arms crossed. The rest of the men are the mayor's bodyguards and other officials. The video lasts eleven minutes and forty-three seconds, and the majority of the time it's Pioquinto who is speaking. "Don't believe this crook," he says. "He uses the army to stop protests against him. . . . He chose to be against the people; he chose the side of the criminals." The video almost seems like a skit. The whole time, the mayor just laughs.

"When I finished speaking we climbed back into the Honda Pilot and headed out fucking full speed back to Chilpancingo. In the car was my son, driving; my daughter-in-law, as copilot; my wife, myself, and our friend Doña Viky in the back; and two friends in the very back row. We were going up to the Parador de Marqués, the first bridge you cross when you're coming from Acapulco, when two SUVs showed up and started shooting at us. My son tried to swerve, but we crashed. The car was a fucking mess. Viky threw herself on top of me trying to cover me, I tried to hug my wife. They fired 180 rounds. My daughter-in-law died, my son's hand was shredded by bullets, and my wife and Doña Viky were each shot in the foot. Me and my two friends came out unscathed, other than totally fucking traumatized." It was a miracle, he said, an utterly historic occurrence.

"Has the mayor tried to find you?" I asked him.

"What's that asshole going to come looking for me for? Here the only reason anyone wants to find you is to fuck you."

○   ○   ○

INSIDE THE SMALL Calipso banquet hall, very near downtown Chilpancingo, live eighty residents of Santa María Sur, in the district of Teloloapan. They came to the state capital nine months ago, when they received an ultimatum: "If you don't get out of here, we're going to steal all of your daughters." Eduardo, the commissioner of the communal lands, didn't want to tell me who threatened them, but two women approached us and accused the narcos, the soldiers, and the police. "They all want land for growing drugs," complained one of them.

In a few minutes, outside the Calipso, I would be surrounded by women and children. I wouldn't take down any names—they asked me not to—but I would hear their stories: "In the sierra a woman can't walk alone anymore; they do things to us. So we always go out together, so that one of us can run for help."

Another woman said, "Up there [in the sierra] shootouts break out all the time. They last for a long while, and the government never shows up."

A young man interrupted, "*La Maña*, the game, it takes everything from you: your life, your animals, your food. Because if La Maña is hungry, your women better cook for it. And then what happens? Other *mañosos* show up, other hustlers, the ones from the rival group, and they kill you for having fed the other assholes."

Another woman: "Over there on our ranches we don't have enough to eat meat, but we still eat well. Here the government gives each of us just twenty pesos a day [less than $2] for breakfast, lunch, and dinner. That's why we just buy forty-five kilos of tortillas a day, so we can at least feel full."

Last August, the state government said that between January 2013 and July 2014, 2,897 people were displaced as a result of the violence. The news agency Quadratín Guerrero, however, did its own count and found that the records showed that more than four thousand people were forced to abandon their villages between July 2013 and July 9, 2014. The majority came from districts in Tierra Caliente, as did the eighty displaced people who are living in the Calipso.

"THIS IS THE WORST CRISIS, and it started over a year ago, when I arrived at the Coparmex. I remember that I did a survey among our members to see what their needs were, and no one mentioned wanting lines of credit or contracts with the government. All they wanted was security. We've taken our own measures—we hired an Israeli anti-kidnapping group, we put up security cameras in our businesses, we have bodyguards, bulletproof SUVs—but that hasn't been enough. The kidnappings and extortions don't stop. A few weeks ago they kidnapped the owner of a cybercafé. His family paid the ransom, and they still killed him. The putrefaction coming out of Iguala isn't unique. Chilapa, Acapulco, Nicolás Bravo, Heliodoro Castillo, and Chilpancingo are all areas full of mass graves, full of dead. Last year, we alerted the CNDH [National Human Rights Commission] to the situation, and by November, the CNDH had sent their observers to forty-six districts in Guerrero. Their conclusion: that the state was on the brink of social collapse. And what did Governor Ángel Aguirre do? He said that the report was a fake, because Raúl Plascencia, the head of the CNDH, is the puppet of the representative Manlio Fabio Beltrones, and Aguirre has had beef with him since way back. This situation gave us no other option than to go to the Senate and ask for the dissolution of the state government.* We really have done everything we could to save ourselves. We businessmen of Guerrero should be given a trophy just for surviving."

I was told all this by Jaime Nava, the head of the Chilpancingo Employer's Association, while he scrolled on his iPad through newspaper articles that supported his claims.

An old taxi driver from Tixtla complained to me about the lack of passengers these days and blamed his bad luck on the normalistas from Ayotzinapa. The manager of the Bancomer bank in Chilpancingo's main square said that "thanks to the teachers" who set up protest camps in the plaza, nobody wants to go to her bank branch, and now she has to call her customers on the phone to offer them mortgage loans and credit cards in order to meet the monthly sales quota she's held to. And in Iguala, a shopkeeper with an extraordinary capacity to maintain total indifference told me that those normalistas were very troublesome.

I wanted to make all of these people understand that the disappearance of the forty-three normalistas was a breaking point for Mexico. What I think I told them was that we should take back our dignity, that the government has criminalized the *escuelas normales* (rural teacher training schools) for as long as I can remember, that President Echeverría

---

* Following the disappearance of the forty-three normalistas, Aguirre has finally given up power and stepped down.

during his term closed twenty of them all at once, that the normalistas are just young people and the sons of campesinos, and that they are ours.

Juan Villoro wrote on October 30 in *El País*:

> The culture of letters has been a challenge to a region that settles disputes with bullets. In the 1960s, two thirds of the residents of Guerrero were illiterate. The Escuela Normal of Ayotzinapa sprang up in order to mitigate this lack of development, but it couldn't turn its back on greater evils: the social inequality, the power of the caciques, the corruption of the local government, political repression as the only response to discontent, the impunity of the police and the increasing meddling of the drug traffickers. . . . The Escuela Normal represents a crucial center of dissent . . . On the night of September 26 there were four different shootings and just one target: the young people. With the support of organized crime, the mayor José Luis Abarca sowed terror that night to intimidate the normalistas who were mobilizing to honor the victims of the [1968] Tlatelolco [student] massacre. Once the repressive mechanism was unleashed, a soccer team also got in its way and was peppered with gunfire. Their crime? Just being youth; that is to say, possible rebels. . . .
>
> Che Guevara spent his last night in a rural school. Already wounded, he stared at a sentence written on the chalkboard and told the teacher, "It's missing the accent." The phrase was "Yo sé leer" ["I know how to read"]. Already defeated, the guerrilla went back to a different way of correcting reality. . . . Forty-three future teachers have disappeared. The dimensions of the drama are encoded in a phrase that opposes impunity, shame and injustice: "Yo sé leer." The Mexico of guns fears those who teach others how to read. This country is missing the accent. The time will come to put it back.

FELIPE ARNULFO ROSA speaks Tu'un Savi, a dialect of the Mixteco (indigenous) language. He learns Spanish. He hires himself out as a laborer in his village, Rancho Ocoapa, in the district of Ayutla. He wants to keep studying; he splits his days between school and working in the fields. Sometimes he works as a blacksmith, other times as a carpenter. He takes the entrance exam for the Ayotzinapa teachers' college; he wants to study for a degree in elementary education, with an intercultural bilingual focus; there are only forty spots available. He's accepted. He arrives at the Normal and has his head shaved, as is the tradition for freshmen. He has a B average, he plants flowers, he feeds the livestock. Felipe Arnulfo Rosa goes to fund-raise in the streets with his first-year friends (before their trip to Mexico City); they arrive in Iguala. They're shot at. They disappear.

Doña Dominga Rosa, Felipe's mother, doesn't speak Spanish, but Kau, a reporter colleague of mine from Chilpancingo, acted as a translator on the morning of October 30. "If I haven't dreamed about him, it's because he's still alive," said Doña Dominga through Kau. "The anguish is killing me; in our village we abandoned our cornfield, we abandoned everything because without Felipe, nothing works." Doña Dominga was sitting at a corner of the basketball court at the Normal. Since the disappearance of the normalistas, that had been the epicenter of their loss: the parents spent hours there, waiting for news, but none came.

Doña Dominga didn't understand why the federal government hadn't been able to find Felipe or the forty-two other normalistas. "They have to be hiding something," she said. Her husband, Damián Arnulfo, had participated in meetings with President Enrique Peña, and Secretary of the Interior Miguel Ángel Osorio and Attorney General Jesús Murillo, but he hadn't heard anything encouraging, just pure rhetoric. "Today I'm going to return to my village for the Day of the Dead, and I'm going to ask my eldest to bring Felipe back."

"Your eldest child is dead?" Kau asked her. They spoke for a while. Then Kau told me:

"They killed him two years ago. He was going to the sugarcane fields when some robbers attacked him. He died right there. She has another child, a daughter. She's in Ayutla, participating in the takeover of the Municipal Palace."

That's Ayotzinapa this year. Look it up on the map. Where forty-three normalistas are missing, that's where you'll find Doña Dominga.

UP UNTIL VERY RECENTLY, Cocula was a town ravaged by the Guerreros Unidos. It's not that Good has triumphed. It's just that the gang decided to leave for now because the town trash dump had become global news: that's where the federal government says the bodies of the forty-three normalistas were burned.

"Just wait for everyone to leave here, and that's when La Maña will return," I was told by a man I can't name. "We've been here for years, with so much violence, so much extortion, so much robbery, but last year I realized that this wasn't going to ever stop, the night that they took seventeen young kids."

It happened on July 30, 2013. A group of gunmen invaded three villages. Among the kidnapped were two high school students and three women. Nobody knows their whereabouts—though in Cocula they say that the women did reappear, but they don't live there anymore. A month earlier, the mayor, César Peñaloza, had been ambushed. He survived. And six months before that, in November 2012, they murdered Tomás Biviano, who had just been named chief of police.

"Cocula was falling apart from one day to the next," I was told by the wife of the man whose name I shouldn't remember. "Shootings, kidnappings, disappearances, everything they say happens in Iguala happens in Cocula and worse. I'm an engineer, and I used to work at the Nuevo Balsas mine; I quit because La Maña takes as much as half of all the workers' salaries. I opened a business here, but I closed it because of all the extortion."

Later, outside the church, I ran into four women who had hung a banner in front of the atrium; on it, four men were shown, three teachers and one youth, and it said that the federal police had arrested and beaten them and were trying to tie them to the disappearance of the normalistas. "They're our relatives. Some of them were detained at a checkpoint and others were pulled out of their homes," I was told by one of the women, the one who was carrying an iPad and looked at it constantly, who knows why. She told me the whole police-abuse story, and when she was done I asked her to tell me about the violence in Cocula. "No, señor," she said. "Our town is very calm. I don't know how anyone can say they brought the normalistas here."

MARIO CHÁVEZ, the mayor of Tlacotepec, was telling me about the man with wings who kept flying through his town when, out of nowhere, he told me, "You've got to come to my town and see the Boeing 737 that they gave me."

"Someone gave you a plane as a gift?"

"Yes, it was given to me by Miguel Ángel Mancera." Mancera is the mayor of Mexico City. "I don't know where he got it from, but I brought it over here on two trailer trucks. Now it's been turned into a computer center for kids, the first of its kind in Latin America," he bragged, and asked the waiter for the check.

"So there's no crime in your town?"

"None. I say that in all seriousness. It's just a bad reputation."

I didn't want to tell him that I had read an article written the past August about how he, the mayor, was asking for help from the state because the narcos had threatened to pick him up.

It was almost midnight when I stopped a taxi. "The bus station," I told the driver, but he didn't hear me at first.

"I'm really out of sorts," he apologized. "I just dropped off a lady, I took her all around, collecting money, but then I made her get out." I didn't understand what he was talking about, until he told me the story from the beginning. That's when I understood that the lady had a clothing business, and her husband, a high school teacher, had been kidnapped. The lady needed to gather two hundred thousand pesos for her husband to be freed. "She wanted me to accompany her to pay the ransom," the taxi driver told me. "Would you have gone with her?" he asked me.

"I don't think so," I said, and felt ashamed. That's why I had to tell this story. +

—Translated by Emma Friedland

ENRIQUE MARTÍNEZ CELAYA, *THE KNITTED FRAGMENT*. 2014, OIL AND WAX ON CANVAS, 50 × 56".
PARAFIN GALLERY, LONDON, UNITED KINGDOM.

BOTH WAYS

Kristin Dombek

This is the second print installment of Kristin Dombek's advice column. Questions can be sent to askkristin@nplusonemag.com.

DEAR KRISTIN,

I don't know how exactly to ask this question. I am a woman who has loved and fucked men and women. I don't love the word *bisexual* for all the usual reasons, but it can be a useful word, and in conveying the equalness with which I have committed myself to men and women it might be useful here. I've tried a couple of times to be in open or less-defined relationships, where I know the other person is sleeping with other people and they know I am too. These have left me feeling unseen and unsupported, like some great one-on-one, "You are my person" intimacy is just not possible, and I am nothing but a big slut. But when I'm in committed relationships, I always feel some part of myself is not welcome, that I am, in some way, too big for our arrangement—too sexual, too wandering, too large in my demands for freedom and creativity. I have cheated on a male partner with a woman, and cheated on a woman partner with a man. I didn't start dating women until college, and I am a firm believer that gay marriage should be an equal opportunity. When advances are made for gay rights, I cry in the coffee shop reading the newspaper. It feels personal. The words *husband*, *wife*, resonate, feel sacred, important. But they feel equally impossible, as if I will never get to either of them.

And here is the problem I'm having. There's a part of me that absolutely wants to get to one of those words, to say, hello, here is my husband, Joe; meet my wife, Jane. My wife, Jane, feels much more possible at this juncture than my husband, Joe; I couldn't imagine living a life with a husband that felt truthful. Part of me thinks I will die if I don't get there, if I don't get a person. But. Another part of me does not want to get there, thinks those words are nothing that could ever be true and nothing I could want. I feel twoness and bothness as the dominant themes in my life right now. If there were a song called "Both Ways Is the Only Way I Want It" after Maile Meloy's short-story collection, I would listen to it on repeat. I want safety and love, I want truth. I want to be settled, I'm always restless.

You told another letter writer that part of her problem was that her story was illegible to other people. There was "no conventional boy-girl or girl-girl true-love story, no Facebook relationship status.... You dared to create another kind of world and then the real one, it must have seemed, crashed down." I think that about sums it up. I feel, in the most boo-hoo queer-me way, that I have so few models to look to for who I can be, in my self and in my relationships. Part of me wants to create another world, part of me wants the true-love story. I want both.

I've started seeing a wonderful woman recently. I care for her so much. We could have the girl-girl true-love story, I think. But do I want it? If I do want it, but want it to look a little different, will I fuck up what we have by trying to get everything I want at once?

Sincerely,
Both Ways

DEAR BOTH WAYS:

Night has fallen on the Help Desk many times since your question arrived. You've put into such clearheaded words a problem so difficult that when I began researching it was Easter Sunday, and Brooklyn was warming. In the spring it seemed clear you should refuse this sacrificial logic of life and love and create another world; in the honesty and generosity of open relationships, I believed, you could refuse all the double binds and find your true love story. But any tragedy will tell you that it's impossible to have anything both ways, that the only alternative to the ambivalence you describe is decision and sacrifice—that such sacrifice is the very lifeblood of social and cultural life. Any romance will tell you that sacrifice is the sine qua non of fidelity: no one else but him, or her, forever. In the heat of summer, I wrote four or five letters to you, each one disagreeing with the one before. Now the snowless sidewalks are lined with dead Christmas trees, put out for garbage collectors whose breath will steam in the frigid air, and the Help Desk is littered with scraps of paper onto which are scratched calculations and schematics, decision trees and flowcharts. I don't know which is more depressing: how hard it is to escape the hegemony of compulsory twoness, on the one hand, or the ambivalence that threatens twoness when we actually have it, on the other. Your question has me reading Emerson, the alternately cynical and exhilaratingly hopeful essay "Circles": "Our moods do not believe in each other."

In a moment of optimism about your question, a friend and I planned a panel on bisexuality, that unlovable word. It wouldn't be on one topic but two: love and justice. The panelists would each have two cups with different beverages in them, maybe a mug of steaming-hot cocoa for warmth and a glass of sweet tea, chilly with crushed ice. We would answer every question both ways, taking sips from both cups, and it would be the funniest and wisest panel ever. Would you like to be on it with us? It would show how our apparent indecisiveness is actually about trying to be true. It would stage the movement expressed in deeply equal bisexuality, the way we try to search out and be and love both this and that, him and her, here and there, the thing and its opposite. How, both loyal and wild, we refuse the sacrifice of one thing for another that lies at the heart of injustice and yet is somehow considered necessary to true love.

Sometimes this feels right, that the ambivalence expressed in loving both men and women holds some revolutionary, world-expanding answer. But it's not that simple, is it? Because you can in fact fuck up what you have by trying to get everything you want at once. There is something inherent in being a bisexual woman, or drawn to nonmonogamy, that does put you at risk of being treated as if you want or are "too much." You can be rejected or held hostage, or hold yourself hostage; you can lose the people you love. And then if you do manage to be intentionally and honestly multiple in sex and love, it turns out to be difficult to do it in a way that's satisfying for everyone involved, and tends to invite even more fear and stigma than being gay. There is a lot at stake in what you ask. I don't know why you've cheated, and you may not either, but these are some of the reasons people do.

Shortly after your question arrived, astronomers discovered infrared traces of the big bang, offering what seemed to be empirical evidence of eternal inflation. I was supposed to be researching statistics on open relationships, affairs, straightness, and gayness, but instead I kept trying to understand one of the stranger implications of this discovery. Nobody really knows how many open relationships are successful, anyway. Most people have cheated on a partner at least once, according to the internet, and half of all romantic relationships suffer from an affair. Most people who identify as straight have been at least partly gay at least once in their life, and most gay people at least partly straight. We know this already. We don't know why the expansion of the universe is speeding up, or why there is exactly the right ratio of dark energy to gravity and the strong and weak forces to allow for life in our solar system, on our planet. A tiny bit more or less dark energy and we'd be smushed or exploded; that is to say, we wouldn't exist in the first place. The shocking thing about this evidence is that some astrophysicists have long argued that if eternal inflation can be proved, there must be multiple universes, existing alongside or even inside ours. One multiverse theory posits that there must be an infinite number of universes, every one that is statistically possible, given the tiniest variations in the expansion of matter and ratio of dark energy to something or other. In this view, there are universes in which every possible version of your life plays out.

This is massively unhelpful, of course. Since even if there is a universe for each possible version of your life—the one in which you make a singular marriage, the one in which you're restless and wild and free, and all the others—you're trapped in this one; knowing they're happening, right now, might even make it worse. In this world, the moment you commit yourself to someone or something you change everything that comes afterward, and live inside it, or so it feels. You also reject or ignore the people who might have been better off if you'd chosen differently. Life feels less like a multiverse and more like the kind of endless sacrificial negotiation Jacques Derrida describes in his little book *The Gift of Death*:

> Let us not look for the examples, there would be too many of them, at every step we took. By preferring my work, simply by giving it my time and attention . . . I am perhaps fulfilling my duty. But I am sacrificing and betraying at every moment all my other obligations: my obligations to the other others whom I know or don't know, the billions of my fellows (without mentioning the animals that are even more other others than my fellows), my fellows who are dying of starvation or sickness. I betray my fidelity or my obligations to other citizens, to those who don't speak my language and to whom I neither speak nor respond, to each of those who listen or read [and so on] . . . thus also to those I love in private, my own, my family, my sons, each of whom is the only son I sacrifice to the other, every one being sacrificed to every one else in this land of Moriah that is our habitat every second of every day.

While some of what you ask is native to bisexuality and polyamory—to sex and the working out of what you desire—the problem is so deep and so familiar to us all that Derrida calls it "our habitat." In every moment we want it both ways, even when we decide how to divide our time among family and friends. We feel it tragic to choose among competing and equally valid beliefs in order to live our one singular life. This problem of desire and commitment is, for Derrida, also an ethical question, perhaps *the* ethical question. The moment we pledge fidelity to another person or people, we make an unethical choice with regard to others.

I'm adding Derrida's avalanche of sacrificial dilemmas here not to overwhelm the problem further, but to say to you, Both Ways: You're not alone in this. The particularities are different, and it's fair enough to wish it were better for queer people already, but this is the problem where we all live. There is a bit of freedom in knowing it: this is all there is. This is where the question of love meets the question of justice.

Derrida mentions the land of Moriah because he's been thinking about Abraham, up on the mountain, called on to sacrifice one great love—his son—for another: the God who demanded the sacrifice. Abraham's choice is validated by a very big story: Because you were willing to sacrifice for me, you don't have to—there's a ram in the bushes—and because you proved your fidelity, you'll be blessed. Your offspring will be fruitful and multiply. In the region of Moriah that is romantic love, we replace God with stories about the other—my husband, Joe; my wife, Jane—and stories about ourselves: I'm too big and wandering. As if in choosing these stories against all others we'll be enchanted. We'll be blessed. But I have a feeling, Both Ways, that whatever story you choose, your longing for bothness will unravel it, until you see that it is you, yourself, who have invested it with its enchanting power.

I used to have a recurring nightmare about a wedding. I walk onto a vast green lawn and see rows of wooden white folding chairs. Suited men clump and scatter across the lawn, and women in taffeta and silk circle up and laugh softly. There are half a dozen bridesmaids in pink dresses puffed by tulle. There are flowers woven cinematically into a fucking white wicker archway. I can feel a hulk of a house off to the right. But I have tunnel vision. I don't know whose wedding it is, and then I feel a rustle, a soft scratching around my legs, a kind of drag when I walk. I look down and I'm in a white wedding dress. In my mind are sentences so loud they feel physical—how did this happen? How do I get out?—but I cannot say any of them out loud; I cannot speak. Even if I had the courage to run I couldn't because the dress is too heavy. I'm pinioned to the lawn and people are beginning to notice me, they turn to look at me, I try to smile, and then I wake up. The worst part of it, when I wake, is the knowledge that even my dreams are clichés.

For years I interpreted the dream as prophetic, as if someday I would be tricked into a marriage from which I could not escape. But I missed the point, I think. We cannot live in all the universes we want to, but neither do we live in that wedding nightmare, a world in which there is only one story, coming for you, and you cannot extricate yourself from it. The dream was pointing out my belief in such a nightmare. Some of the stories you choose will feel like solid worlds and then unravel; some you will unravel, yourself, when you need to. My hope is that you might come to love the unraveling, the way it invites the next story, creates a new world, no matter the relationship structures you choose.

There is a world in which the story is this: you commit yourself to one person after another, a man and then a woman, a woman and then a man, for balance, and when you are with a man, you cheat with a woman, and when you are with a woman, you cheat with a man. And then you find this woman, and something about her stops you. You get to know each other in the way one can only do with another person when there's no one else for you. You see the world through her eyes, and it is like you live in two worlds, yours and hers, rather than one. You learn what it is like to be with her when she is bored, restless, just trying to exist on a Sunday afternoon when she doesn't know what to do, and neither of you has anyone else to run away to, and your own long restlessness helps you to understand and quiet her. In this story, you realize that the cheating, for you, was not so much about bisexuality or ambivalence about monogamy but a way of escaping how embarrassing it is to be seen this way—just trying to exist, yourself. Because you've stopped enough to know her and be known, this ends some loneliness in you. You have the girl-girl true-love story.

In this world, or another, you might decide to have an open relationship with this woman, and after learning to deal with the jealousy and learning to reassure her, you get a boyfriend who knows the deal and wants exactly the freedom and fidelity of loving a woman who is in another relationship. You are, because of the hard work of your honesty, finally yourself in the world: you have it both ways. You have "you are my person" intimacy with both of them; you learn how to divide your life between them, so that you can be present in each place. But your time grows short, and you find yourself weeping inexplicably when you go between them, and you feel you're doing a bad job of caring for each one. In this world, you rewrite the story in one of two directions. In one, you choose between your girlfriend and your boyfriend. Because you've been honest, it is no longer a sacrifice of your identity and desire when you have to choose between them: it is a sacrifice of the life you could have had with either one of them, if there were world enough and time. In another story, your girlfriend and your boyfriend become friends; you begin spending time with them both, together. You come to love your girlfriend's girlfriends; she cares about your boyfriend. Now you have two monogamous relationships each, and a family's worth of friendships, and two or three or four houses, and shared weekends and alone-together weekends, and calendars and schedules and your own shorthand the four of you use to make incredibly complex decisions so that everyone can see everyone. You find that love is not scarce, but like any family, any group of friends, any monogamous relationship, you find that time and space are scarce, and that even here, Both Ways, you may find yourself restless.

But maybe the restlessness is really about sex, and there is a world in which you realize that what you really want is butch women, women with whom you can play with all the impossible twos as a game, inhabit everything, occupy everything yourselves. Or there is a world in which you realize that it's your own masculinity you've been after, that you need to play out that old power yourself, and that you can claim this thanks to some woman or man who loves exactly this about you. Cocks are strapped on or not strapped on, depending on your mood. It is not a girl-girl story or a boy-girl story. You have it both ways. Maybe you need a woman for this, maybe you couldn't have this with a biological man, but if you choose a woman you'll never know. You won't need to: you'll have friends who love men, and in friendship with them, you'll see some of the other worlds through their eyes.

There is a world in which you fall in love with and marry a woman or a man and you have children together, by whatever means, and caring for these children together with your wife or husband expands the circle of people you'd take a bullet for, such that you are living not at the center of the world, yourself, but in all their lives, from all their points of view, and you realize that your restlessness was not about sex, after all: it was about needing to love multiply, rather than in binaries. There is a world in which you do several of these things in succession, failing or feeling you've failed at each, until you hit on one that is not perfect but that you know, in a way you don't know now, is the best bet, and you choose it, knowing that it's not so much about losing these other worlds: you are choosing this one, absurdly, recklessly.

There is, in all these worlds, at least one man or woman who sees the restlessness in you and accepts it. Someone who is more interesting than your ambivalence; who is more interested in you, in all your ways, than in owning you. Who moves with you when you move, who lets you breathe when you need to breathe. Who knows and loves about you that you desire men and women with mysterious, unsettling equality, and seeks to balance out all that is unfair and sacrificial in the world. Who tries out new worlds with you. Because you are fundamentally together, with this person, you can be apart. Because you know you are fundamentally apart, responsible for yourselves, you can be together. Because you think of yourself as no longer alone in the world, no longer the center—you never were, no one ever is—you can make these decisions without seeing them as some kind of sacrifice. And because of this person, you come to understand that your longing for twoness, for having things "both ways," is a desire for love itself, for being really together with another person, for seeing past the illusion that the world you inhabit is the solitary one, and in this way, rehearsing some larger justice. You can do it with several people or you can do it with one, because if you stay long and deep enough, and allow the other to be as restless as you, each other person is a world and, over time, a hundred worlds.

And there is a world—instead or inside of any of these worlds—in which the "true love" story is not the one at the center of your life. You find your place instead among all the people of your town or the world; you love your friends better than anyone has ever loved friends. You change more of the world than most, because you can give your time to more people than those for whom the most important story is having a husband or a wife, children and/or dogs. This is, for you, the bigger love, the most ethical commitment, the least sacrificial fidelity.

However many of these stories you manage to inhabit until they feel like worlds unto themselves, I'm betting that what will matter most is whether you can enjoy the way they change, because they will, from Easter to the dark of winter, on every trip around the sun. Since I started writing to you, that empirical proof of the Big Bang has been challenged, and the hot new theory in astrophysics is that it never happened, the universe has always existed. The stories we research most rigorously always change the most. Truth falls fast on the heels of love, which can't live long without it. Your longing to have things both ways is not some great and secret flaw. There is a creativity in the way you want to commit yourself that will produce something that hasn't yet been seen. Finding the perfect relationship structure means less, I think, than knowing this.

Yours,
Kristin +

ENRIQUE MARTÍNEZ CELAYA, *THE SURROGATE*, 2014. OIL AND WAX ON CANVAS, 72 × 66".
COLLECTION OF THE WADSWORTH ATHENEUM, HARTFORD, CONNECTICUT.

WE FOUND LOVE IN A HOPELESS PLACE

Gabriel Winant

I WAS AT A HIGH SCHOOL friend's wedding in Charleston recently. The wedding itself was harmless and fun, but the city is a haunted place, unrepentantly hawking its evil past as if it were a tourist trap like any other. A city full of gorgeous mansions (who built them?) beside a beautiful harbor (what cargo lined these piers?), it felt like a reunion staged inside a concentration camp. The night before the ceremony, at a place downtown, I made some comment along these lines. A stranger—a white man, obviously—leaned down the bar. "Don't say *slavery*," he said. "Just don't say it. We don't use the S-word here." Here I am, I realized—the death of the party. The next night, a few of us stepped off the dance floor when the band started "Sweet Home Alabama." No one noticed, but it felt like the tiniest victory, a knot of shared bad feeling in the midst of celebration.

The experience of being alienated from common, mainstream ritual, unable to take pleasure in a friend's wedding like a normal person, is something people with left-wing politics will recognize, and not just because of our proverbial social awkwardness. What makes the experience especially painful is not its intensity—often low-level, occasionally rising to the point of rage—but how few others share it. The buzzkill faction is rarely more than a rump. Righteousness, in these circumstances, is a grim pleasure, at best a consolation, never a victory.

Why, then, even bother with such pointless little rebellions? Because the past—the thing that makes it impossible to stay silent, or at least to casually take part—isn't just something one knows. "History is what hurts," as Fredric Jameson wrote. Welling up, often against our own hopes for new beginnings, "it is what refuses desire and sets inexorable limits to individual as well as collective praxis, which its 'ruses' turn into grisly and ironic reversals of their overt intention."

With these lines, written in 1981, Jameson could well have been describing himself or his generation of scholars. Entering what seemed to be an emancipatory era, the leftists of the 1960s and '70s were wounded by the staying power of the past, and by the dark turn events took after the left lost in the streets. In the decades since, this association between pain and powerlessness has assumed an increasingly central place in academic writing and culture. As the pain has grown, so have attempts to analyze it, many clustering around the term *affect*, a more generalized way of talking about the connection between feelings and power. If you hang around academics, especially in the humanities, you've probably heard about it.

You or I can have a particular emotion regarding a particular object. We generate these emotions, but out of what material? Prior to emotions, many of these theorists hold, are affects, which float free of individuals, inhering instead in the atmospheres of institutions and social spaces. Affects reverse the subject-object relationship of emotions: we are their objects, rather than their origins. They are the way social life makes itself felt, leaving deposits in individual people, which we then process into our own emotions. We might even call affects "objective" features of the social landscape, albeit ones that can only be observed and recorded through feeling. As one of this tradition's major theorists, Brian Massumi, writes, affect is "as infrastructural as a factory." By this logic, the power lines of affect running through every office and production facility are as central to our political economy as any physical infrastructure.

Look around the room you are in: there is some way of feeling that is proper to this space. (Most likely, you are in compliance with it, rendering it semi-invisible; it is more noticeable in the breach.) This is affect. The campus library, perhaps, is anxious; the New York party is insecure; the office is alienated. Different individuals will enter these settings in different states and respond in different ways to their atmospheres, but they cannot *not* respond.

What the word *affect* in this sense describes is the inward dimension of collective experience as it is manifested back out to the world and made visible through behavior. Although scholars tend to disagree on how to define the relationship between affect and emotion, the argument for a meaningful distinction comes down to a question of subjects and objects. It is the difference between "I feel terrible" and "this feels terrible." The latter's implicit transitive verb—"this *makes me* feel terrible"—provides much more analytic purchase. It suggests an action taking place, rather than a state being maintained. And if an action is taking place, perhaps other actions could take place. The point of this way of thinking is to make explicit and external something otherwise tacit and internal, and thereby to open a new avenue of critique on the origin point of this particular affect: the institution, the relationship, the object that has generated this feeling.

OUTSIDE OF THE ACADEMY, affect theory's greatest traction has come through its attachment to labor. This also happens to be one of the best ways to get at the origins of affect theory itself.

The idea behind "affective labor," a concept that emerged from the feminist revolution of the 1970s, is that some forms of employment extract value from workers' emotional lives as much as they do from workers' bodies. The argument first directed itself toward the domestic scene, where the ideology of marriage held that women's unpaid work was a natural extension of love. "The literature of the women's movement has shown abundantly the devastating effects this love, care and service has had on women. These are the chains which have tied us to a condition of near slavery," wrote Nicole Cox and Silvia Federici in a classic 1975 essay. At the same time, feminist criticism pointed to the new service workplaces into which women were streaming, where their labor was often an extension of the grin-and-bear-it dynamic of the household. The classic work in this vein is sociologist Arlie Russell Hochschild's *The Managed Heart: Commercialization of Human Feeling* (1979), which took the work of flight attendants as its main object of study. "Seeming to 'love the job' becomes part of the job," Hochschild wrote, "and actually trying to love it, and to enjoy the customers, helps the worker in this effort."

These critics stood at the beginning of a process that has now subsumed us all. Though they differed in their political beliefs—Federici is an Italian autonomist Marxist; Hochschild, an American left-liberal—they shared the kind of ontological optimism that moments of revolution make possible. Hochschild thought the main problem of emotional labor, as she called it, was that it alienated you from your true self. The closing sentence of the book urged readers to ask, as a measure of self-preservation, "What do I really feel?" This humanist position implies that rediscovering your core self—what Hochschild called "the search for authenticity"—is possible. Further to the left, meanwhile, Federici's Wages for Housework movement distributed a pamphlet with song lyrics on it: "We're cooking / We're cleaning / We're looking our best / We're taking a beating / We're faking the rest." Women might have complied, both arguments went, but they did not consent.

Such belief in an authentic and intact subject, perhaps obscured from view by oppression and exploitation but real and uncontaminated at her core, is a relic of a more hopeful era. Its organizing metaphors—authenticity and alienation, surface and depth, consent and coercion—bespoke a belief in the reality of an ultimately resilient individual. And why not? The 1960s and '70s had witnessed the shattering of the postwar consensus by a global uprising of those who had until then appeared subservient. The movements for the liberation of women, black people, and the colonized around the world gave vent to the rage and desire that had bubbled below the surface. This eruptive phenomenon, which historians and sociologists of the time associated with the humanist watchword *agency*, was the way, it seemed, the world changed. People found their voices, and when they did, they made their own history.

But the subsequent story of radical thought amounts, in many ways, to one big crisis of agency. Left-wing criticism has long fixated on the questions of *who* and *how*. Who is the agent of history? How will social transformation come about? The proletariat occupied the position it did in classical Marxism not because of some metaphysical virtue, but because Marxists believed industrial workers occupied a position in society that uniquely equipped them to transform it, and to lead other social elements in doing so. This position faltered over the course of the mid-twentieth-century economic boom, when many radicals came to see the labor movement as complacently accommodating itself to power rather than leading social change. Through the 1960s and '70s, new social movements proposed a series of candidates for the role of the motor of history: students, the postcolonial world (especially its peasantry), African Americans (in the United States), and women. But the defeat or co-optation of these movements, one after another, cast the very concept of agency, premised on the overcoming of alienation and the emergence of the authentic self, into question, and with it went the whole imaginary edifice of collective social transformation. By the 1980s, that model was in ruins, and antihumanist pessimism was triumphant. Agency had proved insufficient as a force of transformation, as the foundations of society, despite the impressive shaking given them by the "new social movements," stood firm and perhaps even strengthened.

In the theory that followed hard on the New Left's defeat, gone was the majestic dialectical unfolding of repressed human freedom that had guided student movements around the world. Gone was the individual itself, the former site and agent of liberation. Flows of desire, the operations of social machinery—these preceded and determined the reasoning individual. As Deleuze, one of the first to make use of the term *affect,* argued in a 1978 lecture: "Inspiring sad passions is necessary for the exercise of power." Rulers, he went on, "need the sadness of their subjects." Here is Deleuze's version of "History is what hurts." Pick a tradition—Deleuze or Jameson, Marxism or feminism—and for all their differences, they arrive at the same place: hurt and sadness.

The sense of a self capable of agency had given left activists a point of entry into political action. Its loss threatened to close off the only known avenue to emancipation—and left these movements and their theorists close to despair. Foucault's 1972 introduction to *Anti-Oedipus* illustrates the problem. There he famously wrote of "the fascism in us all, in our heads and in our everyday behavior, the fascism that causes us to love power, to desire the very thing that dominates and exploits us." But what sort of movement follows from the acknowledgment of "the fascism in us all"? What sort of strategy do you adopt for that? The result, for many if not for Foucault himself, was rather downcast—not to say defeatist.

Affect offers a new approach to this old problem: What latent thing do you and I, two powerless individuals, share that might, if activated, endow us with a common sense of things, and from there a collective potency? Affect theory does not discover an authentic self buried by oppression; it constructs one anew from the wreckage of defeat. In doing so, it assembles collective knowledge against the devil on your shoulder that whispers that you are alone in this—in this dead-end job, in this broken relationship, in debt, in depression, in paralysis.

This political potency comes from another source in affect theory's overdetermined origins—the women and people of color for whom political defeat signaled human catastrophe on an unspeakable scale. The violent repression of black radicalism, the consignment of a generation of gay men to death (Foucault among them), the rollback of victories as basic as the right to birth control and abortion, the criminalization and caging of millions of people of color, the evisceration of the social support on which the poor and the working class, women especially, have depended for survival—mere hurt might not be an adequate response to these occurrences. Sadness is easy: it is the affect of impotence, which is not a position all can afford. Anger is much harder, since it points toward action, even in adverse circumstances.

I began this essay with an account of feeling uncomfortable celebrating a wedding in slavery's theme park. This posture, while probably the right one, comes somewhat easily to me, a white man. What kind of personal vitriol or physical menace would I have withstood, even just muttering complaints at a Charleston bar, if I were a black woman? While Deleuze may have been among the first to speak of affects, radical and black feminists—from Shulamith Firestone to Audre Lorde—proved the decisive origin points for affect theory because the stakes were so much higher. One part of their progeny then crossed these earlier insights with poststructuralism and the traditions of the gay liberation movement, heavily influenced by Foucault, to produce what is often seen as the key to understanding affect: the queer theory of the 1990s. Seen from this vantage, everyone, not just those ruled by the patriarchy, thrums with trapped desires, intensities with nowhere to go. All the world, in other words, is a closet.

The late Eve Kosofsky Sedgwick—best known for her *Epistemology of the Closet* (1990), about the ubiquity of the homo/hetero distinction in modern culture—remains the most immediate reference point for this strand of affect theory, as well as most of the scholarship that has become best known by that name. Sedgwick's work on the psychologist Silvan Tomkins, *Shame and Its Sisters* (1995), is often cited as a key contribution to the field—Sedgwick dates Tomkins's theory of affect to 1955—but it was primarily Sedgwick's work as a literary critic that demonstrated how a more careful attention to affect might rescue theory from political defeatism. As a literary critic, she went against much of the critical current of her time, which tended to search beneath the text for its real truths (somehow already known in advance) and its author's hidden political failures (compared with the critic's superiority). Calling this method "paranoid," she proposed a "reparative" method. This way of reading requires a critic to shed her own hermeneutic biases, or at least hold them at bay. In doing so, she might be able to see "the many ways selves and communities succeed in extracting sustenance from the objects of a culture—even of a culture whose avowed desire has often been not to sustain them."

Affect theorists following Sedgwick are distinguished from many of their feminist and queer forebears because they do not argue that identity or desire has been repressed (a key term in the old theory of agency). Their work approaches the decisions and desires of the apparently obedient victims of domination not through comparison to a presumed true self, but through a much more immediate kind of sympathy, one that need not propose a hidden self in order to acknowledge the humanity of even the most downtrodden. What follows is also a new sensitivity, an openness to surprise, since sympathy may well lead not to a return to the "true self" but to the production of new selves altogether.

What Sedgwick's method also required was a sensitivity to historical time and change, something of little appeal to the post-structuralist sensibility adopted by many of her contemporaries. And while Sedgwick was critical of historicism, what she called "reparative reading" requires a historical imagination; an understanding that the past, as it was lived, was as bewildering and surprising to its writers as the critic's present is to her: "To read from a reparative position is to surrender the knowing, anxious, paranoid determination that no horror, however apparently unthinkable, shall ever come to the reader as New." In her 1997 essay "Paranoid Reading and Reparative Reading, or You're So Paranoid, You Probably Think This Essay Is About You," Sedgwick describes "the dogged, defensive narrative stiffness of a paranoid temporality . . . in which yesterday can't be allowed to have differed from today and tomorrow must be even more so." Noting the "Oedipal regularity and repetitiveness" of such a pattern, in which what happens to fathers is revisited by sons, she moves into a lovely reading of the final volume of *In Search of Lost Time*. Proust's narrator, long a recluse, has gone to a party, and at first thinks everyone is dressed up in old-age costume. But he "realizes that they *are* old, and so is he—and is then assailed, in half a dozen distinct mnemonic shocks, by a climactic series of joy-inducing 'truths' about the relation of writing to time." This revelatory disorientation, Sedgwick points out, "would have been impossible in a heterosexual *père de famille*, in one who had meanwhile been embodying, in the form of inexorably 'progressing' identities and roles, the regular arrival of children and grandchildren." Sedgwick uses the phrase "queer possibility" for this phenomenon—the idea of a break in the transmission from past to future, from fathers to sons.

Contemporary thinkers about affect, a generation younger than Sedgwick, have brought an increasingly explicit historical consciousness to this approach. Where Sedgwick advised an epistemological modesty, her followers suggest a historical modesty. A text might surprise you, they argue, and so, too, might history: it's not just that the reader might pick up on something previously unnoticed (an idea, a fact); she might even discover something new to the world entirely. A Marxian-seeming political hope accordingly crept back into what had been a decidedly non-Marxist tradition. What if the present always contains the possibility of transformation? Perhaps the chain of transmission from one generation to the next can be broken.

It is here that affect theory suggests a new dialectical turn. The growth in affective labor has made possible a form of critical knowledge that begins on the grounds of the conquered self. Vast markets now depend on the successful reproduction of identities: millions of women work in the "caring" occupations, often immigrants, and most often women of color. One major element of the economy of affective labor is thus a mass expropriation of feeling—a flow that runs in aggregate from the Global South to the North, from women to men, from the poor to the rich, and from people of color to white people. The home-care workforce, who occupy one of the fastest-growing job categories in America, is a classic case. But this working class—call it the affectariat—has more proficiency in two skills necessary for political organizing than perhaps any group in history: the creation of fellow feeling and the production of new identities.

If our daily exploitation produces feelings in us that we might turn toward our own liberation, what affect theory seeks to understand is, in effect, why we have been too demoralized so far to do so. It's certainly possible to imagine that being commanded to love on a daily basis might make someone a revolutionary beacon. But it's much easier to imagine that it will make a person depressed or worn out.

Having to spend one's own inner reserves to restitch the fraying fabric of society is exhausting, and poses all sorts of obstacles to collective organization and self-assertion. After a long day spent caring for others, it's hard enough to care for a family, let alone comrades. The spread of capital's reach across all social life has also turned many kinds of human relationships into empty market transactions. Click "Like"; have a good attitude; smile at the customer; establish a real connection with the patient; be an ambassador for the corporate brand. It's exhausting, how the growing immateriality of the economic system depends ever more on the endless work of self-invention. Then there's outright oppression. The shattering of political constraints on the market has seriously wounded democracy, replacing it in part with vicious forms of repressive social control that often act through affective mechanisms: Eric Garner was murdered, recall, for reacting with visible negative feeling to police harassment. It is the interaction of these two dynamics—Facebook and Ferguson—that makes affect so central to the neoliberal order. Capital issues two commands at once: Do what you love, and keep your head down.

The enforcement of these simultaneous imperatives—to both actualize and minimize one's selfhood—depends on a vast, uncoordinated apparatus of powers that regulates contemporary emotional life. Such powers can take the form of institutional authority figures like bosses and police, of course, but also parents, children, friends, and lovers. What's insidious about a system of affective rule is that it doesn't need a center of power. It banks on the fact that it's hard to be defiant when you hear a warning from your parents, feel a chill from your colleagues, or sense sudden distance from your loved ones, who—fearful themselves—are made uneasy by your dissent.

IN HER 2012 BOOK *DEPRESSION: A PUBLIC FEELING*, the feminist theorist Ann Cvetkovich describes the formation of the project Public Feelings, which is more or less the organizational expression of affect theory. "Public Feelings was forged out of the crucible of the long Bush years," she explains. "In finding public forums for everyday feelings, including negative feelings that can seem so debilitating, so far from hopefulness about the future or activism, the aim is to generate new ways of thinking about agency." In a spirit of camp humor that Cvetkovich attributes to the queer-theory roots of Public Feelings, the group's Chicago hub, called the Feel Tank, declared an International Day of the Politically Depressed. They came up with a slogan—"Depressed? It might be political!"—and put it not just on a T-shirt but on the classic garb of melancholy, the bathrobe.

Cvetkovich's book, part memoir and part critical interpretation, represents one of a number of efforts emanating from Public Feelings to inspect sad affects for what they tell us about power relations. How does neoliberalism feel? It feels like shit. "What gets called depression in the domestic sphere is one affective register of these social problems and one that often keeps people silent, weary, and too numb to really notice the sources of their unhappiness (or in a state of low-level chronic grief . . . if they do)," writes Cvetkovich. More empirical arguments have come to register the force of this insight. The sociologist William Davies, in his 2015 book *The Happiness Industry*, argues that depression and stress are the products of the current order, but also grit in its gears: "Since the 1960s, Western economies have been afflicted by an acute problem in which they depend more and more on our psychological and emotional engagement (be it with work, with brands, with our own health and well-being) while finding it increasingly hard to sustain this." We might, then, Davies argues, think of mental-health problems as forms of individualized resistance: "Forms of private disengagement, often manifest as depression and psychosomatic illnesses, do not only register in the suffering experienced by the individual; they are increasingly problematic for policy-makers and managers."

If we can come to understand the negative affects with which we are entangled, these writers suggest, perhaps we can begin to make use of them. Sara Ahmed attacks happiness itself as an expression of normative and disciplinary power in her 2010 book, *The Promise of Happiness*. In her essay of the same year, "Feminist Killjoys (and Other Willful Subjects)," Ahmed goes on to embrace the figure of the stereotypical angry woman as an avatar of feminist willfulness. "Someone says something you consider problematic," she writes:

> You are becoming tense; it is becoming tense. How hard to tell the difference between what is you and what is it! You respond, carefully, perhaps. You say why you think what they have said is problematic. You might be speaking quietly, but you are beginning to feel "wound up," recognizing with frustration that you are being wound up by someone who is winding you up. In speaking up or speaking out, you upset the situation. That you have described what was said by another as a problem means you have created a problem. You become the problem you create.

You know the line: "Why do you have to bring race into this?" Comfort and happiness, in this scenario, are the result of aligning properly with the atmosphere you're in. In other words, they're the affects of obedience: happiness is the feeling that proper behavior generates. "To be willing to go against a social order, which is protected as a moral order, a happiness order, is to be willing to cause unhappiness, even if unhappiness is not your cause."

Affect theory's center of gravity is found near this question of happiness. If there is one contemporary scholar who looms over the field, it is Lauren Berlant, an English professor at the University of Chicago. Her central concept is also the title of her 2011 book, *Cruel Optimism*. It is a distinctively contemporary feeling, Berlant argues, the sticky affective residue left by the slow decay of once-stable forms of the good life: "'Cruel optimism' names a relation of attachment to compromised conditions of possibility whose realization is discovered either to be *im*possible, sheer fantasy, or *too* possible, and toxic." The result is a kind of purgatory. However harmful any individual attachment might be—to a relationship, or an ambition, or a way of life—giving up on it would shatter the personality that has been organized around it. "Whatever the *content* of the attachment is," Berlant writes, "the continuity of the form of it provides something of the continuity of the subject's sense of what it means to keep on living and to look forward to being in the world." Taking on an impossible debt load to buy a house or go to college, because you won't have a stable or normative or meaningful adult life if you don't—this is cruel optimism. The graduate student's single-minded, misery-inducing pursuit of one of the few remaining tenure-track jobs—this, too, is cruel optimism. (It's no coincidence that affect theory so precisely captures academic life; academia, just like the rest of the economy, is undergoing the process of the colonization of feeling.) Perhaps the grandest example of cruel optimism is found in our collective relationship to looming climate catastrophe. What we have done is surely terrible, but apparently we find it less terrible to keep on as before than to imagine other ways of living.

At a more general level, what "cruel optimism" describes is the way life under neoliberalism feels stuck in a stalled-out temporality. Theoretical advances are typically products of moments of great social change. Yet affect theory in general—and some of its sharpest political criticism in particular—emerges from inertia. Cruel optimism flowers in the shade cast by the overhang of an unresolved past over an absent future. We are, Berlant argues, picking over the ruins of a good life that we cannot restore and will not leave behind. It is as if the whole society were living in Grey Gardens.

Berlant's best-known specific case is her reading of mass obesity, which she describes as a form of "slow death." The poor and the working class, she notes, know that they will not live as long as their social superiors. The bourgeois imperative of self-care, the efficient reproduction of one's own body, has become at this point a cruel joke. To eat unhealthily is not simply an act of direct resistance, for Berlant, but a form of "lateral agency." Food is one of life's few reliable pleasures, and its consumption offers a form of community and belonging. "Under a regime of crisis ordinariness, life feels truncated, more like desperate doggy-paddling than like a magnificent swim out to the horizon," she writes. "Eating adds up to something, many things: maybe the good life, but usually a sense of well-being that spreads out for a moment, not a projection toward a future." Berlant's prose, always a bit slanted, seems to enact the kind of lateral agency she describes: "Paradoxically, of course, at least during this phase of capital, there is less of a future when one eats without an orientation toward it."

WHAT BERLANT OBSERVES in her cultural criticism is visible in another strain of social theory. The German economic sociologist Wolfgang Streeck, in *Buying Time: The Delayed Crisis of Democratic Capitalism* (2014), proposes that the wealthy democracies of Europe and North America have been engaged in a delaying operation since the economic crisis of the 1970s. Again and again, these states have pushed forward in time the reckoning building up inside the capitalist order, manipulating the money supply and relying on asset price bubbles to generate "illusions of growth and prosperity."

Streeck's analysis goes like this: As the postwar economic-growth machine sputtered in the 1970s, the legitimacy it had bought for capitalism fell into arrears. Streeck says that from this point, the wealthy capitalist democracies went through three stages of postponement. Each was designed to sustain public legitimacy the easy way, by putting off a resolution of fundamental questions. The first phase came with the great inflation of the 1970s. So long as labor could keep bidding up wages and capital could keep raising prices, both sides could avoid—for a time—the absorption of the underlying losses the economy as a whole had sustained. But this process could go only so far. When the inflationary spiral wore on for a full decade, central banks moved to put it to a halt by hiking interest rates, flatlining economies, and throwing hundreds of thousands of factory workers into unemployment. This initiated the next episode of postponement: the growth of public debt. In the early '80s, high interest rates multiplied the value of the public debt. Meanwhile, the global 1979–81 recession produced large-scale unemployment, forcing governments to take on deficits to finance the social safety net. To escape the recession, the capitalist democracies borrowed, and cut taxes for the rich to spur growth. The state, in other words, took the legitimacy problem onto its own balance sheet. But ballooning public deficits began to spook markets, triggering the retrenchment of the 1990s. The shredding of the welfare state was, of course, largely presided over by center-left social democrats—Blair, Clinton, Schröder, and their ilk. With financial markets liberalized in the '80s and '90s, the state finally offloaded the burden of buying legitimacy onto private creditors. An essentially privatized Keynesianism resulted, in which policy makers encouraged a series of asset-price bubbles—culminating in the housing bubble—in order to maintain overall growth and the consumption levels of individual households. "The securing of a mass base for modern capitalism thus shifted from the sphere of politics to the market, understood as a mechanism for the production of *greed and fear*," Streeck writes.

Although Streeck's argument is as straightforward as that of any other economic historian, we might think of the story he tells, under the sign of affect theory, as a neurotic and incomplete mourning process for the postwar boom—an anguished refusal to say goodbye and move on. Rather than change the organization of our society in response to stagnation and inequality, the wealthy democracies have relied on monetary policy and financialization to delay a reckoning. The consequences are clear in our everyday experience of those markets in which mass participation has been sustained only by the expansion of credit, the debt-financed commodities that we can neither afford nor imagine living without: cars, college, health care, and, above all, houses.

What better represents Berlant's archaic "good life" fantasy than homeownership? At the core of the 2008 financial crisis we find this contradictory arrangement: American society is unwilling to pay enough to significant numbers of its citizens for them to buy houses, yet also unwilling to live with the idea of itself as anything other than an "ownership society," as George W. Bush's 2004 slogan put it. Individuals and households, for their part, cannot bear to break with their aspirations to participate in this version of the good life. The problem, then, is that we are too straight—too bound to failing norms—to attack the forces disfiguring our lives. Desire for the kinds of stability and comfort neoliberalism has dissolved is precisely what makes the neoliberal advance possible.

What radical political economy of Streeck's type lacks is a sense of where to do reparative work. Streeck can survey the landscape and see the aggregate results of cruel optimism, but one dreads the thought of him trying to talk to an underwater homeowner or an indebted college student about the structurally hopeless nature of the situation. Instead, Streeck flatly registers "the destruction of collective agency, and indeed the hope for it, in the neoliberal-globalist revolution." It is to the great credit of Berlant and her colleagues that they have dared to reopen the question of how, without being nostalgic for past movements and victories, we might actually accomplish change in our own time.

Elizabeth Freeman comes closer still to synthesizing queer theory with a sense of political-economic agency in her 2010 book *Time Binds: Queer Temporalities, Queer Histories*. Freeman employs the concept of "chrononormativity," the way that bare and chaotic human bodies are ordered into directional, choreographed lifetimes. This is done through the chronological signposts of an individual biography: "marriage, accumulation of health and wealth for the future, reproduction, childrearing, and death and its attendant rituals." To fail to proceed through the proper stages is, in Freeman's view—an extension of Sedgwick's reading of Proust—a violation of normativity and thus a kind of queerness. To reject marriage, or the future orientation of parenting, or the time discipline of the work ethic, to pursue self-discovery instead of self-denial, is then to refuse capital and heteronormativity at the same time.

If queer sexuality is one version of such asynchrony, another is found in working-class life. "We might think of class as an embodied synchronic and diachronic organization," Freeman writes. "In its dominant forms, class enables its bearers what looks like 'natural' control over their body and its effects, or the diachronic means of sexual and social reproduction. In turn, failures or refusals to inhabit middle- and upper-middle-class habitus appear as, precisely, asynchrony, or time out of joint." Perhaps in the inability to form a nuclear family (or to institute the constitutive rituals of the family, such as the nightly collective meal), or to move steadily forward through a career, or to accumulate savings, working-class people are denied the rewards of "successful" chrononormativity. The working class also looks, to those who do manage such normative goals, off-kilter, queer.

The concept of class has been in fairly wide discredit in much critical theory since the 1980s, thanks to the epochal defeat of the industrial proletariat and the fall of the socialist states that once claimed to speak for it. As an idea, class seemed stubbornly archaic, nearly Victorian, in its fixation on so-called material realities. The rehabilitation of class through the terms of queer theory is a surprising turn of events. The theoretical unity of queerness and class identity in Freeman's account is a record of the defeats of a more fragmentary left and a product of political necessity, to be sure. Yet it represents something more. It is the beginning of a plan.

WHAT WOULD HAPPEN if we could take charge of our own affects? It might be possible to send an impulse back in the other direction; perhaps capitalist institutions are vulnerable at the level of affective struggle.

This possibility gets at one of the strangest and most appealing aspects of academic affect theory: its resemblance, at the level of tone and form—direct appeals to the reader, memoir—to self-help. While odd in the pages of an academic press book, these characteristics shouldn't be all that surprising. For if a downcast affect is a structural component of late capitalism's triumph, one would expect the most depressive of all to be the most defeated people—those who identify with the left. And what is generally the case for radicals should hold doubly for radical academics, who are disempowered twice over: not only identified with a defeated political movement but relegated to doting over the memory of the left and tinkering endlessly with its shrine. The affect of university life—mournful and defensive—would seem to forbid leaps of radical imagination.

Sixteen years ago, the theorist Wendy Brown diagnosed this malaise. In her essay "Resisting Left Melancholy," she described "a Left that has become more attached to its impossibility than to its potential fruitfulness, a Left that is most at home dwelling not in hopefulness but in its own marginality and failure, a Left that is thus caught in a structure of melancholic attachment to a certain strain of its own dead past, whose spirit is ghostly, whose structure of desire is backward-looking and punishing." Today's leftists, as anyone who's done some organizing will know, are still attached to the experience of defeat, since it gives structure to their sense of their own marginal, heroic, and sad position.

Here are some of the times I think of Brown: at the sound of a new repetitious modification of "Hey hey, ho ho"; when I have the same conversation about some irresolvable issue of left-wing strategy for the hundredth time in a union meeting or a Marxist reading group, and I myself have nothing new to add; when an anarchist explains to me that he really would prefer to create communal safe spaces rather than do anything that would make anyone uncomfortable; when a sectarian or an ultra-leftist insists that he is only interested in revolutionary politics and not reform, and therefore will do nothing—call him when the strike starts or the barricades go up. Such is the scale of the defeat inflicted on the radical left that many of its adherents have come to hate politics itself, the site of their sadness, and their aversion has made them sadder still.

An answer to this challenge remains unclear. The case is not helped by the way much affect theory appears incomprehensible and empirically thin outside the bounds of literary criticism. The whole project may be too arcane to have legs outside the academy. Still, in this moment of utopian impoverishment, one could do worse than to begin at the level of fantasy. Berlant herself addresses the question:

> The demands of the present mean protesting not only the state's servility to capital but people's very own fantasies of the good life. . . . The response to a potentially radical reconstruction of the conditions of the reproduction of life ought to be very demanding on everyone, including the resisters. At the moment most resisters are protesting state/capital but not protesting themselves. Without accommodating the affective demands for adjustment to the austere ordinary with which they're being confronted, people need to think about what kinds of good life might better be associated with flourishing, and fight that battle (with fantasy, politically) too.

The content of an affect-theory-driven program or demand would thus seem less important than the form of organization, which would have to be both durable and intimate enough to sustain processes of personal transformation. The project of collective action would then become a project of collective queering. If the aspirations of such a project seem similar to those of the antidisciplinary left of the '80s and '90s, the problem then was that a social basis was not yet in place—nor did the theorists or activists of that era have a sufficiently strong sense of history. The country, as they say, was not ready. It still might not be, but affect theory's promise lies in its belief in the very possibility of positive collectivity: its reparative impulse to generate new fantasies, yet fantasies made practical by their placement in historical time.

Such a political practice ought to terrify its participants as they embark on it, and discomfit those with whom they seek to engage. Like all stigmatized relationships, political engagements adequate to this moment are as likely to feel confusing or frightening as ecstatic or liberating. Affective struggle has to entail becoming connected to the people who can't see past their confusion or fear, and building solidarity where there is none by insisting on a form of relationship to which few are accustomed and that the mainstream neoliberal subject sees as genuinely queer: camaraderie. What's more, the willingness to generate discomfort will require insistence on connection even through multiple rounds of rejection. To lose heart at the first refusal—whether to join a union, attend a protest, or just talk about politics—is one of the indulgences of left melancholy, with its grim satisfaction in defeat. I've been sent scurrying from the slammed doors of many people whom I've tried to recruit to join my union, including countless people who are today members and leaders of the organization. I doubt this process is nearly as painful or costly as coming out of the closet. (Though being queer in America and being a trade unionist may not be so far apart in stigma as they once were.) Still, it does seem to me that the affective kernel at its core—attempting to form new relationships that violate and undermine the collective norm—is essentially the same.

The reparative impulse of affect theory—easily written off as individualist—can in this way give shape to a collective movement. To mount effective challenges the left will have to withstand not only the punishing opposition that descends on any attempt at social transformation but also the more vicious internal mechanism by which power speaks to each of us in our own voice. There may be no authentic self buried deep down, waiting to be discovered, but it might be possible to invent new selves in the crucible of shared struggle. For this, the left may need less of the antinomian radicalism of Foucault and Deleuze, and more of a loving discipline of its own—the kind of social organization that keeps you coming back to the same slammed-shut door, again and again, because you love your comrades more than you're afraid.

There's no way to win any justice without generating tremendous amounts of discomfort, for ourselves first of all. Having a theory for thinking about this is a start. Having some practice at winning will only happen when activists and organizers stop being so melancholy and fearful, and start being more willful, not just in our declarations but in interpersonal relations based on constant unease. This is something that I find few radicals have learned how to do. In our decades of loss, we have become creatures of habit—as is common to exiles. The journey back from the political desert is dogged by the desire to stay and grieve the easier days when we knew we had no chance. To drag our feet or look backward is appealing, given the vast uncertainty of what lies before us. The question ahead is not just where we will arrive, but, more frightening still, who we will be when we get there. Perhaps, if we are lucky and brave, it will be a surprise. +

Admission.
Academic Year, 2015–2016.

CRITICAL THEORY and the ARTS

Robert Hullot-Kentor, chair

ONE-YEAR MA PROGRAM.

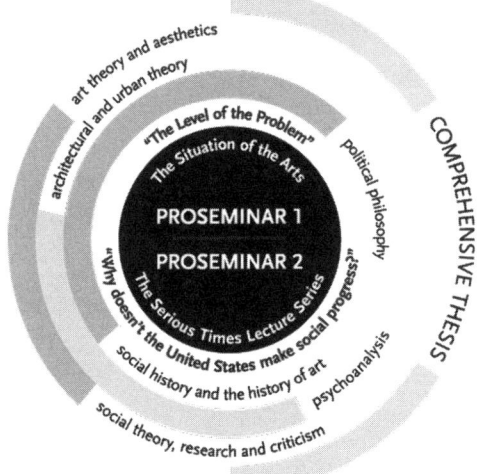

"Artworks ask us to think about them as does nothing else humanly made. An artwork is not founded on any conceptual presupposition or assertion, and this makes it possible for us to experience in it the origin of thinking—as the experience of the need in thinking—which is why art is at the center of the critique of domination. Art that is art is waiting to be understood..."

More about the program: cta.sva.edu.

ENRIQUE MARTÍNEZ CELAYA, *THE SECRET*. 2012, OIL AND WAX ON CANVAS, 44 × 60".
PRIVATE COLLECTION, LOS ANGELES, CALIFORNIA.

THIN PLACES

Jordan Kisner

THE ELECTRODE IS THE WIDTH of angel-hair pasta. A surgeon has threaded it through one of the four dime-size holes in the patient's skull, and it is advancing into her one millimeter at a time, controlled by a small knob that another surgeon is turning and turning with great concentration.

This morning a nurse shaved off the patient's hair, and the surgeon drilled these holes around the crown of her head, two in her temples and two in the back. Then he fastened a metal brace the size of a dog cage around her head to hold the wires steady as they enter her brain. Surrounding the patient, the brace, and the doctor is a giant O-shaped machine the color of tangerine sherbet, which is taking live images inside her head. The patient is awake.

First, the electrode passes through the part of the brain closest to the bone, the part of her that knows the names of things and left from right. Then it bores down through the part of her that knows how to draw, the part that recognizes her mother's face and remembers what she said to the nurse when he asked about the birthmark on her temple. Down through the part of her that likes sex and the part that knows how to talk. Down almost to the deepest part of the brain, the stem, which is responsible for her breath and her heart. This movement, from outside the patient's body through the opening in her skull and into the core of her brain, is called transversal.

The transversal has been plotted carefully. The path of the needle is precise to the millimeter, avoiding important veins and arteries as well as nerve clusters better left untouched. The destination is Area

24, also known as the ventral anterior cingulate. Hers is suffering from either underdevelopment or hyperactivity, depending on which doctor is explaining it. The electrode will stay inside her to deliver electric currents to Area 24 for the next several years, or possibly forever.

The patient finds herself strapped to a gurney with wide belts, naked under her paper gown, because this morning, like every morning, she thought, 117 times, "I am going to kill a stranger." A pacifist by nature and in her politics, she finds this thought sickening and goes to great lengths to ensure that it doesn't come true. An elaborate protocol has arisen: every time the thought "I am going to kill a stranger" pops into her mind she jerks her head hard and declares silently, "I am a peaceful person, I am a peaceful person, I am a peaceful person." This quells the panic that rises—*is* she peaceful? What if she killed someone by accident? What if she flew into a sudden rage? What if she is, at heart, monstrous?—and works like penance: three peaceful thoughts for every murderous one keeps the balance tipped in the right direction. This becomes more difficult when the thoughts come quickly. The number of times she thinks "I am going to kill a stranger" has to be prime or the thought's power increases, so she'll restart the cycle as many times as necessary to bring the count to a prime number. A twenty-minute reprieve is as much as she hopes for in a day.

She has thrown out all her knives, scissors, heavy blunt objects, needles, and sharp pens. She stopped driving a long time ago. She never stands near train tracks or close to people on the sidewalk, just in case something were to come over her and she were to push someone into traffic. Despite being shy, she feels compelled to introduce herself to almost everyone she sees. Once she meets them, they are no longer strangers and therefore no longer in danger of her. This became exhausting—and alarming to the strangers—so a few years ago she stopped leaving her house altogether. Now she lives in terror of what she might do to deliverymen.

Over the years, doctors have prescribed nine medications in various combinations, as well as talk therapy, exposure therapy, cognitive behavioral therapy, and electroconvulsive shock therapy, all with meager results. Her case is, to use their terminology, "intractable." She had to sign all manner of paperwork formally acknowledging this, attesting, for example, that she knows what the word *intractable* means, before she could find herself in this room with Frankensteinian screws in her temples, counting the ceiling tiles. She consented to everything without hesitation.

The first electrode's transversal produces soft, whooshy noises from the monitor in the corner. These noises are her brain waves, tracked by the exploratory electrode, which will forge the correct path before the doctor inserts the permanent electrode. His target is two-and-a-half or three millimeters wide. Once he's reached it, he will remove the exploratory electrode and thread in the one that will be wired to a battery pack sewn in under her collarbone. It will pulse electricity into Area 24 at a constant rhythm for several years, until the battery dies and needs to be changed. She has to be awake during the insertion so that she can tell them what it feels like.

The patient is not altogether articulate about what it feels like. She has been strapped down to prevent her from bolting or fighting or trying to tear the metal cage off her head. This is both terrifying and comforting, as the thoughts are coming in inexorable waves now and she is grateful for anything that will help her keep them from coming true. This is a familiar scene: the afflicted tied down while being ministered to by some credentialed man in a robe carrying an instrument. It used to be books and crucifixes. There used to be prayer and incantation. Now there are only the muted sounds of her brainwaves, the rhythmic beeps and clicks of the vitals monitor, and the voice of the doctor as he murmurs to her through her thought torrent. He sounds calm.

The goal is to alter her experience of reality "with minimal side effects." No one has been able to tell her whether or why this will work. Only a few dozen people have ever had this treatment for a psychological condition, and so every new patient is an experiment. Initially, doctors hypothesized that the electricity would curb overactive neurons; now they suspect it may actually stimulate neurons, or change the types of information neural pathways can transmit, but they're not sure, just as they're unsure precisely where in her brain to place the electrodes for best results. They are learning as they go; once this is all over, her experience will be another data point.

What the doctors do know is what the anterior cingulate cortex does, generally speaking. It houses consciousness, in the existential sense, and emotional pain. It regulates motivation, impulse control, and the anticipation of both delight and catastrophe. Francis Crick proposed it as the center of free will. It's also responsible, in part, for the human capacity for empathy.

There are, naturally, a number of things that could go wrong. Possible but unlikely: hemorrhage, brain damage, stroke, seizure, infection, death. Possible but slightly more likely: memory "problems," trouble speaking, depression, and mania. These latter risks have an aftertaste of irony. The electrode might turn her from a person who speaks compulsively to strangers to a person who cannot speak well at all; it may transform her mind from one reduced to four obsessive thoughts to one hyperexpansive with mania. She wonders what it would be like to go from having one mind to another and then remembers she has already done that.

The doctor in the paper bonnet interrupts this line of thinking to announce that they're ready to begin testing voltages. The electrode has arrived at what they think will be the right place, and now it is time to see what happens to her mind when they turn it on.

She closes her eyes and waits.

This procedure is called deep brain stimulation (DBS). The patient described above is a composite of people I've met, people I've read about, and people whose surgeries I've seen in videos. She is fashioned after the few dozen patients who have undergone DBS to treat severe obsessive-compulsive disorder, an experimental application now in clinical trials at Mount Sinai Hospital in New York, Brown University, the University of Rochester, and a handful of other medical centers. Her symptoms aren't so much fictional as typical: thousands of people are crippled by fears of hurting others. It is shocking how many have thrown out their knives.

Deep brain stimulation has been used for years to diminish tremors in people with Parkinson's disease, but it's experimental and controversial as a treatment for psychiatric disorders.* Only a few OCD patients have undergone it (roughly two dozen so far in the current, FDA-approved study, and no more than a hundred in the US total), and like many historical attempts to alter the mind, it seems halfway

---

* Nevertheless, it's being researched with enthusiasm as a possible alternative to the neurosurgical protocol that preceded it, ablation, in which targeted parts of the brain circuitry are burned by lasers until permanently "neutralized." Deep brain stimulation, for all its echoes of dystopian sci-fi, has the benefit of being adjustable and, for the most part, reversible.

magical because no one really understands its mechanisms. Obsessive-compulsive disorder is not like Parkinson's disease—the symptoms aren't visible and physical (trembling hands) so much as experiential and behavioral—so neurosurgery-as-treatment becomes more existential in its implications. Compounding this is the fact that, neurochemically, obsessive-compulsive disorder bears a conspicuous resemblance to falling in love. Scientists have scanned the brains of the pathologically obsessive and held them up next to brain scans of the love-struck, and the images turned colors in the same places. Doctors drew blood and found the same chemical imbalances—namely, a serotonin deficit. The philosophical distinction between deactivating a part of someone's brain and deactivating some part of their mind or self begins to blur.

I've done months of research about deep brain stimulation—reviewing articles, deciphering studies, interviewing physicians, scrolling through procedure videos on YouTube—for no special reason other than what you might call—ahem—a persistent curiosity. While reading the literature, it's easy to think in clinical abstractions, but then I watched a video of an older woman undergoing the procedure and was struck by the way her voice was muffled by the nest of equipment. The doctors kept having to ask her to speak up during the adjustment phase, when she was supposed to be reporting changes in her psychological state. "I said I almost just laughed," she repeated, gazing at the equipment before her with an expression of wonder. "I haven't laughed in . . . a very long time." The doctor nodded dispassionately. "Can you describe that for us?"

It seems important to cling to the concrete, to remember that illness is not a metaphor or a study but a phenomenon unfolding in (and on) real bodies in real rooms. Its qualia, the crinkly paper hospital gown and metallic adrenaline taste, the mutable and inexpressible shades of pain, demand articulation because they matter. We work so hard at telling others *what it is like* to be sick in whichever particular way we are sick; we are reassured to hear that our particulars fit within larger known narratives of illness. With sickness as with anything else, communicating what it is like so others can know, or understanding others in precisely the way they wish we could, is next to impossible. We try anyway.

Admittedly, most OCD patients are not like my imagined girl. Usually, the disease is damaging but not devastating in a relationship-ruining, inpatient-care, life-disintegrating way. It is considered a less challenging diagnosis than, for example, bipolar disorder, schizophrenia, or any of the personality disorders.* It is "neurosis" not "psychosis," "mental illness" as opposed to "insanity." The existence of the DBS study, though, and the interest it draws from patients and practitioners alike, subtly undermines this differentiation. Extreme treatment reflects the disease's extreme power to cripple. Neurologically, OCD seems to act on similar parts of the brain as schizophrenia; experientially, both diseases are marked by foreign-seeming intrusions on the mind. Both patients are overcome with thoughts, images, and impulses that are, to use the clinical word, ego-dystonic: they feel alien to and in conflict with the self. They feel other. In obsessive-compulsive patients, these thoughts tend to be violent or violating, obscene, immoral, or some other shade of horrifying.

What distinguishes obsessive-compulsive patients from schizophrenic patients is their ability to live inside a paradox: the thoughts hijacking their minds feel urgently not "theirs," but the thoughts are nevertheless something going on in their own minds and bodies. These thoughts are alien, but they have not been planted by aliens. In the medical community, this is known as "insight."

Having insight is not enough to make the thoughts go away. A little while ago, I was talking to a writer who has to touch things—all the slats on the staircase, all the poles as he walks down the street. He knows this doesn't make sense. Sometimes, though not terribly often, he has to go back home to make sure that he didn't leave a cigarette burning, even when he can remember perfectly well that he didn't. He only has to do this when alone. When he's with people, he doesn't have to touch anything.

He told me that since childhood he's been fascinated with the idea that everyone is God. I asked him what he meant, and he said that he had a suspicion that God was everywhere and everyone, and all our souls are the same soul, God's soul, but we're just walking around in different meat suits. That's how he said it: "We're all stuck in our own meat suits."

---

* It's worth noting, though, that OCD has something like a 91 percent lifetime comorbidity with other Axis-I diseases, most commonly depression, generalized anxiety disorder, panic disorder, addiction, and anorexia/bulimia. In a study published in 2008, three-quarters of OCD patients from a clinical sample met the criteria for lifetime mood disorders, nearly 40 percent were unable to work because of psychopathologies, and 14 percent were on disability specifically for OCD. In light of these numbers, a diagnosis of OCD is plenty grim.

I suddenly felt very aware of how different he and I look—his height and beard and age, his ruddiness, his tie; my stringy arms, bitten nails, and freckles. He is older than I am, and bigger, and embodied in a sort of ragged, robust way that I am not. At first I couldn't quite tell whether he was fucking with me when he leaned in and looked into my brown eyes with his blue ones and said, "What I'm saying is that maybe we're all the same, we just don't know it because we're separated into our own bodies," but then I decided that he was not fucking with me and was serious, at least partly, about this hypothetical.

And part of me was thinking, *Get a grip.*

Another part was thinking, *Well, exactly.*

Which did not signal that I was on board with the meat-suit theory per se, only that I was not surprised, even a little, to discover another person with OCD who'd been worrying his whole life about the distinctions and correspondences between himself and other people, and between himself and God. You don't have to have OCD or any mental illness to have concerns like this, but the urgency of locating the boundaries of the self, the distinction between what is inside and outside, you and not-you, becomes particularly acute when your mind seems a little too permeable.

O BSESSION WAS INITIALLY a term of warfare. In Latin, *obsessio* indicated the first phase of a siege on a city, when the city was surrounded on all sides but its citadel remained intact. *Obsessio* was followed by *possessio*, when the attacker breached the walls and took the city from the inside. In *Obsession: A History*, Lennard Davis explains the way these two words were adapted to explain demonic possession in the third century: "In the case of *obsession*, that person was aware of being besieged by the devil since the demon did not have complete control, had not entered the city of the soul, and the victim could therefore attempt to resist." Demonology was, for many centuries thereafter, the only language available for explaining obsession and other insanities. Obsession was understood as a torment of the soul and, often, a spiritual punishment. The cure was exorcism.

This went on for more than a thousand years, until some Protestant churches began to retreat from the idea of possession (piqued at the way the Catholic Church had, per Davis, "the inside track on exorcisms"). In 1731, the English Parliament repealed laws banning witchcraft, which had been the most common grounds for exorcism. Modern medicine was in its nascent stages, and as it developed it annexed mental affliction, recategorizing madness as a physical rather than a spiritual problem. The demonological model was replaced by the medical model. Scientists discovered the nervous system and, with it, "nerves," and the possibility of a physiological source of mental states.* Davis notes, "The nerves are the physical link to the mental—they are dissectible, discernible, and physical, yet their effects are metaphysical, symbolic, and affective."

In the same era, roughly the late 17th to early 18th century, the notion of "partial madness" emerged to accommodate people who were mentally ill but tethered enough to reality to recognize their illness or sane enough to function within society. One could be "a conscious 'I' who is watching an obsessed self instead of a deranged and unconscious self dwelling in a lunatic." Sanity went from a binary category (sane/insane) to a triad: you could be lucid, a lunatic, or a neurotic. The "monomaniacs," as obsessives came to be known, were the stars of this new formulation. The monomaniac tended to be high functioning and highly thought of. Davis writes, "A certain cachet developed, a notion of being fashionable, in having one of these partial, intermittent conditions." Neurosis was constructed as intrinsic to character, but as a possible asset. It was a sign of advancement, complexity, genius, cosmopolitanism, and, so to speak, *heightened sensibilities.***

Such was the case with Sigmund Freud's most famous obsessive. The Rat Man, as Freud nicknamed him to protect his identity, was clever and charming, a successful professional man who was nevertheless ruled by disturbing fantasies of rodents attacking his father and fiancée. Freud, writing in 1909, took a therapeutic approach to the Rat Man that became typical for a time: the man's problems were purely

---

* In the 17th and early 18th centuries, nerves were thought of primarily as connective tissues in musculature. It wasn't until later in the 18th century that the nervous system was understood to have any relationship with emotion. With this switch came the association of the word *nerves* with anxiety, nervousness, hysteria, and other "morbid affections," an evolution to which we owe dubious thanks for the nervous Nellie, Jane Austen's exquisitely irritating Mrs. Bennett (who won't stop mewling, "My poor nerves!"), fashionable neuroses, and Woody Allen.

** The particular metaphors that arose around neurosis, or "nervous diseases," are suspiciously similar to the metaphors that, in *Illness as Metaphor*, Susan Sontag argued were associated with tuberculosis in the 19th century: nobility of soul, creativity, Romantic melancholy, et cetera. Sontag was unimpressed with this

issues of the psyche. His obsessions stemmed from the fact that he'd been punished for masturbating as a child, and had formed as a defense mechanism against the anger, aggression, and anxiety he felt in his adult relationships. The cure: analysis.

A hundred years later, we don't think of the mind as something that can be entered, invaded, or deciphered so much as something that can be altered and adjusted. The mind is less the point, actually—Freud's methods have become passé. Now we talk about the brain, which is not parametric in that our metaphors for it do not indicate that the brain has parameters that can be violated. Insanity is now more biological than spiritual. "Mental illness" is no longer a breach of the self but a neurochemical event happening to—but separate from—the self. Like hypertension, it happens in our cells, and we swallow pills to get rid of it.†

This is more or less how grown-ups talked about what was wrong with me for several years after I was diagnosed with OCD at 13. I was, clinically, a nervous wreck, and many of my fears were about the transformation of my own mind. Was I insane? Was I doomed? Was this who I really was? Therapists and my parents were ready with reassurances that what was happening was only an accident of serotonin, a mysterious but correctable "imbalance" no more essential to who I was than a flu or a sunburn. I balked at taking medication, worried it would change who I was. "You have an illness, and this is just medicine to correct that illness," I was told. "It's like having diabetes. You wouldn't refuse insulin because your body's 'authentic' state is to have diabetes." In the end, I couldn't take the panic attacks, so I took the Prozac and, with it, this narrative of what was happening. It worked. The pills made my hands shake, but my mind was transformed back, more or less, to the healthy, stable state I remembered.

---

equation: "My point is that illness is *not* a metaphor," she wrote, "and that the most truthful way of regarding illness—and the healthiest way of being ill—is one most purified of, most resistant to, metaphoric thinking. Yet it is hardly possible to take up one's residence in the kingdom of the ill unprejudiced by the lurid metaphors with which it has been landscaped." Later in the book, she lambasted the modern impulse to psychologize disease, declaring psychology a "sublimated spiritualism" with such sneering conviction that Denis Donoghue, reviewing the book for the *New York Times*, was emboldened to declare her mind "powerful rather than subtle," a critique it might have been entertaining to witness Sontag read in the paper.

† Incidentally, since the dawn of psychotropic medications, the incidence of OCD in the general population has jumped from .005 percent to 3 percent.

When I was 17, not long after weaning myself off Prozac, I relapsed. It happened sort of slowly. The thoughts came back, but at first I could fend them off. I blew past them with the buoyancy of a teenager whose life was going well. I was a few months away from leaving for what seemed like the most exciting college in the world, and I had my first boyfriend. Gradually, though, I stopped being able to ignore the thoughts. They came too quickly, and one day they seemed to bring real danger with them. Something darkly magical began to happen: I would gaze out at sunny days, beach days, Southern California sunsets, and feel the sidewalks began to warp. The sky was cloudless, but something was terribly wrong. This feeling would steal an hour one day, and then I'd be myself again. The next day, two hours. As weeks passed, the sinister entered, and sick fear took over.

At the time, I worked as a barista for a local breakfast-and-lunch place on the beach, pulling espresso and pouring green-tea lattes in an eight-by-eight-foot alcove off the restaurant's kitchen. A wall obstructed my view of the line cooks, so I spent my shifts in isolation, handing cup after cup out a window the size of a cereal box to a man named Fernando who ate toast with whipped cream for breakfast. I'd be pouring cappuccinos and humming in my little wall-hole and then suddenly, as if from nowhere, a terrifying sentence would appear in my mind. Then another. Then a dozen. Panic attacks rolled in hourly. I began taping poems to the espresso machine to memorize, figuring that if I had to entertain thoughts that weren't mine I might at least try to make them beautiful. I knew what was happening, but knowledge didn't help. Diagnostic categories, the language of treatment—they weren't enough. My teenage hair started to gray; my hands shook at the machine. I was growing desperate. One afternoon, I stepped into the back alley behind the restaurant, dialed my therapist, and told her that I thought I might not survive it.

I was understudying Juliet that summer for a local production of *Romeo and Juliet*, which meant sitting in on rehearsals and learning the lines and blocking. This should have been fun and exciting—and it was some days, particularly when the handsome blue-eyed actor playing Romeo made a point of flirting with me. (The regular Juliet was sleeping with Mercutio.) But most days it felt like something was very, very wrong. People often describe the way your body senses instinctually that you're in the presence of a sociopath or in physical danger. The feeling can be confusing at first, because your body is telling you something that your rational mind doesn't yet know. *Why do I feel so unsettled and skin-crawly when she's so nice? This party is so fun; why do I feel like I have to get out of here?* I spent benign afternoons in rehearsal forcing myself not to bolt from the room. The theater, the restaurant, my bedroom—every place seemed menacing and uncanny. I spent hours in complex, circuitous rationalizations and self-assurances that boiled down to, in endless repetition: "But nothing's wrong, but nothing's wrong, but nothing's wrong."

Of course, something was wrong. The imminent danger was my misfiring sense of imminent danger, the revelation that the stability and habitability of the world can change as the mind changes. Minds are not reliably stable or habitable. They are subject to radical and sometimes horrible transformation. This is a danger of the world that is, as I was discovering, intangible but absolutely real.

Juliet has a monologue in the fourth act, spoken alone in her bedroom as she prepares to take a potion that will plunge her into a sleep so profound she'll appear dead. She and Romeo have agreed that she'll drink this potion, and once she's been mourned and entombed in the family mausoleum he'll come to wake her, and they'll sneak out of Verona under cover of night and begin their life together. She's resolved, even impatient, to go through with the plan and reunite with Romeo, but as she uncorks the vial, a thought occurs to her. "What if it be a poison, which the friar subtly hath minister'd to have me dead?" Fairly quickly she dispenses with this anxiety (the friar is a holy man and a trustworthy friend), but another pops up to fill its place: What if she wakes up before Romeo arrives? What if she suffocates in the tomb? Her nervousness takes on a tinge of panic. What if, worse yet, she wakes too early but does *not* suffocate, and is left alone in the vault "where, for these many hundred years, the bones of all my buried ancestors are packed: where bloody Tybalt lies festering in his shroud?" Then she strikes on the most frightening thought: what if she, surrounded by bodies and smells and "shrieks like mandrakes torn out of the earth, that living mortals, hearing them, run mad," is so overwhelmed that she loses her mind? Will I "madly play with my forefathers' joints," she wonders,

> And pluck the mangled Tybalt from his shroud?
> And, in this rage, with some great kinsman's bone,
> As with a club, dash out my desperate brains?
> O, look! Methinks I see my cousin's ghost
> Seeking out Romeo—

Quickly, she is hallucinating with panic. The loss of her own mind, imagined in the grotesque vision of herself fondling dead bodies in the dark, is made real by her own terror. The figure of Tybalt rises before her to kill Romeo. Desperate to make Tybalt—and the vision—stop, she seizes the potion bottle and, in a gesture that's not a little suicidal, swallows it all. She collapses. End scene.

I dreaded this monologue, but I memorized it, made notes on it, even diagrammed it. I was convinced that the young woman playing Juliet, beautiful as she was in the balcony scene, failed to capture this movement from nervousness to wild, unhinged fear. But I also hoped I'd never have to perform the scene myself. It felt too close. Acting demands letting go of the self in a way that is usually considered self-destructive or pathological in real life; acting demands that you make way for other selves.

But then there's the trick of coming back, of reconstructing the boundaries between your mind and your character's mind. Sometimes this is hard to do. There are characters you don't want to play because you know they'll be frightening to expand into or difficult to come back from.

That summer when I was feeling very much like Juliet holding the potion, the therapist would tell me, "Just know that those thoughts aren't you. That's the OCD, it's not you." It was a kind gesture—she was offering me the illness narrative that reigns now, the one that constructs very, very firm boundaries between brain and self, illness and consciousness, self and other. I clung to that for a while, the notion that the maelstrom happening in my brain was not *of* me but *outside* me, happening to me. That there was a tidy line dividing "me" from "disease," and the disease was classifiable as "other." But then it became difficult to tell whether certain thoughts should go in the me box or the disease box—where did "I want to throw a rock through the kitchen window" belong? Eventually I could no longer avoid the fact that mental illness is not like infection; there's no outside invader. And if a disease is produced in your body, in your mind, then what is it if not you?

Recently I found an image of Juliet and the potion, a film still taken from Franco Zeffirelli's 1968 rendition that is famous even though it didn't make the movie's final cut. Juliet is shown in profile, dressed in a beautiful white nightgown with long sleeves draping to her waist. Her dark hair, a little tangled, hangs loose down her back like mine did when I was 17. She is kneeling at what appears to be an altar but is in fact the carved headboard of her bed; what seems to be the prayer cushion is her pillow, where Romeo's head lay not long ago. We know she's no longer a virgin, but she looks virginal, like one of the saints offering herself up. Her eyes are closed in fear or love or ecstasy, head tilted back in the light that glows down on her wrists and cheekbones. Her hands are clasped at her mouth in what looks like prayer, but if you look closely you can see the vial at her lips. She's imbibing something, but what?

IN A SENSE, what keeps an OCD patient rooted in the world of the neurotic rather than the psychotic, what tethers her to a certain agreed-on reality, the adherence to which seems to be our measure of functional sanity, is her healthy sense of the boundaries of her own ego—her ability to toggle complex and contradictory conceptions of self and other, real and not real, rational and irrational. She is obsessed, not possessed. She has insight. Most patients, though, have moments when their grip on me/not-me slips. In the medical community, this is known as magical thinking.

Obsessions often feel like the work of some cruel and sentient force equipped with its own devious logic, showering you with the exact thoughts and images you find most disturbing and devising new monstrosities as you defuse the old ones. Obsession knows you better than you know yourself. It outwits you. For this reason and others, insight is slippery even for diagnosticians. How is it defined, and how much of it is a patient supposed to have? Are lapses in insight allowed? What sort? How many? In his 1996 book, *Theoretical Approaches to Obsessive-Compulsive Disorder*, the clinical psychologist Ian Jakes writes:

> The absence of reported insight cannot distinguish all obsessions from delusions.... Further difficulties... may be raised by those patients who are classified by some diagnosticians as "partially deluded." These patients are held to have beliefs that would otherwise satisfy the criteria for delusions but do not hold these beliefs with absolute conviction.... How, then, are obsessions to be distinguished from partial delusions, and how are those cases of OCD where reported insight is absent to be distinguished from delusions?

Nearly twenty years later, these categories and definitions are still fluid: in 2013, the *DSM-5* altered OCD's diagnostic criteria to allow for patients who have only "partial insight" or, within certain parameters, lack insight altogether.

Later in this section, Jakes describes a young woman whose case was typical but challenging theoretically. He gives her only five sentences, but the portrait is complex and, in a way, complete. D. S. was 29 and afraid that she might lose possession of her own thoughts, that they might travel from her head down her arms and escape through her fingertips into the world. She worried that she would leave a trail of ideas and images in her wake, clinging like residue to everything she touched. D. S. knew, for the most part, that this wasn't possible, but sometimes she wasn't sure. Her frontiers, the places where she stopped and everything and everyone else began, seemed changeful and pervious. Jakes calls this phenomenon "ego boundary confusion."

I love this young woman with anxious fingers. I wonder about her—what she looks like, where she is, whether she ever got better. If she is still living, she is 47 now. Her fears have such poetic overtones; they riff on common fears of contagion, which are often amplified and uncontrollable in patients with OCD. "Our bodies are not our boundaries," writes Eula Biss in *On Immunity*. "Fear of contamination rests on the belief, widespread in our culture as in others, that something can impart its essence to us on contact. We are forever polluted, as we see it, by contact with a pollutant." This notion extends past the physical realm of germ contamination and into metaphor. We worry about the "bad seed" and fear that someone's awful luck, lousy attitude, or even insanity will "rub off" on us.* At the same time, the things most precious to us often risk—or demand—this kind of contagion. The "sacred" places of the body are the ones where membranes are exposed: our mouths, our eyes, our genitals, the places where we connect with others and make ourselves vulnerable to them.

Accordingly, it is just as common to look for membranes where there are none. We trace our fingers over the faces or bodies of people we love as if we wish we could leave unspoken thoughts and feelings behind like residue. We place our foreheads together and press gently, as

---

* Two roommates, one family member, and a handful of acquaintances have reported to me, independently of one another, that they "caught" OCD after watching the television show *Monk*, by which they usually meant that they'd started buying hand sanitizer and color-coding their folders. These are instances of the way we subtly assume mental states can be "catching," but also examples of the way OCD has become equated with desirable perfectionism, much as it was equated with sophistication in the 19th century. In certain circles, it is now a form of poorly disguised self-congratulation to profess, in confessional tones, that you are "totally OCD" about your work, your house, your record collection, eating organic. Like gluten intolerance, it's an ailment that has taken on chic associations, especially to people who don't really have it.

if to see whether we can merge that way. We struggle toward each other out of our little meat suits.

Sometimes, it works. There is a kind of love where you start to lose track of where you start and stop. It isn't typically sustainable over long periods—it can come and go—but this version of total connection, or total mutual contamination, feels in the moment like the central operating miracle of the universe. Near the end of Toni Morrison's *Beloved*, the prose breaks down in an ecstatic rush:

> I am Beloved and she is mine. . . . how can I say things that are pictures I am not separate from her there is no place where I stop her face is my own and I want to be there in the place where her face is and to be looking at it too a hot thing

This is an exact description of that love. In the book, though, it is also a description of a furious, sublimated obsession, a daughter haunting the mother who killed her. It's a story about love but, just as importantly, about horror; a thwarted love so ferocious it manifests and turns its object from memory to flesh. *Beloved* is in one sense a fable about the chiaroscuro of staying half-merged to someone else, the redemptive power and the unholy danger of "not separate from."

This is one danger that the current, hyperclinical story of illness seems designed to protect us from. If we are permeable the risks are infinite, and it's comforting to imagine firm borders guarding our soft places. Though as Biss points out, when it comes to the body, those borders are largely imagined. For the mind, whose boundaries are literally imagined, the notion of borderlessness, of endless susceptibility to mimetic contagion, is overwhelming. But by denying it entirely, by constructing unimpeachable binaries (me/you, mind/brain, illness/self), we create an experience of the world that's soothing but radically impoverished. If the truth lies somewhere in the middle, then the trick is the mapping. The other day, I found something in an old notebook that I don't remember writing. At the end of a long list of notes I had given up and scrawled, in big letters, *Where do I start and stop, is what I want to know.*

o o o

Sometimes I imagine my fictional girl well again. Out of the hospital, electrodes safely implanted, and responding with promise. Depending on which hospital treated her, she might be sent to an outpatient group therapy called "narrative enhancement."

Dr. Philip Yanos, who developed narrative enhancement therapy, explained to me that its function is to help mentally ill patients overcome internalized stigmas about their conditions. They learn about the ways they have been taught ideas like "I can't have a normal life" or "I'm a bad person" or "There's just something wrong with me." Then they tell the stories of their lives over and over and over to one another. They talk about their lives before they got sick, and they talk about what it was like to be sick, and they talk about now. The therapist and the other patients repeat back to the patient the story she's telling, but suggest more empowering language, and then the patient tells the story again but more like the way they said it.

The goal is to help patients integrate their notions of who they were before their sicknesses with who they are now. The task is to go back and find a thread of a story that can be pulled across the hospitalization or the psychotic break or the shock therapy, from then to now, from "her" to "me." It matters what stories you tell yourself about yourself. When the integrity of the story is violated, people get stuck at the point of fracture. They might re-form themselves around the brokenness, or they might restlessly circle forever, trying to understand what broke and why. The importance of the "coherent narrative self" is paramount: without it, even if the symptoms subside, you might never move on, which is another way of saying get well.

This is the story of how my obsessive-compulsive disorder began: When I was 12, I had a friend who was going through some major psychological disturbance. She was a new friend, because I was new that year in school, and she revealed her problems to me incrementally, each confession like a gift signifying a deeper level of intimacy. First she showed me the box of safety pins and thumbtacks. She pulled them out of her backpack while we sat knee-to-knee on the bus and told me that she used them to cut herself. Next she told me she was bulimic and suicidally depressed. Eventually she told me that there was "a thing in her head" named Ailis, and that Ailis wanted her dead. Ailis, I gathered, was something between a voice and a demon. My friend talked about Ailis all the time, as if she were a mutual acquaintance. On days when I'd been a particularly sweet or loyal friend, she would smile at me meaningfully and say, "Ailis really doesn't like you."

We looked a little alike. (Her breasts were bigger.) We enjoyed the same things. (She turned me on to theater.) Teachers sometimes mixed up our names, and I was quietly pleased at being one of a pair. When she started telling me about thumbtacks and Ailis, I was fascinated and curious and, most of all, thrilled to be brought in. This was interesting, and presented an exciting challenge: I would love her to health. She would ask, "Why doesn't it scare you to hear about these things?" and I would tell her blithely, "Because these problems are yours, not mine. You are you, and I am me." This answer seemed to annoy her, and she would change the subject.

One night, we were up late talking on the phone while I babysat for the neighbors. *Vertigo*, which I'd never seen, was on TV. In the film, Kim Novak's character appears to be possessed by a ghost that is driving her to suicide. "There's a woman in my head who wants me dead," she confesses to Jimmy Stewart after trying to hurl herself off a cliff. "She talks to me all the time." Stewart, a sucker for a blonde with a dark streak, falls in love anyway. Unfortunately, he isn't able to love her to health. He takes her to a place she keeps seeing in her nightmares, an old Spanish mission on the coast, hoping to convince her that she can overcome her fears and exorcise the ghost, but she breaks away from him, dashes up the bell tower, and jumps to her death. This moment at the film's halfway point marks a shift in focus from her possession to his obsession: her madness transfers to him. Unable to let her go, he is ruined by her.

It was during the bell-tower scene—can this possibly be true? This is how I remember it—as Novak dashed up the steps, that my friend asked me again why I was never frightened by her confessions. I repeated my usual answer—you are you, and I am me—and she replied, "You never think you're going to be one of these people, like me, until you are one." Suddenly something came open inside me, and I knew she was right. I hung up the phone and had my first panic attack.

It's uncanny how closely Novak's confession ("There's a woman in my head who wants me dead. She talks to me all the time") matches my friend's description of Ailis as I remember it, and how closely Ailis and Novak's homicidal ghost resemble each other. The synchronicity unnerves me, particularly because I had 100 percent forgotten Novak's imagined woman until I watched the movie again recently. For fifteen years—years during which I carefully avoided *Vertigo*—I remembered only the bell-tower scene, her gray suit ascending the stairwell and then falling past the window.

Did I drastically conflate memories and invent all the details of Ailis in the years since that night? Had my friend seen *Vertigo*, and was it she who suggested I watch it, hoping that I'd see she was not the first person to be visited by an Ailis, perhaps even hoping that I might be visited next—and if so, *why*? I've been asking myself these questions for a while now. Neither scenario makes sense. I am sure I didn't invent Ailis, and yet the diabolical, premeditated manipulation required for the second scenario is so extreme I'd rather find it implausible. Any other possibility demands a coincidence on the level of an act of God. This is a fault in this story I can't overlook and can't heal. It just is.

I've been considering that uncanny confluence for months, but the thing I've been considering for fifteen years is the moment that came next. When my friend said, "You could be like me," and I was plunged irreversibly into a new kind of fear—what was that? In so many ways the moment marks a before and an after, but I don't really know how to talk about it. You could say it was ego boundary confusion. You could say it was mimetic contamination. You could say, maybe, that it was the beginning of real empathy. What I will not say is that it was only a chemical reaction, because while that might be correct, it isn't true.

The summer I was 17 and relapsing, I ran across a moment in the *Phaedrus* when Socrates theorizes that madness "is the channel by which we receive the greatest blessings.... So, according to the evidence provided by our ancestors, madness is a nobler thing than sober sense ... madness comes from God, whereas sober sense is merely human."

Fuck you, Socrates, I thought.

I have said in my darker moments that I would never wish this mess on anyone, even the girl I got it from. (As if that mattered.) I will probably say this again someday, my whining masquerading as largesse, and I will mean it, but it is also true that I know something I did not know before, which is that we are more expansive than we imagine. And this expansiveness is both powerful and frightening. It can ruin you to madness, or fate or God or disease or demons or whatever you call the unknowables. But it is gorgeous, too. It's how the better unknowables get in. I think about being 13 and hanging up the phone, standing frozen in the middle of the carpet in the neighbor's living room while Jimmy Stewart watched Kim Novak's body plummet to the terra-cotta and looking at him and looking at her with my friend's voice ringing in my mind and feeling like I was being cracked wide at the sternum and the top of the head at once, being opened and emptied and invaded, aware suddenly of the way poor, monomaniacal Jimmy could be me and strange, possessed Kim could be me, and my friend with that creature in her head could be me, too.

The warping force of that first panic was truly horrifying. Madness is not some holy blessing; pathology is not the same as pathos. And yet that vertigo has echoes in other rooms and reckonings I've seen, other moments of being opened and emptied and invaded by another person but beautifully, of flinging or being flung wide by radical, magical ego boundary confusions and quiet acts of self-extension over breakfast.

THE OTHER MORNING, I heard a woman on the radio describe her art, enormous conceptual installations that involve manipulations of breath and light. As she was explaining her process, this artist used a phrase I'd never heard before: "thin places." It's a Celtic concept, one that stems from an old proverb that says, "Heaven and earth are only three feet apart, but in the thin places that distance is even smaller." In thin places, the folklore goes, the barrier between the physical world and the spiritual world wears thin and becomes porous. Invisible things, like music or love or dead people or God, might become visible there, or if they don't become visible they become so present and tangible that it doesn't matter. Distinctions between you and not-you, real and unreal, worldly and otherworldly, fall away.

The original thin places were wild landscapes because the idea was born in the heaths of Connemara, a place that's so austere and ancient, so full of twists and hiding places and divots a thousand years old, that it seems somehow likely you might poke a hole through to another reality. But the radio lady said that the delight of thin places was the unpredictability of their location. You can find them someplace with magic written all over it, like Connemara or the Himalayas, but they also pop up in dive bars, bedrooms, hospital rooms. They can appear and disappear.

Because thin places involve an encounter with the ineffable they're hard to talk about. You know something has happened, some dissolution or expansion, but like most things that feel holy and a little dangerous, it just sounds weird in post-factum description. It helps to have someone with you there, someone else to feel what's happening so you can look at each other in awe. Afterward, when you are trying to explain it to other people and sounding like a New Age crank or genuinely insane, you can turn to that person and know that it was real. Or you can choose never to talk about it to anyone else and only sometimes turn to each other and say, What was that? *What was that?*

But then, the thin places I've known aren't always places, per se. Sometimes a thin place appears between people. Sometimes it happens only inside you.

"It could be said, even here, that what remains of the self / Unwinds into a vanishing light, and thins like dust, and heads / to a place where knowing and nothing pass into each other, and through," wrote Mark Strand for his friend Joseph Brodsky:

> What remains of the self unwinds and unwinds, for none
> Of the boundaries holds—neither the shapeless one between us,
> Nor the one that falls between your body and your voice.

Here, transversal takes on a quality of communion, the kind that arises when frontiers fall—a quality that seems inherent, even in the modern transversals of operating rooms where the new exorcism comes in rubber gloves and medical is miracle and knowing and nothing pass into each other and through. Before the word became the name of a medical technique, it was geometry's nod to the importance of the in-between: a transversal is the line that connects other lines. You use it to discern parallels; taking the transverse of two lines reveals whether they'll eventually touch.

After neurosurgical transversal for OCD, the improvements, if they come, will arrive with time. For patients with movement disorders the new world comes all at once, and the first sign is their hands. As the transversal proceeds, the doctors instruct them to hold out one hand and watch the tremors change. The arms start out waving crazily like hoses left unattended but then, within seconds, shudder to stillness. For the first time in years, the fingers can bend to hold a pill or a pen or just to touch lightly. Whatever possessed the muscles is gone, and while it's only electrical impulses, it really does look like a miracle. As a matter of course, the patients weep.

One woman whose name I no longer remember did something extraordinary as she cried. In the recovery room, she sat up immediately without saying a word and extended her new hand to her husband.* Improbably, it stayed obediently outstretched, quivering only a little. The room went still. The doctors and nurses stopped their work and watched as her husband quietly extended his palm toward hers. The air between them grew warm and vanished, and then everyone was weeping in the fluorescent light. +

---

* The exact same gesture sets the events of *Romeo and Juliet* in motion: "palm to palm is holy palmer's kiss." A young man and woman press their hands together at a dance, and whatever happens just then transforms them. I think of the play as orchestrated around two thin places: the holy's palmer's kiss (two hands) and Juliet taking the potion (only her hand).

DANCE! BLOW! ART! LIVE CINEMA! CONVERSATION! SEXY GIRLS & BOYS! ACTUAL REALITY! MUSIC! OPEN BAR!

EVERY SATURDAY NIGHT

GET LOST

AT THE

EVERLASTING
MANUAL ELECTRIC

SHOW

All guest passes $15.00. Special group discounts. TO REQUEST INVITATION, please contact Anna Aiyana (anna@some-more.info) with the subject "Black Kettle 0.2". or call (321)-EXIT-BY-5. Occupancy by more than 500 people is considered unlawful. PHOTOGRAPHY & DIGITAL IMAGING STRICTLY FORBIDDEN. All proposals welcome, contact anna@some-more.info

LOVE YOURSELF VIOLENTLY SHOP FOREVER

HTTP://SHOP.BOYGIRL.XYZ

The Tamiko Grey Collection
New York - Ahmedabad - Manila - Tokyo

Zev Rector
Blonde Jenny, 2014
price upon request
info@tamikogrey.net

SPECIAL ISSUES

/// ELLIOTT CARTER /// A. R. AMMONS /// VERONICA FORREST-THOMSON: UNPUBLISHED ESSAYS /// NEW ITALIAN WRITING///

Subscribe and view our complete list of back issues at CHICAGOREVIEW.ORG.

CHICAGO REVIEW

REVIEWS

DAYNA TORTORICI
Those Like Us

Elena Ferrante. *Troubling Love*. Europa Editions, 2006 (published in Italy, 1992).
The Days of Abandonment. Europa Editions, 2005 (2002).
The Lost Daughter. Europa Editions, 2008 (2006).
My Brilliant Friend. Europa Editions, 2012 (2011).
The Story of a New Name. Europa Editions, 2013 (2012).
Those Who Leave and Those Who Stay. Europa Editions, 2014 (2013).

WHENEVER I HEAR SOMEONE SPECULATE about the true identity of Elena Ferrante, the pseudonymous Italian novelist of international fame, a private joke unspools in my head. *Who is she?* the headlines ask. *Don't you know?* I whisper. In my joke I'm sitting opposite someone important. The person promises not to tell, so I say:

She's Lidia Neri.

She's Pia Ciccione.

She's Francesca Pelligrina. Domenica Augello. Different names, every time, but the reaction is the same: a momentary light in the listener's eyes that fades to bored disappointment. An Italian woman from Naples, whose name you wouldn't know. Who did you expect?

One answer ends in *o*: the first name of a man. Whether to goad Ferrante out of privacy or because they think it's true, the Italian newspaper *L'Unità* has accused the novelist Domenico Starnone of penning her books. If Starnone is behind Ferrante's work, I would like to meet him. No man I know would write so well and not take credit for it.

Since the English-language publication of *My Brilliant Friend*, the first of the addictive Neapolitan novels that have inspired what publicists call "Ferrante fever" in American readers, Ferrante has caused a minor crisis in literary criticism. Her novels demand treatment commensurate to the work, but her anonymity has made it hard. The challenge reveals our habits. We've grown accustomed to finding the true meaning of books in the histories of their authors, in where they were born and how they grew up, in their credentials or refreshing lack thereof. Forget the intentional fallacy; ours is the age of the biographical fallacy. All six of Ferrante's novels published in English to date (translated by the dexterous Ann Goldstein) are narrated in the first person, which invites this kind of reading. Surely work of such intimacy and length must be—as if all novels weren't—*true*.

But there's a greater obstacle still, which is that the novels are *too good*. Book reviewing is a game of outperforming the author, a small and practical agon. A young writer gets an assignment—a poorly written novel or a decent one; if she's lucky, a fairly good one—and to make her name draws life from the host, like a gestating child, as if the goal of reviewing were not to explicate or describe a text but to produce another, better one altogether. Heaping praise is one thing, and praise for Ferrante is not hard to find: she is a master of our time, "the best contemporary novelist you have never heard of," the "Italian Alice Munro." But there is no outdoing Ferrante, and the best critical work on her novels has the humility of someone who knows it. "Writing about the Brilliant Friend books has been one of the hardest assignments I've ever done," Jenny Turner wrote for *Harper's*, and the admission is a relief. The most one can hope to do in writing about Ferrante is to ignore her. Fixating on her identity is one way to postpone reading—to kill time until the words come.

FERRANTE'S FIRST THREE novels, *Troubling Love* (originally published in 1992), *The Days of Abandonment* (2002), and *The Lost Daughter* (2006), are often described as difficult to read. At turns too quick and too slow, they're demanding books, complicated by dizzying ruptures in time and distended by stretches of joylessness. James Wood confessed he struggled to connect "the old work" with the later Neapolitan series, which in contrast was "like water, really, it has a lovely, fresh easiness about it." You could say the old work is more like menstrual blood: clotted, burdensome—not lovely, not fresh.

Troubling Love invites the comparison. The book begins with a period at a funeral: Delia, an anxious but tough woman who draws comic strips, has returned to her native Naples after learning that her 63-year-old mother, Amalia, has mysteriously drowned. There are no signs of foul play—the body shows only some bruising, "a result of the waves that, though gentle, had pushed her all night against some rocks at the edge of the water"—but something doesn't add up. Days before Amalia was discovered floating near the shore, wearing nothing but an expensive new bra Delia doesn't recognize, she had placed a few strange calls to her daughter. She shouted obscenities in dialect and hung up giggling, a man's voice audible in the background; the next day she called to say she was being followed and needed help, only to reassure her daughter, "Go to sleep. I'm going to have a bath now." When the funeral procession begins, Delia is struck by the freedom she feels at her mother's death; as if on cue, she feels "a warm flow" between her legs. The city follows suit, dissolving around her into a scatological stew. The facades of buildings liquefy and sag; the tearful embraces of fellow mourners produce "an unbearable sensation of wetness that extended from their sweat and tears to my groin." Finally she reaches a bathroom and stops the flow, grateful for her black dress. But she's knocked back by a memory of Amalia: "In the shadows I saw my mother, her legs spread, as she unhooked a safety pin and, as if they were pasted on, removed some bloody linen rags from her sex; without surprise she turned and said to me, calmly, 'Go on, what are you doing here?' I burst into tears for the first time in many years." Tired, Delia cleans herself as best she can and goes in search of some tampons. A man inexplicably yells after her "a stream of obscenities in dialect, a soft river of sound that involved me, my sisters, my mother in a concoction of semen, saliva, feces, urine, in every possible orifice."

The novel proceeds as a kind of detective story, as Delia tries halfheartedly to solve the mystery of her mother's death but is distracted by the greater puzzle of her life. Her only clues are Amalia's final moves—where did the bra come from? Who was the man?—and her own memories, which are as useful to her as bits of scrambled tape. Her emotional quest maps neatly onto a geographic one, and certain locations—the funicular stop, the lingerie store—trigger imagistic recollections that are both false and not, like dreams. The deeper she travels into the old town of her youth, the more comes back to her: violent fights between her parents, accusations of an affair. At the end of the road lies a memory of childhood molestation whose sudden revelation usurps the surface plot. It's a satisfying point of closure for Delia, who concedes the impossibility of knowing her mother ("I would never know. I was the only possible source of the story: I couldn't nor did I want to search outside myself"), but a disappointing one for the reader, who's left wanting by the boilerplate Freud. Return to the crumbling remains of home, and there lies trauma.

Troubling Love is Ferrante's weakest novel. Like many classic detective stories, it resolves itself through evidence unavailable to the reader, a trick that compensates for its sleight of hand by restoring confidence in the protagonist. (What makes Sherlock Holmes a durable hero, argues Franco Moretti, is his ability to solve cases the reader literally cannot; linchpin clues are disclosed only in his final monologues.) But this is not what Ferrante is up to, and control seems slightly beyond her reach. Delia's breakthrough offers little reward for the reader's efforts: the conflation of past and present challenges basic comprehension, and unmarked shifts in subject send the reader flipping back in search of a pronoun's referent. This is standard fare for an experimental novel, which a generous reader would say *Troubling Love* is; Ferrante shows chiefly through form how repressed memories can produce false ones, and how stable identities can slip under pressure. (Amalia and Delia appear in queasy double vision, like haloed figures straining to merge.) But the price may be too high for some of Ferrante's readers, especially those spoiled by the clarity of her later work. The writing is also not her best, featuring uninspired metaphors—the unstable streets of Delia's memory are "like a carbonated drink that, if shaken, bubbles up and overflows"—and a predictable refrain of menstrual imagery.

Troubling Love has many flaws, but its ability to elicit strong reactions speaks to its inchoate power. One *New York Times* reviewer confessed he was moved to tear the book in half, presumably out of rage or frustration ("It's the first time a novel ever made me get physical"). The novel also blocks out, as if with a palette knife, themes, figures, and scenes to which Ferrante will return: distrust in physical appearances; fear of regression into the coarse dialect of one's origins; the attempted self-discipline of a woman slipping into madness. "I reproached myself," Delia says. "I had done too many things that I shouldn't have: I had started running, I had given into anxiety, my frenzy had become excessive. I tried to calm myself." This shaky claim on control is shared by almost all of Ferrante's women, who falter and catch themselves: *Focus*, they say. Work—routine—is a detergent for the mind, lifting the stain of another person's unwelcome encroachment.

OLGA, WHO NARRATES *The Days of Abandonment*, is 38 years old. She is living in Turin with her two children and her husband, Mario, when he confesses, on an April afternoon, that he wants to leave her. Her first reaction is muted; she hates spectacles, "noisy emotions, always on display"—the behaviors of her family that as a young woman she defined herself against. "I had learned to speak little and in a thoughtful manner . . . to draw out as long as possible the time for reaction, filling it with puzzled looks, uncertain smiles . . . to wait patiently until every emotion imploded and could come out in a tone of calm." Such manners were indispensable during previous marital crises, but their currency has expired. Mario has left for good, and Olga's veneer of calm is soon corroded by anguish and jealousy. She begins to hiss when she speaks, abandons the careful routine of applying makeup. In the course of a month she gives in to obscenity, which now comes naturally to her lips: "As soon as I opened my mouth I felt the wish to mock, smear, defile Mario and his slut." Her bitterness drives away friends, and the small revenge of her bad-mouthing offers no consolation; her contempt is a check no one will cash. Increasingly worried for her ability to manage her children, she approaches daily tasks with a desperate vigilance: "Be careful to salt the pasta, be careful not to salt it twice, be careful to note the expiration date on food, be careful not to leave the gas on." She nevertheless feels as though she's losing control of her body, her moves like those of a sleepwalker.

Olga's youth, like that of many intelligent women, was marked by contempt for her sex. In the early days of her abandonment she recalls a figure from her childhood in Naples, a neighbor who lost her mind with grief after her husband left her. Every night the neighbor sobbed loudly. Olga's mother and her friends whispered in pity, calling her "the *poverella*"—the poor thing. "The *poverella* was crying, the *poverella* was screaming, the *poverella* was suffering, torn to pieces by the absence of the sweaty red-haired man." As a child Olga was disturbed, disgusted, by this woman. "A grief so gaudy began to repel me. I was eight, but I was ashamed for her." Girls—imperious, unforgiving, not yet women—still believe in the choice to be otherwise. In high school, Olga reacts similarly to a novel assigned by her French teacher:

> I made an arrogant statement: these women are stupid. Cultured women, in comfortable circumstances, they broke like knick-knacks in the hands of their straying men. They seemed to me sentimental fools: I wanted to be different, I wanted to write stories about women with resources, women of invincible words, not a manual for the abandoned wife with her lost love at the top of her thoughts. I was young, I had pretensions. I didn't like the impenetrable page, like a lowered blind. I liked light, air between the slats. I wanted to write stories full of breezes, of filtered rays where dust motes danced. And then I loved the writers who made you look through every line, to gaze downward and feel the vertigo of the depths, the blackness of inferno. I said it breathlessly, all in one gulp, which was something I never did, and my teacher smiled ironically, a little bitterly. She, too, must have lost someone, something. And now, more than twenty years later, the same thing was happening to me.

Becoming the *poverella* was Olga's greatest childhood fear. That she should become this woman who despite her character, her intelligence, her work, constricts her existence to the shallow contentment of marriage—this is the betrayal. "What a mistake it had been to entrust the sense of myself to his gratifications, his enthusiasms, to the ever more productive course of his life," Olga thinks. The novel she hated in high school is the one she now begins to write in her head, though it contains touches of the "vertigo of the depths, the blackness of inferno" she admired. For a moment she narrates her movements in the third person—then stops, fearing madness. "Don't regress, don't lose yourself, keep a tight grip," she reproaches herself. "Above all, don't give in to distracted or malicious or angry monologues. Eliminate the exclamation points. He's gone, you're still here."

Like Delia in *Troubling Love*, Olga finds her physical reality warped by the intensity of her thoughts. Her response is to restore faith in the surface of things, starting with her face. When Mario announces his intention to stop by the apartment, Olga hurriedly cleans the house. She washes off her makeup, applies it again—no use. ("Look, I have pimples on my chin and forehead, I've never been lucky in my life." A touching, insightful detail: so much of beauty is timing and luck.) Her need to look beautiful morphs into a violent need to tear down all that is false. One afternoon, Olga sees Mario on the street with his new lover, Carla. Overtaken by "a black mania for destruction," she slams into him, tears the sleeve from his shirt, knocks him down, kicks him as he covers his face. Glistening at Carla's ears are his mother's earrings, earrings that had been hers and that Mario stole from her house. Olga grabs at the air, determined to rip them from Carla's lobes. Ablaze, her words reel:

> I wanted to rip them off her, together with the ear, I wanted to drag along her beautiful face with the eyes and the nose and the lips and the scalp the blond hair, I wanted to drag them with me as if with a hook I'd snagged her garment of flesh, the sacks of her breasts, the belly that wrapped the bowels and spilled out through the asshole, through the deep crack crowned with gold. And leave to her only that which in reality she was, an ugly skull stained with living blood. . . . Because what is the face, what, finally, is the skin over the flesh, a cover, a disguise, rouge for the insupportable horror of our living nature. And he had fallen for it, he had been caught . . . He had stolen my earrings for love of that carnival mask.

This young woman—so beautiful, so eager to please, who thinks herself the first to be so clever as to win a man by loveliness—what is she but a soft garment of flesh, a sack of wasted guts like the rest? Female ugliness is human ugliness is primordial ugliness, to Olga. As the fight ends, an eerie disembodiment removes her from the scene. Carla is unscathed; Olga sedated by exhaustion. She knows she has reached a point of no return. "What could I do, I had lost everything, all of myself, all, irredeemably."

The *poverella* of Olga's childhood died by her own hand. She drank poison, thinking her husband would rush to her bedside. But he was in another city with his new lover, his new life. She survived, then drowned herself. One day in August, Olga climbs the stairs and hallucinates the *poverella* on the steps—a glimpse into the abyss.

The next morning she wakes to find the apartment has tilted on its axis. Gianni, her son, is vomiting violently; the dog lies in a puddle of shit streaked with blood. Olga finds a can of insecticide and worries she poisoned the house in her sleep. The telephone is broken, she can't work the lock on the front door. It's as if the poison of the *poverella* has seeped into the prison of her apartment. Survival depends on endurance, attention.

This episode spans eighteen harrowing chapters of *The Days of Abandonment*, and they are a painful achievement in style. Scenes begin with short sentences—air between the slats—but then words crowd Olga's head and collide with quickening speed, building up a paratactic velocity: "I began to clean my face with a cotton ball, I wished to be beautiful again, I felt an urgent need for it. Beauty brightens things, the children would be glad, Gianni would draw from it a pleasure that would cure him. . . . What is a face without colors, to color is to conceal, there is nothing that can hide the surface better than color. Go, go, go." Breathless self-interruptions ward off the interruptions of others, real or imagined. At one point Olga hands her daughter a metal letter opener and instructs her to poke her with it whenever she gets distracted. How will I know? the girl asks. "You can tell. A distracted person is a person who no longer smells odors, doesn't hear words, doesn't feel anything." When Olga returns to sense, it is with a deep gash in her thigh.

The Days of Abandonment takes part of a long tradition of feminist writing about "crazy" women—one that runs from Ovid's *Metamorphoses* to Simone de Beauvoir's *The Woman Destroyed*, from Charlotte Brontë's *Jane Eyre* to Jean Rhys's *Wide Sargasso Sea*, from Kate Chopin's *The Awakening* and Charlotte Perkins Gilman's *The Yellow Wallpaper* to Doris Lessing's *The Golden Notebook* and Ingeborg Bachmann's *Malina*, all the way to Kate Zambreno's *Heroines*. Often these works reimagine tragic figures of classic myth, and find in female madness an ecstatic dissolution or transcendence. Hysteria is reclaimed as an affirmation of woman unbound. These stories are fine, but not always for me; like Olga, I have too much pride to embrace the type. In *The Days of Abandonment*, Ferrante offers an alternative—one that doesn't minimize the symbolic power of female malady but captures the double consciousness of a destroyed woman who doesn't want to be "a woman destroyed." Olga is, without doubt, a hysteric: she's nervous, emotionally excessive, and prone to dissociation. But she resists this hysteria with a pride and tenacity I recognize. Becoming the *poverella* doesn't mean breaking like a knick-knack in the hands of a man, as Olga once thought—it means seeking triumph in spectacular self-destruction, like Dido on the pyre. To resist the *poverella* is not to resist her fate, but to pass through it like a crucible: become the *poverella*, then become Olga again. A person with a name, not a martyr.

IN THE MIDDLE OF *The Lost Daughter*, Ferrante's third novel, a young mother asks a middle-aged woman, without inflection, "So it passes." "The turmoil," she adds. They're talking about young children, raising them and the desire to leave them. "My mother used another word," says the other, "she called it a shattering." The Italian word is *frantumaglia*—"fragmentation," literally—and Ferrante returns to it again and again.

The older woman in this scene, Leda, who narrates *The Lost Daughter*, bears some resemblance to Olga. She's 47, an academic, divorced with two daughters: an older iteration of the same character. Now that her children have grown and left the house, Leda

feels newly youthful. In August, she decides to vacation alone on the Ionian coast. There she establishes a simple routine—walk to the beach every day, grade papers under her umbrella, pack up, return to her apartment. One afternoon she sees a young woman, "no more than twenty," playing with a little girl and her doll on the beach. They're part of a big group, a large Neapolitan family similar to Leda's own, but the young mother seems to inhabit another world: she is tranquil and steady amid her family's chaotic activity. Leda begins to watch her day after day, mesmerized by the woman's tenderness toward her child: "They laughed together, enjoying the feeling of body against body, touching noses. . . . If the young woman was pretty herself, in her motherhood there was something that distinguished her; she seemed to have no desire for anything but her child." Naturally it's a projection, but Leda envies the young mother's serenity.

One day she walks past mother and daughter up close. From here the view is less idyllic: the mother is "not as young, the waxing at her groin had been badly done, the child she held in her arms had a red runny eye, a forehead pimpled with sweat, and the doll was ugly and dirty." Leda goes back to her grading, but the beach breaks into panic—the child has disappeared. Leda, who recalls having lost and found her own daughter on the beach years ago, intuitively finds the missing girl and returns her to her mother. Finally, they're introduced. The woman's name is Nina, her daughter's Elena. But the doll, with whom Elena played endlessly and "to whom Nina paid attention as if she were alive, a second daughter," has gone missing, and Elena sobs inconsolably. The family combs the beach but finds nothing. The sky darkens, the sand turns cold. Leda leaves the beach feeling disturbed. In her bag, with her books, is the doll.

Why did she take it? Leda doesn't know. "I saw her abandoned in the sand . . . and I picked her up," she offers. "An infantile reaction, nothing special, we never really grow up." Leda's sympathy for abandoned things runs deep. Her own mother had threatened to leave when Leda was a child, and though she never did, Leda lived in fear of her departure. She was careful never to lose her own doll, whom she called Mina, Mammina, Mammucia—a mother substitute. "My mother had rarely yielded to the games I tried to play with her body," Leda remembers. "She immediately got nervous, she didn't like being the doll." Eager to give what her mother denied, Leda offered herself as her daughters' doll: they yanked combs through her hair, brushed her teeth, gave her "medicine" when she played sick. ("A mother is only a daughter who plays," she thinks.) In taking the doll, Leda may be punishing Elena for her moment of inattention, or the girl's mother for hers. She may be reclaiming her own mother, now dead, in the form of the doll. But above all the episode dredges to the surface, both of Leda's mind and of the novel itself, the time when she abandoned her own young daughters.

Of that time, Leda says, "all the hopes of youth seemed to have been destroyed, I seemed to be falling backward toward my mother, my grandmother, the chain of mute or angry women I came from. Missed opportunities. Ambition was still burning." She felt in love with "anyone who said I was smart, intelligent, helped me to test myself." As she looks at the doll sitting on her couch—slightly deformed, smelling of seawater and dirt—Leda reflects on her own motherhood. She remembers the decisive moment when she and her husband picked up two hitchhikers, a British couple deeply in love who had abandoned their lives to be together. They stayed with Leda and her husband for the night, and the woman, named Brenda, asked Leda about her work on English literature. Leda gave her a hastily photocopied article she'd written, and Brenda took it, circulating it without Leda's knowledge to the academics she knew. The exposure brought Leda unexpected opportunities, and in time she decided to leave her husband and daughters to pursue a career and an affair. She returned three years later and resumed her family life. But to Leda, the rupture feels irreparable.

When Leda runs into Nina again, the mother is exhausted by her daughter's tantrums. Elena won't relent as long as her doll is missing. The two women begin to talk. On an impulse Leda mentions that she once abandoned her daughters, and Nina reacts uncertainly, intrigued. Leda begins to see Nina regularly, always intending to return the doll—she'd found it on the beach, she'd

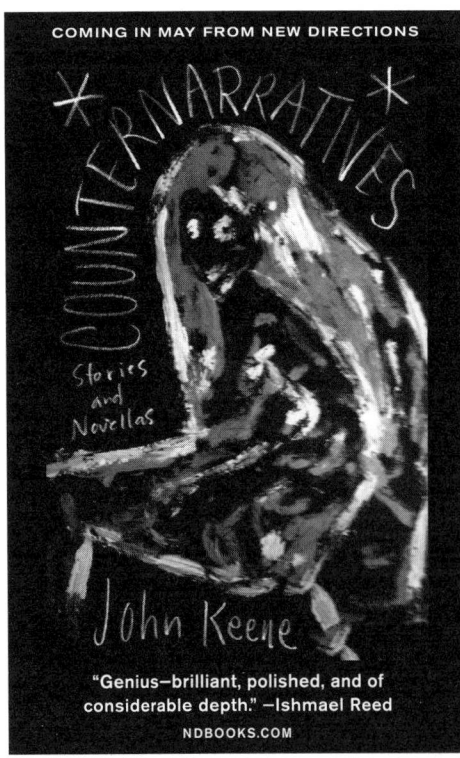

say—but never doing so. She feels a need to maintain their bond, and fears any kind of complication. She hopes to explain herself to Nina in a way she couldn't to her daughters. "How foolish to think you can tell your children about yourself before they're at least fifty," she thinks, remembering the time she tried to speak candidly of her decisions. The girls didn't care, didn't listen; they hardly remembered anything, anyway. "To say: I am your history, you begin from me, listen to me, it could be useful to you. . . . Nina, on the other hand—I am not Nina's history, Nina could even see me as a future. Choose for your companion an alien daughter. Look for her, approach her."

Entwined around the absent doll, the relationship that forms between Leda and Nina is difficult to untangle. Leda sees the doll as "the shining testimony of perfect motherhood," the guardian of the bond between Nina and Elena, mother and daughter. By subtracting it Leda can insert herself—whether as a mother substitute or a daughter substitute is not entirely clear. The erotic power invested in the doll (which, it occurs to Leda, will trump "all the eros that [Elena] would feel as she grew up") is transferred to Leda and Nina. They are drawn to each other's beauty and intelligence, and once, as if by instinct, Nina kisses Leda on the lips. It's possible to glean from this a boring lesbian Oedipal plot, but a truer paradigm lies in a concept from Italian feminist thought of the 1970s and '80s called *affidamento* or "entrustment."

An Italian critic once asked Ferrante, by correspondence mediated through her publisher, "Have you had a psychoanalytic type of education? A feminist kind?" The answer was no. Ferrante denied having any expertise in psychoanalysis, and wrote that to attribute a feminist outlook to her was an exaggeration. She was, she suggested, too shy for strong positions. "Owing in particular to limitations of character, which I've struggled to accept . . . I've never exposed myself publicly, or taken sides: I don't have the physical courage that, in general, is required for these things." But "within this timid frame," she wrote, "I can say that I am slightly interested in psychoanalysis, and fairly interested in feminism, and that I am sympathetic to the ideas of difference feminism." In another letter to her editor, later published in a book of collected interviews called *La Frantumaglia* (2003)—translated this time as "fragments"—Ferrante wrote about her ambitions for *Troubling Love*: "Should I make an offering to the feminine theme of learning to love one's mother? . . . Actually, thinking about it, I'd really like to do this. . . . I'll find a way to develop my theme to the point where I can cite Luce Irigaray and Luisa Muraro." Muraro, an Italian feminist and historian largely unfamiliar to American readers, was a founder of the Libreria delle Donne di Milano, or Milan Women's Bookstore Collective, in 1975, a group whose writings shaped the Italian interpretation of Irigaray's theory of sexual difference. The concept of entrustment was one of their chief contributions to feminist theory.

In the 1970s, American radical and mainstream feminism called for sisterhood. Hierarchies and competition were the constructions of men, went the thinking, and sisterhood was the great leveler. Camaraderie would undo the self-hatred and mutual hostility women had cultivated over centuries of subordination. But differences between women were undeniable, and not only on grounds of race, class, and sexuality. The regime of sameness also failed to comprehend differences in strength and personality, taste and desire. Missing from sisterhood, the Italians argued, were mothers and daughters, and they questioned whether the insistence on sisterhood—to them most manifest in the political fight for "equality" inherited from the youth movement—was a reaction to "the obliteration of the mother in our society." Men were the ones who saw women as equals once the mother was removed: after the mother all women were losers, equally available for domination.

The Milan Women's Bookstore Collective therefore encouraged women to seek out symbolic mothers and symbolic daughters, and to build a tissue of preferential relationships. To entrust oneself, Muraro wrote, meant to "tie yourself to a person who can help you achieve something which you think you are capable of but which you have not yet achieved." (In her introduction to *Sexual Difference*, a collection of the bookstore's writings, Teresa de Lauretis described entrustment as a relationship "in which one woman gives her trust or entrusts herself symbolically to another woman, who thus becomes her guide, mentor, or point of reference—in short, the figure of symbolic mediation between her and the world.") For a woman to entrust herself to another woman—a symbolic mother, likely but not necessarily older, who possesses "something extra"—meant to bridge the gap a woman feels between "her aspiration to a free existence and the privacy of her sexed body." Women did not wish to think about motherhood all their lives, for example, but neither did they want to treat maternity as "a dilemma" in conflict with freedom or deny it as a source of truth. Nor did they want to enter the social world at the expense of their most elementary experiences, those associated with the body and sexuality. Emancipation had created space for women to pursue bigger lives than the ones their mothers had lived, but this required a kind of asexual presence: to be at ease among men a woman had to remove the threat of her body from the scene (unless her body, and its availability, was what she wished to broadcast). Such equality was far from freedom. "Only by reference to those like us," wrote the Milan Women's Bookstore Collective, "will we be able to rediscover and therefore support those contents of our experience which social reality ignores or tends to cancel out as scarcely relevant." The goal was not a static separatism, but a way into the social world of men through a common world of women: a world in which women could aid, validate, and learn from one another as they formed their identities among but independent of men. Even more ambitiously, they sought through the concept of entrustment to create a new symbolic register—one defined not by the Father, the phallus, the singular truth of Irigaray's critique, but by the mother-daughter relationship.

Recall Olga: "What a mistake it had been to entrust the sense of myself to his gratifications, his enthusiasms, to the ever more productive course of his life." What happens when instead a woman entrusts herself to another woman? In *The Lost Daughter*, Leda had once entrusted herself to a stranger, Brenda, whose intervention came as a kind of rescue. Leda recognizes in Nina a similar desire for something more, and envisions herself in the mother role: "I had endowed [Brenda] with a power that I wanted in my turn to have. She perhaps had realized it and, at a distance, with a minimal gesture, had helped me, leaving me then to take responsibility for my life. I could do the same."

If only it were so simple. Under her warmth and familiarity lies something suspect about Leda, making her the first, though perhaps not the last, unreliable narrator in Ferrante's work. The Bookstore Collective hoped that bonds of entrustment would mine "the fertility of the primary emotions linked to the ancient relationship with the mother," and thereby find a means of positive expression. But primary emotions are deep and volatile. Relationships between mothers and daughters are not always beneficial, and one would not need a symbolic mother if one's phenomenal mother sufficed. *The Lost Daughter*, in echo of *The Days of Abandonment*, ends with a stab wound from a domestic object. Mothers and daughters—real and symbolic ones—inflict scars in turn.

There's a tendency to view these three early novels as preparatory studies. To me they're more like Ferrante in concentrate: the dreamlike density of *Troubling Love* is thinned in *The Days of Abandonment* with doses of clarity, and further diluted in *The Lost Daughter* to yield something close to potable. With *My Brilliant Friend*, the blood and poison that threatened to swallow characters whole expands into something voluminous and clear, of staggering depth and breadth: an ocean, in which many people, memories, and emotions—all given frequent breath—can swim.

"IN THE FACES OF THE OLD it's difficult to trace the lineaments of their youth," thinks Delia in *Troubling Love*. "At times we can't even imagine that they had a youth." To do so is the project of Ferrante's Neapolitan series, four novels spanning more than a thousand pages that constitute a single work: *My Brilliant Friend* (2011), *The Story of a New Name* (2012), *Those Who Leave and Those Who Stay* (2013), and *The Story of the Lost Child* (2014), still forthcoming in English.

All her principal figures are here: the *poverella*, the educated young woman who wishes to excise dialect like a tumor, the young mother burning with ambition, the old one who warns of drowning on a full stomach, the thickset husband, the encouraging teacher, the missing doll, the city itself. In the Neapolitan books they coexist not in memory, as in Ferrante's early work, but in the same temporal frame. *My Brilliant Friend* sweeps through a decade with easy intimacy, the kind that makes one feel safe and whole, and with an empathy born of omniscience that none of us has in life. As the books continue—covering twenty, thirty, fifty years—engrossing minor dramas between neighborhood characters play out on a national stage. Exchanges of dialogue are rare, short, and precious; large swaths of the story are paraphrased bits of memory pieced together by the narrator, 66-year-old Elena Greco. She reflects with animating warmth on the history of two women, her and her best friend, Raffaella Cerullo, and the difficult friendship that formed the center of their lives.

My Brilliant Friend begins with a frame narrative—a necessary container. Elena, whom friends and family call Lenuccia, or Lenù, receives a phone call from her best friend's son Rino, who says his mother has disappeared. With her she took every trace of herself: clothes, books, movies, computer. She even cut her own face out of every photograph in the house. Lenù had known for years that her friend, whom others called Lina and she Lila, preferred total elimination to death. But the moment of its arrival leaves Lenù angry. "She wanted not only to disappear herself... but also to eliminate the entire life that she had left behind. I was really angry. We'll see who wins this time, I said to myself. I turned on the computer and began to write—all the details of our story, everything that still remained in my memory."

Their story begins in August 1944—it is perennially summer in Ferrante's novels—when Lenù and Lila are born. Their neighborhood is an unnamed corner of Naples, a site of poverty, madness, and casual violence, associated always with images of poison, muck, dirt, odor, grease, "lavas of water and sewage and garbage and bacteria" that fester in an enervating heat. More than a place, the old neighborhood is shorthand for the generations who never escaped it: women "with tight lips and stooping shoulders," chewed up by men, pregnancy, children, poverty, beatings, and sadness; men ruined by violence and the corruption of neighborhood gangsters, monarcho-fascists with ties to the Camorra who bleed the city dry. "Men returned home embittered by their losses, by alcohol, by debts, by deadlines, by beatings, and at the first inopportune word they beat their families, a chain of wrongs that generated wrongs." From a young age Elena dreams of escape, investing all her energy and self-worth into her performance in school. She pays attention, does everything with great diligence, takes pride in being the smartest in her class. She likes pleasing the teacher, "pleasing everyone." But her sense of self is destabilized when the teacher discovers that Lina Cerullo, daughter of the shoemaker and most hated child in the neighborhood—an insolent girl with skinny limbs marred by cuts and bruises—had taught herself to read and write. Lenù is wounded by the demotion, but what haunts her is greater than jealousy; following the revelation of Lila's brilliance, Lenù begins to fear that she will wake up crippled like her mother, whom she sees as a lopsided collection of flaws: a lame leg, a large body, a wandering eye. To ward off that fate she attaches herself to Lila: "If I kept up with her, at her pace, my mother's limp, which had entered into my brain and wouldn't come out, would stop threatening me. I decided that I had to model myself on that girl, never let her out of my sight, even if she got annoyed and chased me away."

Lila possesses a quick and natural intelligence, which manifests in feverish spurts of

Fiction Titles out this Spring from Henry Holt!

A hilarious, tender, gut-punch of a debut about a man flailing wildly after losing his mom to cancer. "Sumell's shrapnel-sharp sense of humor is never more than a sentence away. By the time you're finished, you'll want more."

— *GQ*

After nine year old Eli's mom walks out on him to live in the woods with a sasquatch, Eli devotes his life to hunting down this mythical creature. A novel deemed "deeply strange and strangely moving."

— Richard Russo

imagination and cruel capability: "Her quickness of mind was like a hiss, a dart, a lethal bite," Elena recalls. Elena's mind is more mimetic and persistent. She has an immense memory bolstered by stubborn self-discipline and an ability to expand on what she reads with great eloquence. Both girls possess an organic brilliance, but Lila's is more entrancing to Lenù, and Lenù's to Lila. Their insecurities follow predictably: Lenù fears that she is incapable of original thought, her mind a repository for other people's words. Lila fears that her natural facility will cease to suffice and that she will fall behind her friend. Their anxieties both enable and hinder their intimacy. Each guards her privacy carefully, sometimes to protect herself from the other's influence and sometimes to obscure the differences between them. Each, assuming the other is ahead, pushes herself beyond the boundaries of the familiar. School, maturity, love, and sex become games of escalation, part of a lifelong cold war that drives them to both great achievement and emotional darkness. But their competitive energy can also take the form of eager collaboration, as they restore to each other an authentic intellectual energy that wanes in the other's absence. In elementary school, Lenù is mesmerized by a "book" Lila writes called *The Blue Fairy*—a story written on a few pages of graph paper bound with a dressmaker's pin. They read *Little Women* together and make a plan to write a novel and get rich. Writing, they imagine, will be their way out of the neighborhood.

But writing will prove a way out only for Lenù. At the end of fourth grade, both girls find themselves qualified to attend middle school, but Lila's parents won't allow it and Lenù goes off alone. Lila stays involved in her friend's education and life: she becomes Lenù's tutor, drilling her in Latin and Greek, encouraging her through high school, pushing her to pass the exams that will allow her to go on to university. Meanwhile, Lila throws herself into her father's shoemaking business, establishing a pattern she will persist in for decades. Whenever her world narrows, Lila seeks freedom in her confinement. She pours her energy into a constricted space and makes it feel large, enchanted by the enthusiasm only she can generate. She can convince Lenù of the importance of any activity she's immersed in, so much so that Lenù feels her own life small by comparison with Lila's grandeur.

Lila wins the race to maturity among the girls of the neighborhood by marrying at 16. In *The Story of a New Name*, she struggles to free herself from the victory that has become a cage. She trains her mind on passionate work: the grocery her husband owns, the shoe store he financed, the language of computers that might spell her way out. "Whatever happens," Lila says to Lenù, "you'll go on studying." Lenù laughs nervously and says sure, but at a certain point school is over. "Not for you," Lila says, "you're my brilliant friend, you have to be the best of all, boys and girls."

Some readers have described the bond between Lila and Lenù as familiar but ineffable, and in the absence of adequate vocabulary call it "female friendship"—an ambiguous catchall that's slightly evocative of a slumber party. The phrase doesn't do this psychically complex relationship justice, and though perhaps "entrustment" doesn't either, it comes closer. Lila and Lenù wish to break the mold their mothers made for them, and to model themselves after what they imagine each other to be. Over the course of their "long sisterhood," as Elena calls it, they alternate between playing the symbolic mother and the symbolic daughter. The story this dynamic produces is all too rare: a fully embodied heterosexual bildungsroman for women, in which sex and love and intellect are given equal space, with no two-dimensional heroines, no religious redemption, no suicide.

Such an outcome would have pleased the Italian feminists. *My Brilliant Friend* and *The Story of a New Name* offer proof that mining the symbolic wealth of the mother-daughter relationship can inscribe in the world of men—the world of books, of fame, of world-historical significance—the social existence and worth of women: what kindles their intelligence, what will they possess beyond the will to subservience and procreation. But as in *The Lost Daughter*, entrustment is a difficult road toward a sense of ease. The mother-daughter relationship, in its symbolic and material manifestations, is nurturing, formative, enabling—but it's also obstructive, scarring, parasitic. Like real mothers and daughters, Lenù and Lila need distance from each other to disentangle their identities. Like real mothers and daughters, they police each other: each feels resentful, even paranoid, when the other steps outside her established identity. Like real mothers and daughters, each expects the other to live the life that she, owing to inevitable compromises, could not. And like real mothers and daughters, Lenù and Lila take things from each other—sometimes unintentionally. Shortly after Lenù publishes her first novel, at 23, her elementary school teacher dies, leaving to Lenù all her old school notebooks and the only copy of Lila's *The Blue Fairy*. Flipping through the pages of her friend's story, Lenù feels sick to her stomach: she realizes Lila's story was the secret heart of her book. "Anyone who wanted to know what gave it warmth and what the origin was of the strong but invisible thread that joined the sentences would have had to go back to that child's packet, ten notebook pages, the rusty pin, the brightly colored cover, the title, and not even a signature." Even the pact of their friendship is sealed in childhood by an act of mutual theft: Lila throws Lenù's doll Tina into the cellar of a neighbor's building, and so Lenù throws Lila's doll Nu. "I felt an unbearable sorrow," Elena remembers. "I was attached to my plastic doll; it was the most precious possession I had.... For me the doll was alive." From the moment they surrender their dolls, those first mother substitutes, they live for and against each other.

For a while, they try not to. Some of the most affecting scenes in *My Brilliant Friend* and *The Story of a New Name* are those in which Lenù molds her interests after those of men and teachers she wants to impress. In high school, a professor invites her to a party at her house, to which she brings Lila for company. The atmosphere dazzles Lenù, but Lila feels estranged; she stands alone and stares at the books on the living-room wall, uneasy among these traces of middle-class wealth. Leaving her friend behind, Lenù joins a group of boys on the balcony for an animated discussion of politics she doesn't understand. "I listened spellbound," she remembers. "Their words were buds that blossomed in my mind into more or less familiar flowers, and then I flared up, mimicking participation; or they manifested forms unknown to me, and I retreated, to hide my ignorance." The debate is a wash of proper nouns: colonialism, neocolonialism, Gaullism, Fascism, France, Beirut, Algeria, Saragat, Fanfani, Moro, the Christian Democratic Congress, Sartre the pessimist. How much the boys knew: "They were the masters of the earth," Lenù thinks. "What were Gaullism, the O.A.S., social democracy, the opening to the left; who were Danilo Dolci, Bertrand Russell, the pieds-noirs"? Despite her unsure footing, she leaps in to speak:

Then I heard myself utter sentences as if it were not I who had decided to do so, as if another person, more assured, more informed, had decided to speak through my mouth. I began without knowing what I would say, but, hearing the boys, fragments of phrases read in Galiani's books and newspapers stirred in my mind, and the desire to speak, to make my presence felt, became stronger than timidity. I used the elevated Italian I had practiced in making translations from Greek and Latin.... I said I didn't want to live in a world at war. We mustn't repeat the mistakes of the generations that preceded us, I said.... Lila, who was next to me, didn't say a word.

The outpouring suspends Lenù in elation and fear; to participate this way is all she wants. But Lila insists they leave, and only later in the privacy of her notebooks does she admit her humiliation that night—she felt stupid, invisible, unremarkable. When her husband arrives to drive the girls home, Lila mocks Lenù mercilessly. "So they all talk just so, so they dress and eat and move just so. They do it because they were born there. But in the heads they don't have a thought that's their own, that they struggled to think.... You, too, Lenù, I have to tell you: Look out or you'll be the parrots' parrot." She turns to Stefano, laughing. "You should have heard her, she said. She made a little voice, *cheechee, cheechee.*" The words burn, marking the beginning of the "first break and long separation" between the two friends.

Years later, Lenù reflects that Lila was right. "*Become*," she thinks. "It was a verb that had always obsessed me.... I had *become*, that was certain, but without an object, without a real passion, without a determined ambition." What were those years of education but an effort to become unlike herself? "No one knew better than I did what it meant to make your own head masculine so that it would be accepted by the culture of men," she thinks. "I had done it, I was doing it." At 29 years old, encouraged by her sister-in-law, Lenù reads for the first time Carla Lonzi's 1970 feminist pamphlet, *Let's Spit on Hegel*:

> Every sentence struck me, every word, and above all the bold freedom of thought. I forcefully underlined many of the sentences, I made exclamation points, vertical strokes. Spit on Hegel. Spit on the culture of men, spit on Marx, on Engels, on Lenin. And on historical materialism. And on Freud. And on psychoanalysis and penis envy. And on marriage, on family. And on Nazism, on Stalinism, on terrorism. And on war. And on the class struggle. And on the dictatorship of the proletariat. And on socialism. And on Communism. And on the trap of equality. And on all the manifestations of patriarchal culture. And on all its institutional forms. Resist the waste of female intelligence. . . . Restore women to themselves. . . . How is it possible, I wondered, that a woman knows how to think like that. I worked so hard on books, but I endured them, I never actually used them, I never turned them against themselves. This is thinking. This is thinking against. I—after so much exertion—don't know how to think. . . . Lila, on the other hand, knows. It's her nature. If she had studied, she would know how to think like this.

The self-recognition is overwhelming. Like an incantation, Lonzi drains all the terminology Lenù admired as a student of its enchantment: spit on colonialism, neocolonialism, Gaullism, Fascism—on all the manifestations of patriarchal culture, even its language. Lenù feels an urgent need for words that describe her life—the life of a writer with two young daughters, with education but no knowledge, a husband but no happiness. She calls Lila, eager to talk about her reading. "But it was a fiasco," she remembers. "She listened but then she laughed at titles like *The Clitoral Woman and the Vaginal Woman*, and did her best to be vulgar: What the fuck are you talking about, Lenù, pleasure, pussy, we've got plenty of problems here already."

Lila's inability to understand is partly the product of an emerging class difference, one that widens between the women as they age. But it also feels generational, as if Lila, trapped in the old neighborhood like Lenù's mother, has joined the ranks of mute and angry women who know firsthand the condition their daughters describe but feel alienated, even enraged, by the obfuscating theoretical language they use to dissect it. Of all the women pained by this discrepancy, Lenù's mother, Immacolata—mentioned by name only once in the first three books—is the most furious. "My dear," she hisses at her daughter one morning, "you came out of this belly and you are made of this substance, so don't act superior and don't ever forget that if you are intelligent, I who carried you in here am just as intelligent, if not more, and if I had had the chance I would have done the same as you, understand?" The only way she can understand her mother is through understanding Lila when Lila says, in different words, the very same thing.

IN 1980, FIVE YEARS after the Milan Women's Bookstore Collective first opened its doors, its members started a reading group. They were still in search of "a female symbolic"—a language through which they could describe their newfound knowledge without bending to the demands of a borrowed one. Without a female language, women's politics was weak: endlessly forced to justify itself according to "the politics of victimization and vindication," unable "to speak starting from itself." Novels, they thought, might contain a solution. Perhaps sexual difference expressed itself in "special linguistic forms in the writing of female authors," even those who defended themselves against gendered interpretations of their work. They set out reading their favorites: Jane Austen, Emily Brontë, Charlotte Brontë, Gertrude Stein, Sylvia Plath, Ingeborg Bachmann, Anna Kavan, Virginia Woolf, Ivy Compton-Burnett, and Elsa Morante. The list came to be known as "the mothers (of us all)."

Reading "the mothers," the women developed an idiosyncratic reading style. Wiping away the distinction between life and literature, they substituted themselves for characters, authors, and figures in the authors' biographies, "giving birth to new, strange novels: we kept searching for the right combination" that would tell them what it was they were looking for. The answer came during an argument about Austen. Over time, two camps had emerged within the group: the strong readers, or "scholastics," who offered the most convincing interpretations and argued hardest over what to read next, and the rest, who waited for consensus to emerge before giving an opinion. One meeting, a woman who didn't want to read Austen but again found herself among the minority interrupted the debate: "The mothers are not the writers; they are really here among us, because we are not all equal here." These words at first "had a horrible sound"—"sour, hard, stinging." Like many feminists, the members of the Bookstore Collective had learned to fear hierarchies, and they wondered whether this rupture spelled the end of their political work. But after the fear came relief: it wasn't a coincidence that the disparities between the women had been named in relation to the mother. *This* was the "symbolic" they'd been searching for—a source of authority of female origin. Women who succeeded, dominated, or loomed large were not "honorary men," leaving the others to languish in weakness and passivity. Rather, mothers and daughters existed in a separate sphere, one that counted the achievement of one woman as a validation of all. Without such "gendered mediation," as they called it, "the wealth possessed by one woman might be resented by another as something stolen from her." Reconsidered in the context of the mother, however, "disparity, made recognizable and usable, becomes a means of enrichment."

I confess that this anecdote and its contents—the theory of the "symbolic mother," the concept of a "female symbolic," the school of difference feminism (unfashionable in egalitarian America), and *écriture féminine* in the French tradition—made no sense to me until I read Ferrante. Not that it's so crystalline now: a convenient difficulty of difference feminism, for anyone asked to explain it, is its insistence on being inexplicable in legible ("male") terms. But Ferrante's novels animate these ideas with a generous clarity. In her work, you can see how the mother-daughter paradigm operates in all relationships between women without reducing them to cardboard. You can feel the inefficacy of words that structure but don't describe your world. Even Lila and Lenù's power struggle is mediated, like that of the women of the Bookstore, through their understanding of literary texts: so much of their friendship is contained in that first imbalance in skill, when Lila learns to read and write before Lenù. Ferrante writes some beautiful sentences, but it's almost her ordinariness—the middlebrowness of her writing—that allows her to carry such theory so far. The Neapolitan books are riddled with formulas: love triangles, sudden reversals, fabricated cliffhangers marking the return of tertiary characters. Strings of commas generate an unstoppable forward momentum—the reader doesn't read so much as fall through the pages—and much of what grips our attention could be called gossip. The Turin daily *La Stampa* called the novels "a soap opera," a telling if unfair accusation. In the hands of a gifted writer, it's sometimes the most conventional stories—those that bear the features of pleasure genres, including their much-hated feminine strains "chick lit" and "soap opera"—that make the best vehicles for radical thought. With this Ferrante has given intellectual and literary women an invaluable gift: books that speak to them in a language their mothers can understand.

In this Ferrante is not without precedent. Among the "mothers" of the Milan Women's Bookstore Collective reading list was the novelist Elsa Morante, from whom Ferrante takes her name. Morante's most famous book, *La Storia*, or *History* (1974), was an unorthodox historical novel spanning 1944 to 1948. Its novelty was in its structure: each chapter begins with a time line of History in the grand sense—scientific discoveries, declarations of war, the decisions of Great Men. The section marked 1941 opens with "JANUARY: Continuation of the disastrous winter campaign of the Italian troops sent to invade Greece" and ends with "DECEMBER: Leningrad does not surrender.... This further extension of the world conflict will increase to forty-three the number of belligerent nations." What follows are ordinary stories—histories with a small *h*—of women, children, peasants, animals. Morante dedicated the book with a line from the Peruvian poet César Vallejo's "Hymn to the Volunteers of the Republic": *Por el analfabeto a quien escribo*, "For the illiterate to whom I write." She wanted the book to reach beyond elite readers and "be accessible to and read by the general public—the poor general public," as Lily Tuck writes in her foreword to *History*. Morante released it in paperback, fixing a low cover price at the expense of her own advance. Within a year, the book had sold hundreds of thousands of copies. Tuck describes a *New York Times* article reporting on the sensation in Italy: "For the first time since anyone can remember, people in railroad compartments and espresso bars discuss a book—the Morante novel—rather than the soccer championship or the latest scandal. The critics write endlessly about the meaning of *La Storia*, and the reasons for the exceptional stir it is causing."

The Morante novel, the Ferrante novel. By the time *The Story of the Lost Child* appears in English this fall, with its comically ditzy cover—two girls in fairy wings sitting on the beach, facing the shore—the Neapolitan books will likewise have reached hundreds of thousands of readers. And like *History*, the Neapolitan novels will form an unorthodox piece of historical fiction, a chronicle of postwar Italy with almost no dates, few intrusive headlines, and no Great Men. Here, too, history is only a shadow: where Morante extracts the record of textbooks and offers it to the reader like a supplement, Ferrante removes it almost entirely, leaving only the margins, the losers, the women, their fragments. Both Ferrante and Morante wish to make their work accessible, and they do so with a conviction that suggests deeper motives than faux populism and guilt. As writers, they understand that all histories—even fictional ones—are indebted to the living actors whose names never made the record: the people, like Lila, who wrote history through the movements of everyday life.

In *Those Who Leave and Those Who Stay*, during a period of separation, Lenù suspects that Lila is behind a recent spate of bloody antifascist actions in Naples. Out of poverty Lila has taken work in a sausage factory, and with the encouragement of some students has begun to organize the workers. Lenù imagines Lila reappearing "triumphant, admired for her achievements, in the guise of a revolutionary leader, to tell me: You wanted to write novels, I created a novel with real people, with real blood, in reality." The fantasy contains something of the truth: the authorial power that Lenù wields over characters, Lila wields over people. Occasionally, when Ferrante returns to the frame narrative and allows Lenù to reflect on her writing, Lenù considers this. "I wish she were here," she thinks of Lila, "that's why I'm writing. I want her to erase, add, collaborate in our story by spilling into it, according to her whim, the things she knows, what she said or thought." But they have already collaborated in the creation of their shared history, as Lenù knows well. Once, presumably after reading the sex scenes in Lenù's first novel, a bully of the neighborhood says, "In my opinion you and Lina made a secret agreement: she does nasty things and you write them, is that right?" Though Lenù is offended, the man is right, if in a different way than he means. Without Lila, Lenù would have nothing to write.

Like Lenù, Ferrante knows that authorship is never the isolated work of an individual artist; the author owes everything to those she remembers. "There is no work of literature that is not the fruit of tradition, of many skills, of a sort of collective intelligence," she told the *Paris Review*. "We wrongfully diminish this collective intelligence when we insist on there being a single protagonist behind every work of art." No doubt the media will take her words literally and accuse Elena Ferrante of being a group of writers. But she already is, and this is her point. The name Elena Ferrante is not a credit but an homage—to Elsa Morante, to the feminist collectives, to the literary tradition before her, to her mothers. There's more truth in this name than any other she could give. +

BRANDON HARRIS
Blood Couple

Spike Lee (director). *Da Sweet Blood of Jesus*. 2014.

ON A SUNDAY NIGHT LATE LAST JUNE, I stepped into the School of Visual Arts Theatre in Manhattan for the world premiere of Spike Lee's *Da Sweet Blood of Jesus* with a sense of foreboding. It was in the air of the place, a mild gloom, despite being packed with well-dressed and excited negroes of every shape and size and color, the ebony and the high yellow, most of them notably well-off. For my part, I was less than casket sharp, as they say in parts of the South, but playing the schlubby journalist at festivals is something I've grown accustomed to. Soon enough I spotted other members of that schlubby tribe, in T-shirts and poorly fitting jackets, clutching their press tickets. Those pale journalists and a smattering of indie-film folks, lackeys for the small and midsize distributors still interested in a new Spike Lee joint, made up most of the whites in attendance. In these parts, they seemed exotic.

It was the American Black Film Festival's first year in New York, and it had a lot riding on this screening, perhaps even more than Mr. Lee. One of the country's most venerable auteur brands, Spike Lee is the most famous African American filmmaker the United States will likely ever produce. He doesn't need the American Black Film Festival to survive, but the Festival does need him. No one gives a shit about the American Black Film Festival. For most people, Spike

Lee is American black film, and where he goes, critics will follow.

Da Sweet Blood of Jesus was financed largely through a controversial Kickstarter campaign that Lee, who is reportedly worth $40 million, undertook the previous summer. His bankroll padded by $1,418,910 from more than six thousand contributors, Lee made the film quickly and without fanfare. He needed a comeback. His previous feature, a 2013 remake of Park Chan-wook's elegant and hyperviolent Korean grindhouse hit *Oldboy*, skipped festivals altogether, probably because its distributors didn't want it to be thought of as a "festival circuit" film. Lee seemed unhappy with the effort; he dropped the "Joint" branding at the end of his credit for the first time since his earliest films.

Except for the commercial success of his first foray into pure genre filmmaking, 2006's heist and hostage thriller *Inside Man*, Lee has not had a real hit since 1998's *He Got Game*, which debuted at number one at the box office and grossed $21 million in theaters. Since then, returns, both financial and aesthetic, have been diminishing. Is Spike Lee still a major American artist? Was he ever? The self-satisfaction and intellectual malaise of his most recent works is troubling enough to warrant some skepticism and soul-searching, even among his fans.

In the '80s, Lee found his niche speaking for black middle-class audiences in pictures that seemed, given the climate of the industry, more or less impossible before his arrival. No one was making movies about middle-class black hipsters (*She's Gotta Have It*, 1986), Greek life at historically black colleges (*School Daze*, 1988), or the causes of Brooklyn riots (*Do the Right Thing*, 1989). Displaying a black-American-centric sensibility absent from the indie sector and the studio world, these films signaled the dawn of a career unlike any American film had ever seen. Along with the Nike commercials he was making a fortune on, these films gave Lee an importance few directors achieve in a lifetime, much less after three features.

His next three films, *Mo' Better Blues* (1990), *Jungle Fever* (1991), and *Malcolm X* (1992), the last of which I saw on the big screen as a 9-year-old with my entire family, elevated Lee to the first rank of American auteurs. Had he never made another film, like other black directors who showed early promise only to find their careers at the mercy of Hollywood executives uninterested in marketing their visions and a black community unwilling to support its own stories financially, we might still think of Lee as the greatest black American director. But instead Lee continued with the lucrative side gigs, and continued to make movies of interest and quality—*Clockers* (1995), *Get on the Bus* (1996), *He Got Game* (1998), *Summer of Sam* (1999), *Bamboozled* (2000), *25th Hour* (2002)—until just after the towers fell. *25th Hour*, about a convicted drug dealer (Edward Norton) making the rounds on his last day of freedom before serving a seven-year sentence, is shot through with disorientation, fear, and uncertainty. It remains one of the most evocative American films to grapple with the larger urban mood in the wake of 9/11.

Inside Man, the last financial success and first deeply impersonal work of Lee's career, was well made but slight, with purely commercial aspirations. The troika of *Miracle at St. Anna* (2008), *Red Hook Summer* (2012), and *Oldboy* have few partisans; meandering, overlong, and unfocused, they're all hampered by a sensibility that feels wrong for the material. *Miracle*, Lee's picture about black GIs, has scenes of great emotional weight, but its structural coherence is torpedoed by a silly present-day framing device that makes the film a Russian doll of flashbacks. It's also overburdened by self-righteous writing

("We served our country too," one character says, in one of the many speeches about racial injustice), and, in what's since become a bad habit for Lee, excessive musical cues. Lee's bombastic style—already straining against his material in *She Hate Me*, with its animated sperm shooting out of Anthony Mackie's cock—overwhelms *Miracle* with sentimentality and smugness.

In the '90s, Lee was too big for festivals. Not anymore. In 2012, *Red Hook Summer* premiered to mixed notices at Sundance, a place Lee had never felt the need to take his narrative films before. It was the first narrative Lee shot digitally without a name cinematographer, and his crew consisted largely of recent alums from his NYU graduate filmmaking class, not the union vets he was used to. He came to Sundance with something to sell, but no one wanted to buy it: *Red Hook Summer* was released through a service deal with a small start-up distributor called Variance Films, to whom Lee paid an undisclosed sum to distribute the film. There were subway ads, but no televised trailers, no billboards. The movie quietly disappeared from view in a way none of Lee's narrative films have since the dawn of his career.

DA SWEET BLOOD OF JESUS might be just another dud if it weren't also a remake of Bill Gunn's *Ganja & Hess* (1973), a legendary film in certain cinephile circles, especially black ones; the mere fact of a remake represents a bold claim by Lee. Rumored to be the lover of several white-boy starlets of the '50s, such as Montgomery Clift and James Dean, Bill Gunn was for a short while a darling of the New York theater world before he began his varied career as a novelist, playwright, and filmmaker. Like so many fascinating black actors from the era, Gunn was never blessed with roles that spoke to his talents. Nor was his motion-picture work granted the distribution and cultural platform it deserved. After adapting Kristin Hunter's novel *The Landlord* for Hal Ashby to direct (resulting in one of the earliest narrative films to document the gentrification of Brooklyn), Gunn made his directorial debut with *Stop* (1970), which made him one of the first four African Americans to direct studio films, alongside Melvin Van Peebles, Ossie Davis, and Gordon Parks. That of those four filmmakers' work only Gunn's is now unavailable is no accident of history. Beloved in neither gay nor black circles, *Stop* has all but disappeared. It was pulled from theaters following a brief run in 1970 and never released on home video. It last screened in its original 35mm in 1990, following Gunn's death, at a Whitney Museum retrospective of his work curated by his publisher and collaborator Ishmael Reed.

In retrospect, Gunn's next feature, *Ganja & Hess*, should have made him America's

first broadly celebrated black auteur. The first film directed by a black American to screen at Cannes, the 1973 picture was, like *Stop*, vigorously suppressed before it could make an impression. Its backers anticipated a *Blacula* redux, a cheap vampire movie with brown faces to satisfy the grindhouse crowd. What Gunn delivered instead was a brooding and mysterious film built on erotic lyricism and the parochial aspects of black American life. At Cannes it was greeted by a standing ovation. Its backers at home were less enthusiastic. They angrily seized the film from Gunn, and it was recut several times into bastardized versions that later crept into B-cinemas and home video under lurid titles like *Blood Couples* and *Double Possession*. It was re-released in the late '90s at the behest of its producer Chiz Schultz, who spearheaded a reconstruction of the director's cut from materials found in the attic of the film's editor. By then the legend of *Ganja & Hess* had spread, though its stylings and concerns were still too baroque, and too negro, for the sort who put the cult in "cult film" to latch onto completely.

Like Gunn himself, the film is an unclassifiable piece of work. Gunn's symbol-heavy narrative creates a world in which the word "vampire" is never used, and the usual tropes of the genre are discarded (daytime really ain't no thang for negro bloodsuckers). Shot in hazy Super 16, the opening sequences glide from frozen tableaux of neoclassical European sculpture to extended, documentary-like scenes of a Pentecostal church, replete with speaking in tongues and lustily belted spirituals. It's a vampire movie that feels at once like a vaguely remembered daydream concerning negro church life, post–Civil Rights black class consciousness, and lucid erotic nightmares. While Gunn's film focuses on a wealthy black man, and so raises questions about the travails and wages of black assimilation, its interests are opaque and only incidentally political. Bill Gunn, unlike the most prominent black American directors of his era or afterward, had no desire to make everybody's protest movie.

In the film, Duane Jones is memorably assertive and taciturn as Dr. Hess Green, an anthropologist living in a gothic Hudson Valley mansion and studying a long vanished (and fictional) African civilization known as Myrthia. Hess reads as self-made, a man with one foot in and one foot out of the larger black community. Though he attends a black church where his chauffeur, played by the musician Sam Waymon (better known as the little brother of Nina Simone), is a pastor, he also has a self-consciously aristocratic mien and a son expensively educated in private schools, who is most comfortable speaking to his father in French.

Trouble begins when the local archaeological museum assigns him a new research assistant named George Meda, played by Gunn himself in a memorably animated and feline manner: his high-pitched voice and unruly shock of negro hair make him come across like a haunted, less-jheri-curled Lionel Richie. After spending an odd evening together getting acquainted, Hess discovers Meda sitting in a tree behind his home with a noose in his hand, threatening to hang himself. Convincing the man not to kill himself on his property is paramount to Hess. "Mr. Meda," he pleads, "I am the only black man who lives in this neighborhood, so if another black washes up ashore I can assure you the authorities will drag me in for questioning."

The drunken Meda comes down from the tree, and, after indulging Meda's bizarre, obliquely self-revelatory conversation for a while, Hess goes to bed, crisis seemingly averted. In the middle of the night, however, the formerly suicidal Meda turns homicidal, bursting into Hess's room and stabbing him with a Myrthian dagger. Meda follows his attack with a bath—after which he shoots himself in the chest. Hess wakes up following the attack unharmed, with a dead research assistant in his bathroom and a new thirst for blood, which he immediately whets by licking Meda's off his bathroom floor. At first he robs blood banks to feed his thirst, but soon his cravings lead him to the seedier parts of New York City—the negro night spaces in which so many blaxploitation fantasies were lived out—to seduce victims for his fix.

When Meda's wife, Ganja (Marlene Clark), a nouveau riche arriviste, comes looking for her husband, she falls swiftly in love with Hess and his haute bourgeois lifestyle. "I'm very valuable," is how she introduces herself to Hess, and when he asks her straightforwardly why she came to his estate, she replies, "Money." They begin a torrid relationship, and even after she discovers her husband's body, hung frozen in Hess's cellar, she marries Hess in front of a small crowd of mostly white people. (One of them is William Gaddis, a friend of Gunn's.) In the midst of one of their sexual encounters, Hess makes Ganja into a vampire. They soon find themselves luring young men to their home to extract their blood.

Hess comes to rue his lifestyle. It's a lonely and morally degrading slog, killing for blood, not to mention the tedium of being physically cold all the time. Despite what might promise to be the eternal companionship of Ganja, he finds himself seeking redemption in the arms of the Christian God. Standing shirtless in his basement, in the shadow of a cross that hangs from the ceiling, he drops dead. Gunn, whose film treats both the teaching of black Protestantism and the myth of vampirism literally, saw the irony of casting the salvation of Christ as freedom from immortality as opposed to the doctrinaire Christian reading. Ganja, however, lives on, and the last image of the film is of a new young man rising, undead, to join her.

The association of the vampire with the aristocrat is as old as *Dracula*, and has always implied the extraction of vital life forces by the wealthy. *Ganja & Hess* adds another layer by making its well-heeled vampire a serial perpetrator of black-on-black crime. In Gunn's film, when Hess exclusively attacks poorer negroes, images from pastiched African ("Myrthian") rituals flood the screen, accompanied by a ominous, horror-movie drone of synth strings; it's as if Hess's vampirism were a way of forming a connection to an atavistic past, one he could only study at a cold distance as long as he was fully human. It is as strange a portrait of the

ADJUNCT COMMUTER WEEKLY

AVAILABLE THIS SUMMER FROM DME.

black bourgeoisie as has ever been offered on film, and for his pains the film brought Gunn obscurity and neglect.

NO SUCH FATE WILL likely visit Spike Lee. It took a combination of luck, talent, and unyielding ambition for Lee to become the face of whatever we speak of when we speak of black cinema. He is now etched permanently in the national memory as a rabble-rousing cultural touchstone. As he has grown older and richer, his relevance as a media persona hasn't waned as much as his reach as a filmmaker. Lee's increasingly tone-deaf and heavy-handed narrative filmmaking is antithetical to Gunn's mix of lyrical, moving camerawork and biting cynicism. A telling contrast lies in their use of music: where *Ganja & Hess* unfolds largely without a score, *Da Sweet Blood of Jesus* is plagued by desperate underscoring through music—a never-ending sound track of neo-soul and neo-Tropicália, crowdsourced through Twitter, that strains to save the movie from its jerky pacing.

Things are similarly awry in the design and aesthetic of the film: what's veiled or suggestively opaque in Gunn's film is dialed up and garish in Lee's. Lee's overly crisp, wide depth-of-field digital sheen replaces the gauzy Super 16 of Gunn's gloomier telling. A modern beach house on the shores of Martha's Vineyard—the island where Mr. Lee and many other members of the negro elite, including the 44th President, "summer" in the wispy confines of Oak Bluffs—stands in for the Hudson Valley mansion. The home becomes something to scrutinize (how much those curtains must have cost!), and the lush colors of the décor, lighting, and costumes—deep browns, reds, blues, and yellows—provide too much visual information, running counter to the mystery of the story. Ganja and Hess, played by the Broadway actor Stephen Tyrone Williams and the British-Iraqi actress Zaraah Abrahams, are ten or so years younger than in *Ganja & Hess*, and much more flamboyant. They get married wrapped in Kente cloth, ride in private jets, and put on designer clothes even to go to the bathroom. Where Hess in the original was ecumenical in his tastes, Lee's version makes him out to be a high-class pan-Africanist only interested in collecting African art. Even the recondite "Myrthia" is transformed into the real—and therefore implausible—Ashanti.

What Lee's remake handles most clumsily is class; it is as if Lee's own astronomical wealth has blinded him to its essential meaning. Lee's need to underline everything with a thick political marker gets in the way of the point he appears to be making. In the original, Hess's wealth was shrouded in mystery; in the new version, it turns out that his family owned "the first black firm on Wall Street." On his large estate, which Hess claims measures "about forty acres," he holds forth about the ills of contemporary society: "We do live in a blood society. The United States is the most violent country in the world." But violence appears not to be the issue so much as "addiction"—as vague an idea as Lee has ever put on screen. "Change is impossible because we're addicted to our society," one white woman tells Hess at a party, "especially the upper middle class, because they've taken the damn thing in such large doses." "What decides whether one is a criminal or not is which side of the law your fix is on," says another. Lee has always been heavy-handed, but in the past he tempered his didacticism by threading through ambiguities and political impasses that made lessons hard to extract. It's hard to view *Da Sweet Blood of Jesus* and remember the deeply felt paradoxes that made his best work so watchable.

Four Brooklyn artists whom I met over the past 25 years helped us celebrate the 25th anniversary of the brewery. All gave me artwork for special labels adorning our 25th Anniversary Lager Beer. Our great brewmaster, Garrett Oliver, developed the beer, a double-bock version of our first and best-selling beer, Brooklyn Lager. The first label released was done by Fred Tomaselli, a now famous painter who I met many moons ago at Kasia's, the diner that was for many years the only meeting place in Williamsburg. The second label was done by Joe Amrhein, founder of one of the first galleries in Williamsburg, Pierogi 2000. The third label was done by Roxy Paine, a world-renowned sculptor who was the only other tenant in the old Otto Huber Brewery in Bushwick, site of our first warehouse. The fourth was created by Elizabeth Crawford, a painter of very fine still-life oil paintings that depict household objects, like a bottle of Brooklyn Lager. I think this is a fitting way to celebrate our success, and the wonderful renaissance in Brooklyn that has spawned so many important contributions to American culture.

Steve Hindy
co-founder & president

BrooklynBrewery.com • BrooklynBloggery.com
Facebook.com/TheBrooklynBrewery • @BrooklynBrewery

Lee's sloppy approach to class issues ends up straining the plausibility of his film. In Lee's film as in Gunn's, Hess seduces and kills ghetto women, but here all of them are light-skinned and well-dressed. The scenes of seduction and murder reach such queasy unreality that it's clear Lee sees these events as simply fodder for an exploitation flick he can only commit to halfheartedly. Hess meets one victim, a crisply enunciating mother—she unspools dialogue like "You ask mad questions! Dang!" without a shard of credibility—minding her own business on a park bench outside the projects with a baby in her arms. Inexplicably, he convinces her with little difficulty to go upstairs with him so he can bleed her. It's hard to believe a child-rearing, light-skinned, stately-looking black woman would be sitting on that park bench in the first place, let alone allow a total stranger into her home to have sex with her in the presence of her child. Nor does it seem plausible that Lee's Hess, fed with silver spoons since childhood, would know the first thing about the Fort Greene projects where he scores his victims.

After the ABFF screening, the baffled audience stuttered their questions. "What message are we supposed to take from this film, Spike? And my second . . .'" one audience member said before he was cut off by the director, who exclaimed, "I don't talk about the meaning of my films anymore, I haven't for fifteen years, I stopped doing that." Lee, with his trademark intimidation, stifled debate over his intentions before it even began. The director was willing, just barely, in the most canned responses, to allude to the film "being about addiction" in an ever more addiction-prone world. Perhaps these banalities hid a deeper problem—that the movie was an allegory of Lee's own addiction to high society, his need to preserve himself above the black filmmakers whose work he wouldn't abide. Or, perhaps, an allegory for the New York he helped turn into a luxury product he neither desires nor understands.

THE SO-CALLED "NEW BLACK CINEMA" of the early '90s didn't yield many lasting directorial careers, save those of Lee and John Singleton. Where have you gone, Julie Dash? Leslie Harris? Matty Rich? Darnell Martin? These young black filmmakers made celebrated debuts in late Bush or early Clinton years only to, for the most part, disappear.

White studio execs were largely to blame. But black audiences were partly responsible, too; they didn't show up for the best of these films. Charles Burnett's *To Sleep with Anger* (1990), a masterpiece on par with his revelatory student film *Killer of Sheep* (1978), found audiences that were overwhelmingly small and white. Burnett, considered by many the greatest American black filmmaker, has had only one widely distributed feature since, 1994's *The Glass Shield*. A flawed but potent movie set in the immediate aftermath of the LA riots, it was taken away from him and recut at the behest of Harvey Weinstein, likely to its detriment.

Lee's celebrity, which grew exponentially while he shucked and jived with Michael Jordan during his Mars Blackmon years, shielded him from such indignities. For much of his career in the studio system, Lee received final cut, giving him the authority to make his films as he wished. In an America that seems to prefer a single black arbiter of negro feelings and beliefs, his career and public persona have eclipsed everyone else's. It has also, somewhat dispiritingly, eclipsed his own filmmaking.

In many ways, this state of affairs seems to suit Lee just fine. He, too, seems to prefer a single black arbiter. More than a few young filmmakers Lee has mentored at NYU, black and white, have offered casual anecdotes of his evasiveness and defensiveness when dealing with potential heirs. One ex-student of Lee's once bemoaned at a party how his professor would read the scripts of students who were the sons of white billionaires but not of those like him, who'd grown up on the streets of black Bed-Stuy (unless they were gay and female, a baffling wrinkle). "A sucker move," the student said. Another, a documentary filmmaker, went so far as to say that his mentor was happy to help cinematographers, actors, and documentarians who were black, but male narrative directors were another story; he liked being the only iconic American film director among black males and wished, in his heart of hearts, to stay that way.

The morning after the premiere, I took the subway from my apartment in the Bronx, where I've settled since Bed-Stuy became too expensive, to the Forty Acres and a Mule offices in Fort Greene to interview Lee. A neighborhood long lost to most of the middle class through gentrification, Fort Greene is still home to poor folks who reside in the Whitman and Ingersoll projects just north of Fort Greene Park, where Lee shot much of *She's Gotta Have It*, and near where his father, a jazz musician, has lived since 1969.

The original home of Forty Acres and a Mule, which relocated five years ago to South Elliott Place, was in a firehouse on the southeast corner of Fort Greene Park. In my early years in the city, as I would pass it while riding a bus down DeKalb Avenue, its imposing African-themed flag billowing above the street always seemed to me a beacon of hope, the shining star of black filmic achievement. The flag, which had been relocated, too, didn't hold quite the same power in front of 75 South Elliott.

Lee had caused a stir the previous February during a Black History Month–themed appearance at nearby Pratt Institute, where he was asked to address "the other side" of the gentrification debate. In blue Nikes and a hoodie emblazoned with the slogan DEFEND BROOKLYN, he said:

> Why does it take an influx of white New Yorkers in the south Bronx, in Harlem, in Bed-Stuy, in Crown Heights for the facilities to get better? The garbage wasn't picked up every motherfuckin' day when I was living in 165 Washington Park.... What about the people who are renting? They can't afford it anymore! You can't afford it. People want to live in Fort Greene. People want to live in Clinton Hill. The Lower East Side, they move to Williamsburg, they can't even afford fuckin', motherfuckin' Williamsburg now, because of motherfuckin' hipsters. What do they call Bushwick now? What's the word?

"East Williamsburg," someone called from the audience.

I was ushered into Lee's second-floor rehearsal space, which was serving as a staging area for journalists. I sat at a small table in the middle of a building-length room with wood flooring, its walls stocked with memorabilia: the pizza box Lee carries in and out of Sal's Famous in *Do the Right Thing*, a gargantuan one-sheet from the Italian release of Scorsese's *Mean Streets*, signed by Lee's fellow NYU alum. The other journalists and I made small talk, scanned emails on our phones. I checked the early reviews. My pallid interlopers from the night before had mostly given it a pass. Richard Brody praised it on his Front Row blog for the *New Yorker*, saying that "Spike Lee has entered his Mannerist period, which, in movie terms, can be defined as making a film on the basis of images rather than experience." No kidding. Scott Foundas from *Variety* had clearly found the film wanting, but he didn't bring the knives out. It was too loaded for anyone outside the tribe to pour salt on the wound of a filmmaker who had so lost his way.

When I arrived on the third floor, it was mostly silent except for Lee yelling at one of his staffers for leaving a stack of boxes unattended in a hallway. He spied me quickly, out of the corner of his eye, and immediately ceased his theatrics; the media was watching. I followed him into the editing room, its blue walls covered, floor to ceiling, with paintings and images of Michael Jackson. It was the single creepiest room I entered in 2014.

I sat on a leather couch and produced my laptop, making small talk as I prepared to record the conversation. Mr. Lee's legs were crossed, one orange-Nike-bearing foot perched not far from my computer. "What you got for me?" he asked.

Although he spoke lovingly of Gunn, he spent the better part of the next thirty minutes bobbing and weaving around my questions like Floyd Mayweather. He wouldn't address whether there was latent meaning in Hess's newfound class status and youth, or in his preference for mulatto victims ("I'm just trying to cast the best people, I wasn't trying to find the most light-skinn'ded actresses I could!"). He cared not to elaborate on how his methods have changed or evolved as he's grown older; whether he enjoys the newfound freedom of not having financiers to answer to; if, indeed, he has any more original stories he's dying to tell, themes he's hankering to explore. He seemed, in many ways, resigned.

It is odd to see Spike Lee, a filmmaker who came to prominence as someone with a bold and uncompromising voice, become, in his midfifties, something resembling a hack—a Jay-Z and Beyoncé–era rich black navel gazer. This is an intelligent and remarkably accomplished man who seems to have little or nothing left to say in his films and has abdicated control of their meaning. I was more than a little sad.

After we mercifully concluded, he grew somewhat more magnanimous, for a second. He stood as I was putting away my computer. "Thanks for coming all this way," he said.

"I used to live down the street in Bed-Stuy until recently. Got rent-sabotaged out just last month," I replied. He asked where I was currently living, and I told him the northern Bronx. Suddenly the wall of defensiveness he'd erected as soon as he stopped yelling at his employee fell away. His face softened. I watched him utter a brief but full-throated laugh. I couldn't tell if it was schadenfreude or a jadedness that he normally kept to himself.

"Just give it some time. Pretty soon, you won't be able to afford to live there either."

FUCK GEORGE JEFFERSON, it's Spike Lee who has moved on up. He didn't want to be like Melvin Van Peebles, trumpeting the accomplishments of one movie he made forty-five years ago in some tattered sweatshirt he wore around the apartment — a nice one in Columbus Circle, bought with Wall Street speculation money. He didn't want to spend thirty years trying to get his first movie distributed and bumming around Africa, as Charles Burnett has, asking dictators and strongmen for funding. And he didn't want to be like Bill Gunn, thumbing his nose at the genres he was expected to make. He wanted to be noticed, to make a lasting impact on a broader cultural stage. He wanted to gentrify Black Brooklyn himself. He didn't want slumming, Sundance-hungry white filmmakers — like Oscar nominee Benh Zeitlin, or Slamdance winner Keith Miller, or filmmaker-brand Quentin Tarantino, or any other white liberal making inauthentic stories about black poverty or bondage or struggle — to do it for him. Then he gave up. He moved to the Upper East Side, the story goes, and got citizenship in the Republic of Jaguar commercials, the brand of "Brooklyn" emblazoned on limited-edition Absolut Vodka bottles with his name underneath.

But these days Lee — minus the fame, fortune, and ritzy address — is just like the rest of us. In mid-January, a full month before its "theatrical release," *Da Sweet Blood of Jesus* was released through Vimeo on Demand for a fraction of what a new videocassette of *Clockers* would have cost in 1995. The film will grace a few coastal theaters and fade into oblivion along with most of the other movies given weeklong runs in New York City in 2015, a number which will likely exceed the 950 the *Times* reviewed last year.

It might not feel this way because of the recent successes of Steve McQueen, Ava DuVernay, and Ryan Coogler, interesting black directorial voices all, but black movies by black people that are not beholden to the desires of white audiences — black films in which the characters are, you know, *alive*, as opposed to symbolic stand-ins — have always been exceedingly rare. "Black cinema" is no better off than it was in 1984, just after Lee debuted his senior thesis film and Gunn finally gave up directing for good, while his novel *Rhinestone Sharecropping*, about how nearly impossible it is for negroes to make nondegrading work in Hollywood, gathered dust on bookstore shelves. "I want to say that it is a terrible thing to be a black artist in this country," Gunn wrote in the *Times* in 1973, "for reasons too private to expose to the arrogance of white criticism."*

---

* In the same letter, he wrote, "When I first came into the 'theatre,' black women who were actresses were referred to as 'great gals' by white directors and critics. Marlene Clark, one of the most beautiful women and actresses I have ever known, was referred to as a 'brown-skinned looker' (*New York Post*). That kind of disrespect could not have been cultivated in 110 minutes. It must have taken a good 250 years."

How is it possible that this still rings true? How likely is it that Charles Burnett, Haile Gerima, Julie Dash, Wendell B. Harris Jr., Tina Mabry, Dee Rees, Dennis Dortch, Billy Woodberry, Larry Clark (the black one), Leslie Harris, Darnell Martin, Rashaad Ernesto Green, Michael Schultz, Kasi Lemmons, Barry Jenkins, Shaka King, Damon Russell, or Moon Molson will get a directing job on the kind of topical, studio-financed film that Lee, for more than a decade, made seem commonplace?

And so we wait. We wait for a black public to find ways to pay for its own media, and for its stars—like Will Smith, or Robert Johnson, or DuVernay's industry midwife Oprah—to start their own studios with their own ambitions and novel ideas for reaching black (and nonblack) audiences. We wait for athletes like Baron Davis and Chris Webber, who have already begun financing films, and wealthy negroes you and I have never heard of to provide a more muscular financial backing for specialty films with content that speaks to the concerns of the African diaspora. For indie-film prognosticators to stop doubting the ability of films with black characters to perform overseas. For young white studio heads with a love of hip-hop but no middle-class black friends to stop telling seasoned negro filmmakers something is or isn't "black" enough for their studio to produce, market, and distribute. A man can dream, can't he? +

OUR CONTRIBUTORS

Alejandro Almazán is a journalist and the author of two novels. His essay "No Luck Narco" appeared in Issue Nineteen.

Philip Connors's second book, *All the Wrong Places*, was published by Norton in February. His essay "So Little to Remember" appeared in Issue Eight.

Cosme Del Rosario-Bell is the business manager of *n+1*.

Kristin Dombek is *n+1*'s resident advice columnist. Her first installment of The Help Desk appeared in Issue Nineteen.

Emma Friedland is a translator living in Los Angeles.

Brandon Harris is a writer, film director, and visiting assistant professor of film at SUNY Purchase. His essay "Bed-Stuy" appeared in Issue Eighteen.

Lawrence Jackson is an English and African American studies professor at Emory. His essay "Slickheads" appeared in Issue Fifteen.

Jordan Kisner is a writer living in New York. Her essay "Jesus Raves" appeared in Issue Eighteen.

Elias Rodriques is a teacher living in Philadelphia.

Christine Smallwood is a contributing editor of *Harper's*, where she is a New Books columnist.

Doreen St. Félix is a writer and activist living in New York.

Gabriel Winant is a graduate student in history at Yale, and a member of the steering committee of the Graduate Employees and Students Organization (GESO), UNITE HERE. His review "Slave Capitalism" appeared in Issue Seventeen.

RENT ROULETTE!

Roulette, the site of *n+1*'s 10th Anniversary Benefit, is an arts non-profit and performance space in Downtown Brooklyn. Our Art Deco venue is well equipped to host: readings, conferences, film screenings, weddings, office parties, galas, and more.

For more information, please visit **www.rentroulette.org** or email **events@roulette.org**.

SUPPORTERS

SPONSORS

Judith Keenan
Anthony Jackson
Andrew Delbanco
Anders Widebrant
Justin Bailey
Samuel Popkin
Bill Lambert
Adam Max
Eric Sumner
David Nachman

ADVISORY BOARD

Kate Bolick
Georgia Cool
Patrick Garrison
AJ Glusman
Adam Gunther
Edward Joyce
Allison Lorentzen
Christopher & Whitney Parris-Lamb
Gary Sernovitz
Ben Wizner

INSTITUTIONAL SUPPORTERS

The Baskin Family Foundation
Prince Charitable Trusts & Scott Wood-Prince

Special Thanks to
Carla Blumenkranz
Maxwell Donnewald
Joseph Frischmuth
Frank Guan
Adam Plunkett
Kathleen Ross
Becca Rothfeld
Samantha Schuyler
Jordan Sjol
Eddie Zhang

n+1 is published with the support of the National Endowment for the Arts, the New York City Department of Cultural Affairs, and the New York State Council on the Arts.

THE BOOKS of SUMMER

NEW FROM NELL ZINK
AUTHOR OF *THE WALLCREEPER*

A SHARPLY OBSERVED, MORDANTLY FUNNY, AND STARTINGLY ORIGINAL NOVEL ABOUT THE MAKING AND UNMAKING OF THE AMERICAN FAMILY THAT LAYS BARE ALL OF OUR ASSUMPTIONS ABOUT RACE AND RACISM, SEXUALITY AND DESIRE.

"Zink is a writer of extraordinary talent and range. Her work insistently raises the possibility that the world is larger and stranger than the world you think you know."
—JONATHAN FRANZEN

ALSO NEW THIS SUMMER:

A DEFT AND HILARIOUS EXPLORATION OF THE SIMMERING TENSIONS BENEATH THE SURFACE OF A MARRIAGE, THAT EXPLODE IN A SMALL TOWN OVER THE COURSE OF A LONG, HOT SUMMER.

"Everything [Bakopoulos] writes is full of insight and inspiration and the best kind of divine comedy."
—LORRIE MOORE

A RAVISHING FIRST NOVEL, SET IN VIBRANT, TUMULTUOUS, TURN-OF-THE-CENTURY NEW YORK CITY, WHERE THE LIVES OF FOUR OUTSIDERS BECOME ENTWINED, BRINGING IRREVOCABLE CHANGE TO THEM ALL.

"Irresistible."
—EMMA DONOGHUE

A THOUGHTFUL, POIGNANT NOVEL THAT EXPLORES THE CREATION OF ARTIFICIAL INTELLIGENCE—ILLUMINATING THE VERY HUMAN NEED FOR COMMUNICATION, CONNECTION, AND UNDERSTANDING.

"Speak is that rarest of finds... complex, nuanced, and beautifully written."
—EMILY ST. JOHN MANDEL

A TENSELY DRAWN LITERARY THRILLER THAT GETS TO THE HEART OF WHAT DEFINES US AS HUMAN BEINGS AND THE SINGULAR IDENTITIES WE CREATE FOR OURSELVES.

"Part glamorous travelogue, part slow-burn mystery, this full-bodied tale of a runaway is at once formally inventive and heartbreakingly familiar."
—LENA DUNHAM

ecco an imprint of HarperCollins Publishers

FOLLOW US! EccoBooks on Twitter, Facebook, and Instagram

LETTERS

Labor, Letters, Interns

Dear Editors,

I wonder if any other reader was as gripped as I was by your series about the problems of paying writers and editors at big and little magazines ("Labor & Letters"). I couldn't put it down, and felt I had been waiting about thirty-five years (since the founding of the *Threepenny Review*) to read such a thing. Thank you!

—*Wendy Lesser*

Dear Editors,

In her otherwise enjoyable article about the recent history of *Harper's* ("Easy Chair"), Gemma Sieff gets wrong the reason for my resigning as its editor. She has me compelled to fall on my sword in 2004 because of a misused past tense in an essay about that year's Republican nominating convention in New York City. The mistake passed uncorrected through the hands of two copy editors and four proofreaders. A grammatical slip of the pen, it was not an error of fact or interpretation likely to prompt falling on a sword. I retired from the magazine two years later to start up the publication, *Lapham's Quarterly*, that had been six years in the planning.

—*Lewis Lapham*

Dear Editors,

I worked at *Harper's* during the union negotiations that Gemma Sieff chronicled in her article. While there is much truth in her account of those trying times, I take issue with several crucial items relevant not only to that story, but to all stories of those who work with words.

The sentence in the piece that stopped me, and stops me still, is this one: "All this talk of salary seemed in poor taste." Talk of salary is tasteless only to those for whom salaries are unimportant. To me and many others at the magazine, the low salaries we were earning, with increasing duties and dwindling prospects of cost-of-living raises, let alone promotions—and a new fear of being suddenly fired—shaped our lives. Fighting for something better was not a matter of taste but of dignity.

This notion isn't new or particularly radical. Many editors and writers have been unionized for years. The *Nation*, the *New York Times*, *Time*, radio producers, television and film writers: they all settled this question decades ago. Some editors may fancy themselves "delicate orchids" or "thoughtful starfish," but editing is work. It is labor. It is, to be sure, quite specialized labor. It requires skill, passion, good judgment, and a level head—all things that are greatly aided by a peaceful, which is to say a reasonably secure and remunerative—working environment. It is true that the union drive disrupted the workplace, disrupted relationships. Yet, just as truly, low wages disrupt morale, cause turnover, and disrupt plans for a normal life.

It can be difficult for white-collar intellectual workers to identify as workers. We fretted over this most of all: if it came down to it, would we be able to walk out, miss the close, and allow the magazine not to come out as it always had? No one wanted that, but merely considering and discussing the possibility was eye-opening.

Like all workers, editors are vulnerable to exploitation by management; like all workers, we need to pay rent, taxes, and medical bills. Previous to the union at *Harper's* I did not have a reasonable expectation of job security and fair pay. Once the union was achieved, not everything improved, but some things did—salaries and job security among them—and among the most valuable was the recognition that our labor was worth defending.

I no longer work at *Harper's* and cannot judge the current vitality of the union. I do not know if the future will judge the union to have been the surest way of securing our goals. But we unanimously determined that it was a worthwhile gamble. I joined the union gladly, because I was proud to consider the work I did as work.

—*J. Gabriel Boylan*

Dear Editors,

I recently read the symposium on unpaid or underpaid labor, a series of essays by dedicated editors of independent left-leaning magazines, who also happen to rely on unpaid and underpaid labor. It reminded me of a feeling I had constantly as an intern: that of being meaningfully included yet alienated.

For the most part, it is refreshing to read these somewhat confessional pieces by editors who have themselves navigated unpaid or underpaid work. When I feel part of a shared struggle as well as a shared project, I feel proud of my work, and I am no doubt privileged to have experienced something that few have the means to experience. This makes it all the more disappointing that the symposium understates the political implications of this privilege. It's not enough simply to admit, as the editors do, that the financial arrangements of small magazines are exclusionary to so many.

In fall 2013 I was an intern at *Dissent*, working unpaid for sixteen hours a week until, partway through my internship, *Dissent* reinstituted a stipend equivalent to minimum wage. In the spring of 2014, I was an unpaid intern at *n+1*, where I generally worked twenty hours a week. After leaving *n+1*, I interned part-time at a nonprofit organization and an independent publishing company. I finished my most recent and most highly paid internship at the *Nation*, working forty hours a week and making $8 an hour.

I've been thinking a lot about why I so readily chose unpaid or underpaid work. Sometimes I feel a twinge of shame when I picture myself complacently grabbing on to the short end of a shrinking stick and refusing to let go. Though I've accepted unpaid and underpaid work gratefully, I've also incubated some resentment. When I'm by myself I can act out my catty feelings toward others. I try hard to keep my small amount of spite private, both because I don't want to alienate some of the wonderful friends and allies I've made along the way and also because it would be ungracious—a toxic quality in a community that sometimes feels as competitive as it does socially meaningful.

Many of my choices no doubt derive from my generation's work ethic, or at least the version that I've found is common in other interns in this field. Contrary to many claims about our disenchantment with labor, the idea of working for work's sake becomes more integral to our self-perceptions than ever when we fail to find paid work. This kind of worldly asceticism isn't new, though it's shifted from its classical formulation toward a more romantic one. The Protestants, according to Weber, saw work as a tool to sublimate anxieties about a possibly meaningless and godless world: work was about maintaining the faith that was necessary to prove yourself before God. Today, we work to prove our worth to our profession, we work so that we may feel genuine, and we do so by trying to make work into something that it fundamentally isn't: a calling.

The idea of unalienated labor—of producing something because you want to, because it's fulfilling and it reminds you of your individuality—has been co-opted by managers to justify increased hours without compensation. People deserve and should ask for better-quality work, but to do so can affirm the wrong idea that relatively better work can redeem the fundamental limitations of work itself. It often leads to the feeling that to make work better requires one to commit more fully to work, and to work harder. In this confusing situation, it becomes difficult to advocate for yourself and at the same time to ask for less work, especially when we increasingly think of work as a form of self-expression. As the literary critic Kathi Weeks has argued, the "bad dialectic" of arguing for better work only to find ourselves accepting more work puts us in an uncomfortable position, which may require that we refuse to work outright. (In the case of unpaid internships, what's the worst that could happen?)

This response, like much of the symposium, is confessional. I don't want to be unfair, and resentment is a turnoff, especially considering all that I owe to *n+1* and *Dissent*. I'd like to be honest about how I think many interns feel: that they are pulled in two directions, between the dream of being fulfilled by your work and the disenchantment that often paves the way to it. This first desire is aptly conveyed by Keith Gessen ("Brief History of a Small Office") and Maxine Phillips ("The Mission and the Movement"). They express a volunteerism that is also antiprofessional. They write as if to say: We are all simply trying to express ourselves (and, occasionally, our politics) through our work, and if some of us make mistakes along the way, then we are sorry. Gemma Sieff's writing triggered that second frame of mind, the unapologetic don't-give-a-fuck savvy, which comes from having seen enough to know that succeeding while taking care of yourself often requires dissociating from the work you love and accepting the culture of mutual paranoia that it occasionally involves. I have felt both of these sentiments, and I believe many other interns have as well.

It seems inevitable that some will read this as petty. After all, I could have said this directly to the editors. I didn't, because it didn't feel like it was my place to do so. *n+1* has been phenomenal at flipping the respectability politics of literary commentary on its head, encouraging honesty about the ungracious emotions that often empower us to critique. And yet I'm wary of expressing these feelings here. I believe my anxiety reflects something common to many workplaces—that feeling of being split against yourself in your work, especially when so much value is placed on being unapologetically honest and authentically yourself. This unstated demand from "creative" workplaces ignores the fact that most of us already don't feel like ourselves at work.

Political magazines face contradictions when they devalue labor in the name of producing something of cultural and political value: what one *Washington Post* piece on the symposium called "eating your young." In their rush to accept unpaid work by a limited and often privileged population, magazines—especially left-wing magazines—limit the quality and relevance of their own work. It was shocking to me that reflections on this problem weren't more present in the Gessen and Phillips pieces in particular, given their reverence for independent journalism.

Ironically, I often hear interns complaining of the existential angst that comes with trying to make meaning out of really limited internships, and how they dream of a well-paid, mindless job that would somehow make their own private pursuits feel more deserved. What else explains their nostalgia for an older work ethic, if not the stress of trying to do what you love while maintaining your integrity? It seems related that so many professionals and would-be professionals submit themselves to punishing workout routines.

Labor law dictates that interns are exempt from common labor standards so long as they do work that would not otherwise be paid for. Taking the legal definition at its face value means accepting the idea that the only legally defensible internship is one in which the intern is completely superfluous. And yet interns are among the few who can touch the dream of a job that is self-affirming—a feeling that becomes immediately hollow if you feel completely useless. Many interns will tell you that the most fulfilling internships they've had are ones in which they were actually put to work—an example of labor exploitation according to the National Labor Relations Board. And so when you rely on un- or underpaid work as a means of self-expression you often experience the odd combination of feeling useless and used at the same time.

But let's shift the conversation to concrete discussion of what could be done to democratize internships. I'll start with a few basic suggestions, certainly not comprehensive enough to be a program, but general enough to apply outside of our institutional bubbles.

1. Transparency. Many interns, especially those working outside of the mainstream, are used to hearing euphemisms about austerity privately at the same time they are lambasted publicly. I'm not saying we should ignore scarcity, and I appreciate the avoidance of worn-out references to belt-tightening. But it is tone-deaf to restrict oneself to an apologia on this issue instead of making it part of a dialogue with the interns. In his piece Keith begins to answer a number of my own questions, many of which I wanted to ask while I was an intern, but which I never felt comfortable asking. I often wondered: If you paid me a living wage, if you paid me at all, how quickly would it all go under? Would it mean the end of left-wing literary journalism? If we agree that in theory I should be paid, then why is it never completely clear where my theoretical money is going? A new printer? Higher fees for writers? Another fund-raiser? I was not privy to these discussions when I was an intern, so I'm naturally cynical when I see them published in the magazine, and I wonder if it reflects any real dialogue. Were any interns involved in the making of this symposium?

2. Pay Your Interns. I can't really speak to your ability to do this, but if you can, you should. It is also important that interns feel comfortable making this demand. You should pay your interns because it will help ensure that there will be a generation of writers who are committed to your project, and who did not have to feel hazed or demeaned along the way. You should pay your interns because it will avoid hypocrisy and because it will improve our work, assuming that we remain committed to injecting dissenting, experimental, and radical voices into the mainstream.

3. Expand Your Internship, or Abolish It. If we continue to follow the legal definition of an unpaid internship, then creating one actually requires extra work. In theory you would have interns so that you may open them up to experiences and skills